D0041979

THE

Wealth CURE

THE
Wealth Cure

Putting Money in Its Place

Hill Harper

GOTHAM BOOKS

GOTHAM BOOKS
Published by Penguin Group (USA) Inc.
375 Hudson Street, New York, New York 10014, U.S.A.
Penguin Group (Canada), 90 Eglinton Avenue East, Suite 700, Toronto, Ontario M4P 2Y3, Canada
(a division of Pearson Penguin Canada Inc.); Penguin Books Ltd, 80 Strand, London WC2R 0RL,
England; Penguin Ireland, 25 St Stephen's Green, Dublin 2, Ireland (a division of Penguin Books
Ltd); Penguin Group (Australia), 250 Camberwell Road, Camberwell, Victoria 3124, Australia
(a division of Pearson Australia Group Pty Ltd); Penguin Books India Pvt Ltd, 11 Community
Centre, Panchsheel Park, New Delhi—110 017, India; Penguin Group (NZ), 67 Apollo Drive,
Rosedale, Auckland 0632, New Zealand (a division of Pearson New Zealand Ltd); Penguin Books
(South Africa) (Pty) Ltd, 24 Sturdee Avenue, Rosebank, Johannesburg 2196, South Africa

Penguin Books Ltd, Registered Offices: 80 Strand, London WC2R 0RL, England

Published by Gotham Books, a member of Penguin Group (USA) Inc.

First printing, September 2011
10   9   8   7   6   5   4   3   2   1

Gotham Books and the skyscraper logo are trademarks of Penguin Group (USA) Inc.

LIBRARY OF CONGRESS CATALOGING-IN-PUBLICATION DATA
Harper, Hill, 1966-
    The wealth cure : putting money in its place / by Hill Harper.
        p.   cm.
    Includes bibliographical references.
    ISBN 978-1-59240-650-0
    1. Well-being.   2. Wealth.   3. Self-realization.   4. Satisfaction.   I. Title.
    HN25.H367 2011
    178—dc22   2011015530

Printed in the United States of America
Set in Bulmer MT   •   Designed by Spring Hoteling
Chapter opening maps by George W. Ward

This publication is designed to provide accurate and authoritative information in regard to the subject
matter covered. It is sold with the understanding that the publisher is not engaged in rendering legal,
accounting, or other professional services. If you require legal advice or other expert assistance, you
should seek the services of a competent professional.

While the author has made every effort to provide accurate telephone numbers and Internet addresses
at the time of publication, neither the publisher nor the author assumes any responsibility for errors,
or for changes that occur after publication. Further, the publisher does not have any control over and
does not assume any responsibility for author or third-party websites or their content.

Some names and identifying characteristics have been changed to protect the privacy of the individuals
involved.

This book is dedicated to a dear friend I know very well and to thousands of men and women I do not know but respect a great deal.

First, to my friend Tracey who was recently diagnosed with breast cancer. Tracey, I love you and I'm praying for you.

And second, to the men and women of the U.S. Armed Forces. You are heroes, and I thank you for serving our country and fighting for our freedom. God bless our troops.

CONTENTS

Prologue: Putting Money in Its Place   xiii

PART ONE
The Diagnosis   1

Am I Using Money or Is Money Using Me?   3

Enough Is Enough   7

Shelter from the Storm   10

The Pot of Gold at Rainbow's End   14

Things Fell Apart   17

My Storm Clouds   20

PART TWO
Treatment Options   25

My North Star   27

Beginning the Journey   35

Create a Blueprint for a Wealth Cure   39

How High Is the Cost of Being You?   44

Achieving Unreasonable Happiness   47

Money Is Energy   50

Building a Valuable Financial Framework   56

PART THREE

Compliance: Sticking with a Treatment Plan   63

Courage Is a Muscle   65

Smart Money Versus Dumb Money   70

Purchased in a Blur of Endorphins   77

Servant to the Credit Card   79

Credit Fix-up   86

The Biggest Purchases You Are Likely to Make   89

Deals on Wheels   92

Learning to Surf   95

You're in This Together—Resolving Oppositional Money Styles   101

PART FOUR

Maintaining Your Health and Wealth   105

Put Your Money Where Your Mouth Is   107

I Am George   116

Follow Your Heart   120

A Leap of Faith   125

The Path to Being Unreasonably Happy   132

Who Teaches Us About Money?   136

Hailing Happiness   140

Standing on the Shoulders of Dred Scott   144

Which Wolf Are You Feeding?   149

You Are Your Own Lottery Ticket   158

Your Personal Board of Directors   171

You Decide Where to Go   180

PART FIVE

Masterminding: Thrive and Survive   183

"Satisfactory" Is Not Enough   185

Investing in You   194

Investing in Life Insurance, a Will, and an Emergency Fund   201

Filling the Bucket   206

Investing by Giving Back   209

Chi-Town Bound   212

A Fast Nickel   219

. . . Versus the Slow Dime   223

Our Debt to Our Past   227

Taking Stock   236

Forming Your Mastermind Circle   243

CONCLUSION

Life Account Versus Bank Account   247

Epilogue: Successful Surgery   256

Resource Bibliography   259

Acknowledgments   263

"The search for love and the search for wealth are always the two best stories. But while a love story is timeless, the story of a quest for wealth, given enough time, will always seem like the vain pursuit of a mirage."

—Mark Kurlansky, *Salt*

Prologue
Putting Money in Its Place

"The most creative people on the planet are
those who frame the biggest, hardest questions
and then gather the resources necessary to find
the answers."
> —Rob Brezsny, American astrologer,
> writer, poet, and musician

Wealth. To most of us this doesn't sound like something we need to be cured of, right? In fact, most people would love to get infected with a "wealth virus." I am not suggesting that wealth is a sickness. Rather, I believe that we—as a culture and as individuals—must reexamine, alter, and then cure what has become a debilitating relationship with money and wealth.

Our society is addicted to debt, and, exacerbating that problem, we live in a culture that associates material objects—"bling"—with success. Those two factors have led us to overvalue money. So much so that in many ways we "chase paper" just as intently as substance addicts chase their next fix. Our relationship with money borders upon addiction, and so many of the problems we see today, individually and collectively, are the result of this craving. **We make irrational and often destructive choices because we have given money and its pursuit too much value.**

I thought I understood the meaning of wealth. When I was a kid I saw a *Mad* magazine cartoon of a man holding a sign that said, MONEY IS THE ROOT OF ALL EVIL. And right behind him stood another man, holding an almost identical sign with just a slight adjustment in wording and a drastic adjustment in message: THE LACK OF MONEY IS THE ROOT OF ALL EVIL.

Now don't get me wrong; I'm not saying money is not important. Of course it is. Let's be real. We need it to acquire goods and services; it's the compensation we receive for our labor and ingenuity. Money also enables us to take care of loved ones, be charitable with the less fortunate, invest in people, or simply throw crazy fun parties. It's easy to see how many of us came to believe that money equals happiness. But money is *not* wealth. This is a book about money *and* wellness. I believe that money plus wellness equals wealth.

In early 2010, I began writing a book about money and financial literacy. Since so many people I met were struggling with issues related to their personal finances, I thought it would be a valuable topic to explore. Oftentimes I choose to write about issues that I personally want (and need) to understand better. But what started out as a very straightforward book about budgeting, savings, and debt evolved as the result of a life-changing experience in July of 2010.

As so often happens when you start out on one life path, unforeseen events affect the route you end up taking. Sometimes you get a short cut, other times a detour that takes you way, way out of your way. For me, the unexpected came in the form of a parallel path, one that brought me to the same point but that offered unexpected scenery and in many ways changed the way I looked at life around me.

A sudden and unexpected health crisis became the background against the book I was writing about money. And as I thought about the physical challenges I faced and how in many ways they paralleled the challenges we all face when it comes to our financial health, I realized that the roadmap to physical well-being was much like the one to financial well-being: from health cure to Wealth Cure.

Health and healing concerns come naturally to me and it may be genetic since so many family members on both sides are deeply rooted in medical fields. On my father's side I count at least six Harper healers. My grandfather, Harry Harper, a general practitioner who focused on obstetrics; his two brothers, also general practice physicians; another brother who was a dentist; my dad, Harry D. Harper Jr., a psychiatrist who guided patients toward mental health; my Uncle Frank, a family practice physician devoted to promoting health for his patient's entire family circle.

The Hill's (my mother's side) medical interests started with my grandfather, Harold Hill, a pharmacist who provided medicines and advice to his clients. My mother, Marilyn Hill Harper, practiced anesthesiology, spending her days ensuring that surgical patients moved safely through their procedures to recovery. My first cousin Joe Pinckney is a family practice physician who directs a clinic for underserved populations in North Carolina. From all these health-oriented relatives, I learned that a series of steps is required to facilitate healing and I adapted these strategies to wealth management. These are the Wealth Cure stages: Diagnose / Treat / Comply / Maintain / Thrive.

The first step in assessing the health of your wealth is to do what you would with your body: get a physical, have it checked out to make sure everything is working as it should, at its optimal level. For most of us, there's bound to be something that needs adjusting—either minor or major. **A DIAGNOSIS** of your fiscal health is the first step on the road to a Wealth Cure.

Any diagnosis should be followed by a second opinion to help develop **TREATMENT OPTIONS**. When it comes to health, there are many experts, all with different sets of experience and with different perspectives. It's true with money, too. Maybe even more true! Everyone you know—from your brother-in-law's financial advisor to your mother—has something to say about money. Not all of it is right or good for you, but sorting through their perspectives and pulling together a team you trust is a must for long term financial health.

Once you've gathered all the information you need, the next step is compliance with **THE TREATMENT PLAN**. It's one thing to buy that treadmill, it's another to get on it every day and work on your cardiac health. And so it is with your financial health: having a great plan isn't worth much if you don't stick to it.

Anyone who's worked to lose that extra twenty pounds will tell you they feel great once they've hit their goal. They'll also probably tell you that staying at that target weight takes as much effort as getting there. Paring back your credit card debt is a great way to cut your expenses and get your financial ship righted. The hard part is resisting the temptation to run up the next bill now that you're out from under a cloud of debt. So **MAINTAINING YOUR HEALTH AND WEALTH** is vital to long term well-being, whether physical or financial. Ultimately, all of this is to **THRIVE AND SURVIVE**.

I give speeches all over this country and many of the people I speak with these days say they feel exhausted, overwhelmed, and even defeated when it comes to money and personal finance. Why are so many people discouraged? Is it the decimated real estate market? Is it the financial meltdown that erased life savings? Or is it taxes, the deficit, health care premiums, rent or mortgage payments, high unemployment, or credit card debt? The most important question is, do we have the education and tools to effectively manage our money and our life choices?

On the macro level, many are frustrated because our government seemed to stand idly by and allow a massive economic meltdown, causing the worst job losses and recession since the Great Depression. And although both government and businesses were wildly irresponsible, no one appeared to be appropriately punished, and it was back to business as usual.

On the micro level, many are suffering right now with the aftermath of that recession. Scores of individuals have overextended themselves with oppressive credit card and mortgage debts. Debt issues cause a huge amount of stress, particularly in an uncertain job market. **Problems with debt can poison every aspect of our lives.** The number one thing that couples argue about is—you guessed it—money.

Beginning around 1980, our values began to shift in catastrophic ways. Credit card use expanded rapidly, resulting in an exploding personal debt that rose from $355 billion in 1980 to $2.6 trillion in 2008. Financial institutions collect billions of dollars in credit card, debit card, and late fees because we spend more than we have. And, to make matters worse, while personal debt is exploding, savings have plummeted. The savings rate was seven times lower in 2008 than in 1980.

Our society has become steeped in *hyperconsumerism*. Advertising and the pressure it creates to own the latest model or name brand have led us to believe that acquisition is the only representation of abundance. As a result, we are buying more and more and attaching an elevated importance to these items. The irony is not lost on me that my paycheck from *CSI: NY* is due to those same advertisers that buy time on our show.

Through pop culture we are bombarded with the message that **cash is king**. Even when we turn on a sports report, we hear more about the players' salaries and contract disputes than their performance on the field. At times ESPN sounds more like CNBC. It reminds me of how I used to sway to Wu-Tang's anthem "C.R.E.A.M." (Cash Rules Everything Around Me).

Many of the problems we have witnessed in the world during the last number of years are a result of people chasing money at all costs, looking for quick, easy gains, even at the expense of their morals or integrity. Rather than coming up with new ideas, products, or services, many individuals and businesses just focus on creating new "schemes." We devote our energy to devising intricate plans for how to separate other people from their money. We have placed such a disproportionate value on wealth that we have made it acceptable to take other people's money if we're clever enough to trick it out of them. The attitude seems to be, "What's the least we can provide, yet charge the most for it?"

I often hear elders talking about "the good ole' days" before predatory lenders, hedge funds, derivative contracts, and house flippers. That's selective memory. The original Ponzi scheme happened back in the 1920s, and snake oil salesmen were defrauding folks decades before Mr. Ponzi. But the recent real estate crisis created by predatory lending practices and the problems on Wall Street exacerbated by credit default swaps were considered to be more than A-okay. In fact they were rated AAA.

Caveat emptor—"let the buyer beware"—is a saying we often hear. But what about *aequitas equitas*—which means the quality of "fairness" or "values." We must reassess the exalted place that we award to money and stop worshipping "Benjamins." It's okay to appreciate money; the challenge is to make sure its *value* is in balance with the other sources of wealth in our lives.

Redefining our proper relationship to money and wealth—participating in what I call the Wealth Cure—requires a return to some fundamental values that have been discarded. Sometimes we think we're in touch with what matters, but then something unexpected happens, a change takes place that propels us to reexamine our hearts to uncover what we truly value. **We can create a new definition of abundance, which will lead us to a new way of living.** This awareness and shift of focus form the basis of the Wealth Cure.

The pages that follow tell the story of a recent journey. And although most of my trip was spent alone, in a real sense, I had lots of company:

— The wisdom of inspirational people whose stories help guide and instruct me

— My memories of loved ones who are no longer alive but whose words, and deeds, helped shape me

— Old friends, whose own journeys helped clarify mine

— And a couple of new friends who enriched my life in unexpected ways

My trip was transformational.

In sharing this story, I hope to pass on what I have learned. I hope to dispel some of the confusion and anxiety around money and show how it can be an effective tool. But most important, I want to help reinvent the fundamental understanding of wealth in order to help us achieve a balanced happy and healthy life.

PART ONE
The Diagnosis

diagnose \dī-ig-nōs\: the identification of the nature of an illness, or other problem by examination of the signs and symptoms

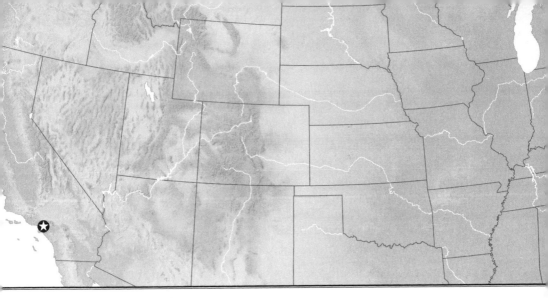

Am I Using Money or
Is Money Using Me?

"Money and success don't change people; they
merely amplify what is already there."
—Will Smith, American actor

Just as my plane from Dallas touched down in Los Angeles, I switched
my BlackBerry on, and a message from my friend Andre popped up.
"Hill Harper! Me/You *The Henry* tonight! DJ Ruckus is spinning. They're
opening the patio. Let's get a table, some bottles, and hang!"

Andre often invited me to go out with him, which served a double purpose for him. First, I am one of his few friends who can pull him back from
the edge when he starts spending money like water. We all need a friend like
that. And second, I am one of his few friends who can afford to split the bill
with him. Andre, like a lot of us, overspends when he's having fun. Once
Andre starts, he has a tendency to keep buying expensive drinks for more
and more people. I understand the impulse—you just don't want the fun to

3

stop. But I worry about my grandparents, reaching out from their graves, grabbing me, and then slapping me.

I've been in a number of circumstances where I've watched celebrities spend money like they're printing it. One case that magnifies this for me was a night a group of us went out in Vegas. Around midnight a prominent athlete who was a part of our group whispered to me that he was gonna "make it look like Chinese New Years up in here" and proceeded to spend $30,000 in under three hours. The "Chinese New Years" referred to a line of ten waitresses walking toward our table carrying bottles with sparklers affixed to the bottle tops, making it look like a parade. It was breathtaking and heartbreaking to watch. The money was flowing so fast, he was like the Usain Bolt of the cocktail lounge. When the bill came and he put down his card, I couldn't help thinking how many school uniforms, musical instruments, or computers that money could have provided. This type of conspicuous consumption bothers me especially when it's obvious that a lot of this floss is more than likely covering up a deeper insecurity that spending money isn't about to fix.

I'm hoping that with my buddy Andre that's not the case. When I asked him, he explained that this was simply the cost of doing business. In his mind, you have to spend money to make money. "It's all about relationships and perception, Hill Harper." Andre always used my first and last name as if I were Charlie Brown or Ronald Reagan.

Andre was a good friend, and I was proud of him. He had taken a decent mortgage broker business and built it into an extremely successful mortgage broker business. He assured me that he was still doing well, even in the midst of the economic downturn. And Lord knows, he liked being out and about in Hollywood.

Usually Andre had to guilt me into hitting the clubs until all hours of the night. "Hill Harper, if you don't come, I'll have to spend all that money on my own. Don't do that to me, man."

But tonight was different. I'd been on the road the past month, in and out of hotel rooms. Forget what you see in those vacation commercials. When you're living in a hotel room for long periods of time, it gets lonely. This time I was the one needing company.

"Don't leave me hangin', Hill Harper!" was his last text to me.

As the plane pulled into the gate, I decided that getting out could be just what the doctor ordered. At times I'd been accused of being too serious, but there was no doubt I enjoyed a good party. In fact, it was too long since the last one.

As I sat in *The Henry* later that night surrounded by friends, music, bottles of Patron, Belvedere, and lovely women, I wondered how I could feel so lonely surrounded by two hundred people, who seemed so happy. Ruckus was spinning a Juelz Santana/Curtis Mayfield mash-up, and the room was rockin'. In spite of the energy, a wave of sadness washed over me. The words people were shouting over the music were beginning to sound like all the adults in a *Peanuts* cartoon: "Whah, whah, whah." Was it the tequila, or something else? Instead of acknowledging how I felt, bowing out and heading home, I motioned the waitress to keep the drinks pouring. My credit card joined Andre's, even though I wasn't feeling a part of the same party everyone else was enjoying. At that moment, it hit me. Money can buy you access to places like *The Henry*, but it can't buy a real connection to "real" people. I definitely wasn't feeling any connections to this crowd. In fact, I'd say I was feeling pretty disconnected.

As I gathered my things to leave the club, I pulled Andre to the side and said, "You know how you can go get your car washed and waxed, but underneath the car, in the wheel well, if you stuck your hand in there, it would come out grimier and dirtier than your car's exterior ever was . . . that's how I feel right now."

Andre looked at me with a confused expression and said, "What the hell are you talking about, Hill Harper?"

"Never mind," I responded. "I'll hit you tomorrow." I went home and went to bed.

> We often make external choices that have internal consequences, and here I was feeling the sting of mine.

A few weeks later, when I opened my credit card bill and saw the charges from *The Henry*, I felt sick to my stomach, because I couldn't help realizing, on that night, I had become "*that guy*" and the evidence was right there in my hand. All that money, and not only did I *not* have a good time, but worse still, I didn't actually help anyone else with the thousands that were spent. **We often make external choices that have internal consequences, and here I was feeling the sting of mine.** I knew I needed to make some changes.

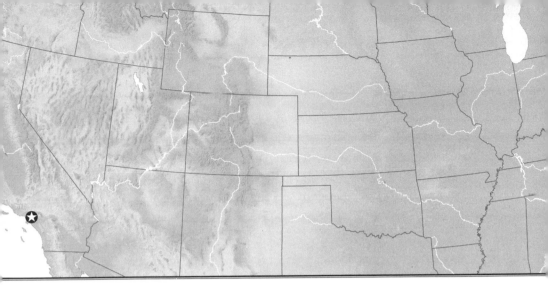

ENOUGH IS ENOUGH

"Money never made a man happy yet, nor will
it. The more a man has, the more he wants. Instead of filling a vacuum, it makes one."
—Benjamin Franklin, American statesman,
scientist, philosopher, writer, inventor

How do we know when we have enough? "Enough" is a funny word.
It's used in so many different ways:

"I've worked and studied hard enough . . ." as in an adequate amount.

"I just wish I had enough money . . ." as in a comfortable amount.

"He doesn't love me enough . . ." as in an abundant amount.

"Enough" is one of those words that carries within it a value judgment.
If you use it in one way, it conveys something of tremendous worth. If you
use it in another way, it conveys something that is acceptable but maybe not
preferable. To say, "His/her love is enough," is not at all the same as "His/
her love is good enough."

And then there is "Enough with this rain already!" as in fed up. Now that's something my parents and grandparents heard me say often. **It took me years to finally realize that storms are a necessary part of nature and of our lives. Some storms are real, some metaphorical, but they all have the power to be a catalyst for change.**

When I was a young boy, growing up in Iowa, I hated storms, especially thunderstorms. First, there'd be dark, ominous clouds, followed by the severe weather warning on TV, with a banner of words across the bottom of the screen announcing a tornado watch. I *really* hated those kinds of storms. They were the worst sort of intrusion; they stopped everything. All plans changed; no hanging out in the neighborhood with friends, no school field trips, no riding around town with my father and watching him tend to his business. I would be stuck indoors, sometimes for days.

Whenever it rained during the day, I'd kneel on the couch closest to the window, put my folded arms on top of the couch's backrest, and watch the drops fall slanted against the windowpane. The rain always seemed to fall sideways in evenly spaced intervals during those storms. It was mesmerizing and kind of fun to watch, though I would have never admitted it back then. I was too busy being angry about all the things the rain was keeping me from doing. I'd just sit there on that couch for hours, pouting and staring as though staring long and hard enough might magically make it stop. It seems that as adults many of us do the same thing. **We believe that if we just think about a problem long enough, it will somehow be solved or cured, as if we can simply wish it away.**

> We always have a choice between a perspective of gratitude for what we have in the present or a perspective of constant longing for the things we think we may never get.

When I look back on my youth, those storm-filled hours stand out as among the most memorable but also the most meaningful. I realize now what I couldn't appreciate then. I was so focused on what I wanted, whether it was playing with a friend outside or going somewhere with my dad, that I wasn't able to see what I already had—the warmth and safety of home and the love of my family—all the things that I relied on to shelter me from the storm. I didn't realize the value of what I already had. I could have benefited from a shift in perspective. **We always have a choice between a perspective of gratitude for what we have in the present or a perspective of constant longing for the things we think we may never get.**

I had grown to love storms as an adult, or so I thought. Then came Hurricane Katrina. I was nowhere near the storm, but I spent hours, days, sitting on my couch, as though I'd suddenly been transported back to my boyhood, watching on television as the falling water claimed not just an activity or an afternoon but the lives and homes and futures of an entire community.

"Whew," my grandmother used to say, shaking her head when she came inside from the rain. "I sure hope Aunt Tiki doesn't get caught in that mess. She said she was going to do her shopping this morning." If she wasn't thinking of Aunt Tiki—who wasn't my biological aunt at all, but loved me as if I were blood family—it was somebody else. And if it wasn't my grandmother doing the hoping, then it was my grandfather or one of my elders. The point was that they wanted to make sure the people they cared about were dry and safe and out of harm's way. As I watched the news reports and the footage about Hurricane Katrina, I found myself doing the same.

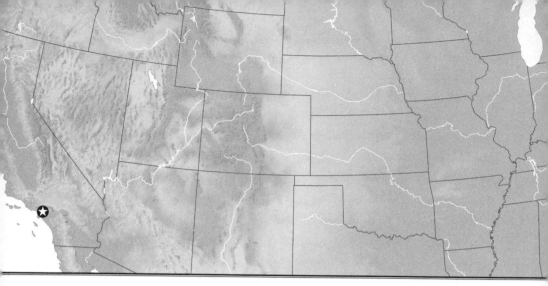

Shelter from
the Storm

"Clouds come floating into my life, no longer to
carry rain or usher storm, but to add color to
my sunset sky."
>   —Rabindranath Tagore, Indian poet,
>   playwright, and essayist

S ean Lombard, my best friend from college, was from New Orleans,
and I had grown to love the Crescent City from my frequent visits
with him and his family. In the late '90s he convinced me to join an investment group with him that would open a hotel near the French Quar-
ter. My connection to New Orleans and its people deepened through my
friendship with Sean and the hotel investment.

Sean lived with his family in the Lower Ninth Ward. To me, he was as
cool as New Orleans jazz in a Herman Leonard photo. Sean seemed very
laid-back, but at the same time, he had a fire in his belly. He was the type of

man that the author Dan Millman would call a peaceful warrior—a gentle man who lived life with a warrior's spirit. As soon as I heard the news about Katrina, I immediately prayed for his family's safety. "Please don't let Sean, Lorraine, and their kids be caught in that mess," I'd whispered to the television, sounding an awful lot like my late grandmother. The more news I saw, the more my spirits waned. The Lower Ninth Ward was among the hardest hit during the storm. It was completely submerged. I made frequent calls attempting to check on Sean and the well-being of the hotel's eighty-eight employees, many of whom, along with their families, used the upper floors of our hotel for shelter.

Even if Sean and his family had managed to escape the levee breaches, surely their house would be lost to the flood. That thought alone was devastating. I knew how much Sean loved that house. Three generations of Lombards had grown up there. It was big and stately, much like Sean himself. The house was a part of their family. Well, Sean's family anyway. His wife, Lorraine, had never been a big fan of the neighborhood, which was old, transitional, and divided by invisible boundaries of class and caste.

Sean used to tell me stories about growing up in the neighborhood, about how he'd borrow books from the poet Kalamu ya Salaam, bump into R&B singer Fats Domino, and even catch the Marsalis brothers" impromptu jam sessions. I used to love Sean's stories so much I started going to visit him there in New Orleans, where he introduced me to Mardi Gras, zydeco, and second-line dancing.

I kept calling Sean's house, even though I figured the lines were down and cell towers not working, and I got a busy or no-service message every time. His phones were probably underwater, like everything else he owned. The very idea of it created an image so disturbing that it gave me chills. **Imagine what it would be like if everything you owned was**

> Imagine what it would be like if everything you owned was floating in the water—photographs, CDs, computers, clothes, keepsakes, art, jewelry, deeds, titles, birth certificates—everything except what was on your body and in your pockets.

floating in the water—photographs, CDs, computers, clothes, keep-sakes, art, jewelry, deeds, titles, birth certificates—everything except what was on your body and in your pockets. It makes you wonder how important all of the things we keep and worship really are, but more on that later.

When the phone rang the next evening, the last person I expected to hear on the other end of the line was Sean.

"Hey, Hill," he said, his voice sounding surprisingly normal. "Got any vacancies in Newark?" Sean was referring to a twenty-three-unit apartment building that I co-own in Newark, New Jersey. There was a fully furnished two-bedroom unit in the building that I sometimes used as a getaway, a place to go to escape. Several times in the past, I'd let friends stay there. Some of them were in between homes, in between jobs, or just in between the person they used to be and the person they were in the process of be-coming and needed a place to perch for the duration.

"Sure," I told Sean, not even sure where to begin asking questions. "Are you—what happened? Lorraine—the kids . . ." I could hear that I wasn't making any sense.

"We're fine. We're fine," Sean assured me. "We went on vacation. We're still in Orlando, at Disney World." For a moment I wanted to let out a laugh, because the situation was so surreal. Disney World . . . the happiest place on earth? I was relieved, but I didn't know what to do with all the worry, fear, and anxiety that had built up.

"Man, I was really worried about you guys," I said to Sean, my tone hanging somewhere between annoyed and ecstatic.

"I know," he said. "I'm sorry. It's been a crazy couple of days." A mo-ment of silence passed between us on the line. Sometimes silence between friends can communicate more love and support than words are able to. In this instance, silence was enough.

Hurricane Katrina had arrived in late August. Sean, Lorraine, and their two kids, Clare and Tony, ended up flying from Orlando to my place in Newark and staying until the end of the month, and then they rented a home in Los Angeles. L.A. seemed like the best choice because Sean is a sound engineer, and he often worked there. After they'd settled into their new place and Tony and Clare were enrolled in school, Sean planned to go back to New Orleans to begin fixing the house so that they could return as soon as possible.

Then came Hurricane Rita to finish what Hurricane Katrina had started. Sean's family home for three generations was completely destroyed. One day Sean said to me, "It's not the house, the TVs, jewelry, or clothes that I miss, I don't even remember most of that stuff. It's the smell and the sound of the floors creaking when we walked and the reverberating laughter of my kids from upstairs that I miss the most."

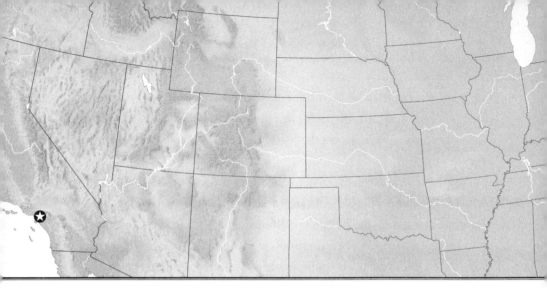

The Pot of Gold
at Rainbow's End

"May God give you . . . For every storm a rainbow, for every tear a smile, for every care a
promise and a blessing in each trial. For every
problem life sends, a faithful friend to share, for
every sigh a sweet song and an answer for each
prayer."

—Irish blessing

In the summer of 2010, I was feeling fantastic! I had just wrapped another successful season of *CSI: NY,* and I'd recently been cast as a
character in Tyler Perry's film adaptation of Ntozake Shange's choreo-
poem *For Colored Girls Who Have Considered Suicide/When the Rainbow
Is Enuf,* a collection of twenty poems, performed as monologue narra-
tives. Through these poems, each of the five African American women
characters let us into their lives, providing poetic images of the storms

that have wreaked havoc in their worlds. *For Colored Girls* is a poetic tapestry that illustrates the mountains that each woman climbs and the valleys she digs out of to emerge reawakened on the other side of her journey once the skies have cleared.

I had read the book upon which it is based during my college years, and one of the first things I did to prepare for the role was read it once more. Once again, I was deeply moved by the rawness of the emotions expressed and by the courage of her conviction that each of the women had to employ in order to find a path, however difficult that might seem, toward happiness. **I've always been a huge proponent of not only seeking happiness but aiming for *unreasonable happiness*, the sort of joy that is not predicated on any person, possession, or accomplishment, but the sort of joy that exists for its own sake.** The energy of unreasonably happy people makes others ask, "What is it about their life that makes them so happy? . . . That's unreasonable." The fact that these characters facing so much difficulty choose to strive toward happiness is incredibly life affirming.

In Atlanta to shoot the film, and working with Kerry Washington, Janet Jackson, Phylicia Rashad, Whoopi Goldberg, and many other talented and amazing women, there was no other way you could define my mood and demeanor than as "unreasonably happy." Life was good. God was good. It was all good, all the time. There was nothing that I wanted or needed—and to be truthful, money had very little to do with that. Yes, I was being paid to work on the film, but the point was that I was doing what I loved, what I'd set out to do all those years ago when I'd made the decision to pursue acting. And by no means has that pursuit been easy. It's been one storm after another. But this was a beautiful summer in the ATL, and no storm clouds were on the horizon.

Every day of filming, I thought about the last part of the play's title, . . . *When the Rainbow Is Enuf.* It seems like we all get so caught up in the concept of more. More money. More fame. More food. More clothing. More friends. More opportunities. More, more, more. When does the understanding of "enough" come into play? What *is* the understanding of enough? And is the rainbow ever enough?

Lynne Twist, in her wonderful book *The Soul of Money*, writes about what she calls "the great lie of scarcity," the feeling that dominates our thinking that there is never enough. Whether it's time, sleep, exercise, or money, the idea that we are lacking something, a sense of inadequacy, underlies everything. The consuming sense that there is not enough drives us to look outside ourselves to be fulfilled. We spend, spend, spend in a frantic attempt to find relief and comfort with the things money can buy. **Searching outside of ourselves for fulfillment can oftentimes be as futile as chasing the ever-shifting pot of gold at the end of a rainbow. We never quite get it, and even if we do, it's never enough.**

Perhaps the most extreme example of this from my life happened in May of 2000 when my father passed away. He lived in Sacramento, California, and I had been there for weeks caring for him and helplessly watching him deteriorate from pancreatic cancer. The morning after my birthday, while holding his hand and crying and praying, he looked me and my brother in the eyes and took his final breath. I watched the life drain out of his eyes and squeezed his hand more tightly.

I inherited my love of cars from my father. He loved new and vintage cars—the faster, the more beautiful, the better. He and I would often sit together and look through the classified section for vintage cars for sale. As my brother and I began the sorrowful task of making funeral arrangements, every morning I continued our tradition and one day I saw a listing for a mint condition 1957 Corvette convertible that was red with white side panels. At that moment, I decided to buy that car. I used almost all of my savings and paid cash. What is so clear to me now wasn't at all clear to me then. I was attempting to use this huge purchase to fill a hole that couldn't be filled.

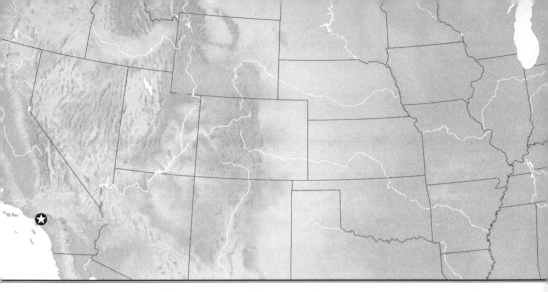

THINGS FELL APART

"When wealth is lost, nothing is lost; when
health is lost, something is lost; when character
is lost, all is lost."
　　　　—Billy Graham, American evangelist

I n between days of shooting, I was scheduled to attend the annual Essence Music Festival, where I was a featured speaker. It's held every
year in New Orleans on the Fourth of July weekend. I'd been many times
since the hurricanes, but without Sean there, it just never felt the same.
Each time I was about to go, he would always ask me to stop by his property and take pictures for him, as he was rebuilding little by little, but I
wasn't able to get there as often as he'd like. Coincidentally, Sean called
while I was at the airport waiting to board my flight to New Orleans.

　　"Hey, Hill," he said in an upbeat voice that sounded a little forced. "Got
any vacancies in Newark?"

I was confused, speechless. Had something destroyed their home in L.A.? Had there been a quake?

"Lorraine and I are getting a divorce," he added.

I couldn't believe what I was hearing. "No way," I said, emphatically. "Why?" I'd always thought that Sean and Lorraine were one of the most solid couples I knew.

"Things just fell apart, man."

"When? When did all this happen?" I wanted to know. In Sean's voice, I heard what I imagined to be suppressed tears. My eyes started to tear up as well, but I was in a very public place, so I did my best to keep it together.

"Disney World," Sean blurted out without a hint of humor or irony. "Hill, this thing ended the day of that damn storm. It just took five years for it to rot and fall apart."

It was the last thing I expected to hear. I told Sean that my Newark building had no vacancies. With the foreclosure crisis, many people were in need of affordable rental units.

"That's okay. I just need to get out of L.A. for a while . . . to someplace where I don't know anyone and clear my head a bit. Lorraine understands, she's got the kids," Sean said. He sounded like the weight of the world was on his shoulders. My mind was racing. I desperately wanted to help my friend, and then it clicked.

"Hey, what about Chicago? You know anyone there?" I asked.

"No," Sean replied. "That'd be perfect. You got a hookup there?"

In fact, I did. I have a buddy, Randy, in Chicago who is a real estate developer. I knew that he had many furnished units throughout Chicago, and I hoped he had a vacancy. "Call you back in five," I told Sean.

Randy took care of me and said that Sean could stay in one of his vacant units in the South Side neighborhood of Hyde Park.

"How much?" I asked Randy.

"Free. I just went through a divorce; I know how tough it can be. But do me a favor and pay for a cleaning lady when he leaves, and when I come visit you, I want you to give me and the kids a tour of the *CSI: NY* set."

"Absolutely," I said, laughing, "Thank you."

I called Sean back. "I hope you like deep-dish pizza," I said, trying to get him to laugh. My little joke was met with silence on the other end. "Man, I'm really sorry you're going through all this," I said.

"Yeah." Sean sighed. "I think I've about had *enough* for one person. But, hey, at least I've got my health, right?"

We both laughed at that.

"True, true," I agreed. **"The greatest wealth is health,"** I added, quoting the Roman poet Virgil. "You'll be fine. You can stay in the Chicago apartment as long as you

"The greatest wealth is health."

want. Listen, they're calling my flight, but I'll check in with you when I land and give you the details about the Chicago place."

"Sounds good," Sean said, "and hey, thanks, Hill."

"That's what friends are for, man. I love you, brother."

We signed off and I got on the plane.

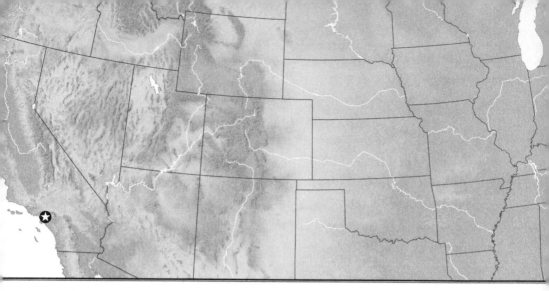

My Storm Clouds

"Sometimes God calms the storm. At other times, He calms the sailor. And sometimes He makes us swim."

—Unknown author

A few days later, I woke up and realized that I could barely swallow. There was discomfort in my throat, but nothing that I would characterize as severe pain, and my voice was slightly hoarse. Other than that, I felt all right. I couldn't understand why I was having so much difficulty swallowing. I didn't have a fever or a headache or anything else that might be indicative of a cold. I knew something was off, but I didn't know what. This feeling was very unfamiliar. I've always bragged to my friends that "I never get sick."

I may not be a doctor, but I've played one on TV enough times to have developed friendships with a number of actual doctors along the way. For the CBS television series *City of Angels*, I was cast in the role of Dr. Wesley Williams, a hotshot, egotistical, super-talented surgical resident.

To learn how to play a doctor authentically, I wanted to shadow a surgical resident, observing every aspect of his professional life as well as some aspects of his non-professional life. Every profession has its idiosyncrasies. Beyond the actual nuts and bolts of the job are little nuances that go along with it. Those are the things that actors try to embody in order to bring their characters to life.

The doctor that I was assigned to shadow was Dr. Romeo Walker, a resident trauma surgeon at the Martin Luther King Jr./Drew Medical Center in Los Angeles, more commonly known as King/Drew. The facility was named after MLK and Dr. Charles Drew, the late physician who is widely credited for developing the first working method for storing and transfusing plasma.

King/Drew was a prominent trauma-medicine teaching hospital. In fact, it was where the military sent its trauma teams to get practical experience because of the unusually high number of gunshot victims the hospital regularly received. For weeks, I followed Dr. Walker around as he diagnosed and treated his patients. The knowledge I gained from him was crucial to the success of my role. More important than that was the respect I developed for him and his expertise, and the friendship we've maintained through the years, long after the television show had been canceled and both of us had moved on to other jobs.

As luck would have it, Dr. Walker was working in Atlanta. I phoned him and explained that something strange was going on with my throat. He listened to the symptoms and told me that he wanted me to come in to see him. After examining me, Dr. Walker determined that I needed to see an endocrinologist.

In life, our intuition is often sparked in the most unexpected ways. Although my friend Dr. Walker wouldn't say what he suspected was wrong, I knew he was holding something back because the normal joking way we related to each other became much more matter-of-fact almost immediately.

Dr. Walker did not go to the most expensive medical school, but I would trust him over any doctor I know. It was so comforting to have him overseeing my situation. I knew he would make sure I was in the care of the best possible physicians. So often we rely on blind trust when dealing with professionals—doctors, lawyers, contractors, bankers, anyone with a degree, license, or fancy title. We assume that they know better than we do, and, without question, we give away our power. Though degrees can be a sign of the quality of an education, they are not necessarily indicative of the wealth of an education.

Without a doubt, Dr. Walker possessed not only a wealth of education but also a wealth of experience. And to me, after I had woken up hoarse and unable to swallow, that was better than money in the bank. Truth is there are plenty of people I went to Harvard with whom I wouldn't want as my doctor, lawyer, or anything else. **Just like money, a prestigious degree is simply a piece of paper;** it's all about how both are used. A friend of mine used to say jokingly, "Have you ever asked yourself, what if the pilot in the cockpit of the plane I'm in was the slacker? What if that guy was the class clown who barely got by?"

The endocrinologist ordered an ultrasound of my thyroid to determine if I had nodules and, if so, how many there were. Then, an ultrasound-guided fine-needle biopsy was performed to extract cells from the nodules to see if they were cancerous. Sixteen different needles stuck into my neck. I hate needles. After that, all there was left to do was wait for the pathology report.

Cancer has claimed the lives of many of my relatives, distant and close. My grandfather died of cancer when I was ten. My uncle died of cancer when I was in grad school at Harvard. My father died of cancer in 2000. Those were tremendous losses that I am not sure I will ever make sense of, no matter how hard I try. Nevertheless, I don't believe we are destined to follow in the footsteps of our parents or our forebears. **We have the**

> We have the will and the power to create our own destiny.

will and the power to create our own destiny. Science has proven that this is true, even when it comes to biology. **If we can't altogether change our physiological makeup, we can certainly change our lifestyle and how it influences that makeup.**

"At least I have my health," Sean had said to me when we'd last spoken. I suddenly envied his confidence. I'd been just as confident, assuming that I had my health as well. Now I wasn't so sure. I tried as hard as I could to stay positive, but it was difficult. I had five nodules in my thyroid, and I was waiting to hear if they were malignant. I was afraid.

One of my favorite sayings is that **"FEAR is an acronym for 'false evidence appearing real.'"** In this case, I had a sinking feeling the evidence coming back could be very real, just as it had been for the men in my family. Each of them still had so much more to offer the world and to offer me. I'd felt cheated out of the love I could have shared with them and the time I could have had with them.

Part of staying positive meant constantly reminding myself that I am not my father or my uncle or my grandfather or any other relative who had succumbed to cancer. I had to remind myself that I didn't even know if I had cancer. The future could hold anything. I had no idea how it was going to turn out. Nobody did. The only time we have is the time in which we are living. The now. The rest is yet to be discovered, something we move slowly but steadily toward with each breath that we take. I wanted to call friends and talk about it, but something stopped me. Truth is, I tried to fool myself; maybe if I didn't talk about my diagnosis, it wouldn't be real, just like people who don't open their bills when they don't have enough money to pay them. I needed to admit that ignoring the problem would never get me closer to resolving it.

So much of the culture we live in is fear based. We are all inundated with messages telling us what we can't do. Yet technology allows us to have amazing access to almost infinite amounts of information. This entices us with the false notion of being well informed, when in fact we are often misinformed. When acting out of fear, we use the information to convince ourselves of our inevitable failure or demise. **Fear is a way we sabotage our** dreams because we often forget that we are capable of achieving *whatever* **we want, of doing whatever we want.** We spend too much time living in the past, holding it up as proof. Proof of what isn't possible. Proof that we are not capable. Proof that we are doomed to the same fate as our parents.

As I sat in the doctor's waiting room feeling very much alone, I thought about how wealth and value are both entirely relative. **Cancer, an unwelcome visitor, can quickly remind us that each moment is more valuable than we thought and that true wealth does not simply mean having money in the bank.** Without one's health, the cash reserves are meaningless.

So often we take for granted that we can wake up and move through our day in a manner we're accustomed to, without interruptions from doctors' appointments, medicines, aches and pains, or surgery. It shouldn't, but sometimes it takes a wake-up call to make us realize that when we have our health, we are truly wealthy. And when we don't, no amount of money can make up for it. Yet many of us don't exercise regularly, eat fried and fatty foods—my personal weakness is the delicious "bear claw"—and still *expect* to be "healthy."

In my first book, *Letters to a Young Brother*, I wrote:

> Your wealth in life is made up of a number of components. . . . To give you an example, I'll break down the key wealth components in my life. The first key wealth component for me is good health. See, there's no way I can win in any area of my life unless I have the wealth of health as a starting point. . . . Without health, all of our great plans and future goals are meaningless.

And here I was, waiting for test results and not feeling very wealthy at all.

PART TWO

Treatment Options

treat \trēt\: therapy used to remedy a health problem

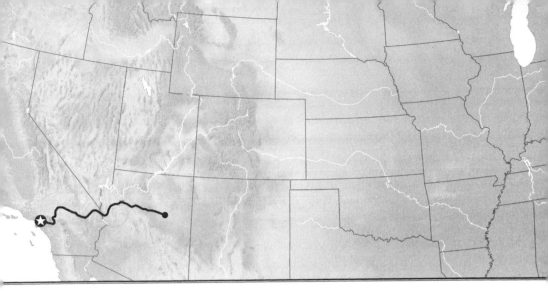

My North Star

"People take different roads seeking fulfillment
and happiness. Just because they're not on your
road doesn't mean they've gotten lost."
  —H. Jackson Brown Jr., American author

W hat happens when one of your worst nightmares comes true?

"Hill, we believe you have thyroid cancer. And it looks to be follicular—the worst kind," the endocrinologist said.

I had no idea what "follicular" meant, but it didn't sound very good. "What the hell is follicular, Doc?" I said as I tried to deflect the idea of even having cancer.

"It's the type of cancer you don't want to have," he responded.

"As opposed to the type of thyroid cancer you *want* to have?" I joked.

But the doctor was serious. "Okay, Hill, let's talk about next steps . . . your treatment options."

I had finished shooting the film in Atlanta, and I was back in L.A. The various papers my doctor sent were spread across my kitchen table. The pathology report indicated that I had a 50 to 75 percent risk of malignancy. Surgical removal of my thyroid was recommended. They wouldn't know until after my surgery if I would have to undergo any radioactive iodine treatment. If health is our greatest wealth, I felt entirely bankrupt when I read that pathology report. How could I have so quickly gone from being unreasonably happy to being unbelievably sad and feeling so vulnerable?

Two weeks before I'd seen that pathology report, if you'd have asked me to name one thing that I most wanted for myself, I would have said, "Not a thing, I'm all good." If you'd have asked me that right after I'd read the pathology report, I would have merely said, "To live." How easy it is to take our most precious gifts for granted.

My friend Tracey's new house was in Malibu, right on the beach. You could sit on her deck and stare at the ocean. Maybe that was why I drove there. Or maybe I drove to Tracey's house because I knew she would listen to what I was going through without adding any more stress or fear or anxiety to my situation. In a way, she'd been there herself. It had only been a year and a half since her husband, Jarrett, had died.

Jarrett had fallen ill one day. He had pancreatic cancer, the same cancer that took my father's life. Since pancreatic cancer is very difficult to detect, it is often discovered at a very late stage. Jarrett's illness progressed quickly and he died less than a month after his diagnosis. For a very long time, even though she was still breathing air, it seemed Tracey had died with him. She barely ate or went out. She rarely allowed friends to visit. At first we thought it was a normal reaction, given the situation. Once a year had passed, and she still hadn't gotten any better, we grew concerned and tried to get her to see a grief counselor. She'd refused and locked herself up in the tiny apartment that she and Jarrett had shared.

"The bat cave" was what Tracey used to call the place, because it got so little light. "See what happened when I trusted him to find us a place to live?" she would tease Jarrett. They adored each other, and the fact that they often struggled to make ends meet didn't seem to bother either of them at all.

I had been amazed by how transformative love had been in Tracey's life. Before she met Jarrett, she kept a wish list of achievements and acquisitions taped to the refrigerator door, but once they got together it was their list, not just hers.

After Jarrett passed, we discovered that they so fully supported each other in their desire to fulfill each wish on that list that they'd each taken out life insurance policies with unimaginably high benefit amounts so that on the off-chance anything happened to either of them, the other could still move forward with his or her plans. Tracey didn't care about the money. She would have given it all back to have the life she'd built with Jarrett. For more than a year, she stayed in that bat cave and hid from the world. And then one day, motivated by the simple realization that her life was passing her by, Tracey finally emerged. We picked up our friendship where it had left off.

When I walked in, I said hello and hugged Tracey, then I handed her a copy of the pathology report and headed straight out to the deck. It took about ten minutes for her to join me back there. By then I had already been transported to another world by the soothing sounds of the ocean.

"I've seen worse," she said breezily, before handing me back the report. I laughed, knowing I had, indeed, chosen the right person to talk to about what was going on.

"I'm scared," I admitted to Tracey.

"Me, too," she said, looking up at me. "But you can only take on what you can take on, then you've gotta let the rest go."

It sounded a little old-timey, like something my grandmother would say, and I told Tracey as much.

She responded with a laugh, "Oh! You're knocking my advice? Okay then, how about I throw some of that advice you gave me last year back in your face." I tried to think back to what I might have said to her, but I couldn't remember saying anything to her during the time after Jarrett's death that would have remotely seemed like advice.

"You don't remember, do you? It was the last time you came to the bat cave. You looked at me, you looked at the place, and you said, 'What a disaster.'"

I immediately felt ashamed of myself. I didn't remember doing that. Why would I have said something that insensitive to a woman who'd just lost her husband?

"I am so sorry. You must have thought I was a jerk," I muttered.

"Not at all," Tracey said. "Okay, maybe at first, but then you went on and talked about what that word 'disaster' means."

The instant she said that, it all came rushing back to me. Of course I remembered. I'd told her that the word "disaster" comes from the Latin prefix *dis,* which means "apart," and the Latin word *astrum*, which means "star." Centuries ago, when something went wrong in a person's life, it was blamed on the stars. **In Italian the word *disastro* means "unfavorable to one's stars."**

"Yeah, you explained all of that to me," Tracey recalled, "but do you remember what you said afterward?"

I shook my head; I really didn't.

"You said, '**Don't lose your North Star.**'"

For centuries, throughout the world, people looked toward the North Star for direction. The North Star enabled them to position themselves. Without it, they were lost. It was disastrous. Nighttime shipwrecks were always called disasters because people felt that the errant ship's captain must have lost his direction by losing the North Star. I remembered telling Tracey that, because I could see that she was allowing herself to be engulfed by darkness. **I wanted her to know that she could look into that darkness, the same way so many people on journeys have looked into the night sky, and find the light they needed to guide them to their destination.**

"Hill," she said softly, "don't lose *your* North Star."

I've never really been good with astronomy. I still don't understand why some stars reveal themselves on some nights and allow the sky to remain black on others. My former girlfriend, Nichole, loved stargazing. I admired her ability to recognize and name all of the constellations. She taught me how to use the Little Dipper to find Polaris, another name for the North Star.

"And what's that one called?" I asked Nichole one night as we were walking along the Georgetown Canal in Washington, D.C., where she lived. "It looks like a shooting star." The star I was pointing to was shining extra brightly, and it seemed to be moving, pulling the other stars along in its wake.

Nichole shot me a sarcastic look. "Hill, that's not a star. It's an airplane."

How do we know what our North Star is? Is it something *inside* of us, like an emotion, a certain knowingness? Or is it something *outside* of us, like a person or a profession? Actually, it's a delicate balance of both, the intersection of passion and purpose with profession, as well as love and happiness in connecting with a particular person. All I know is that **when you do find your North Star, all the other elements in the universe seem to magically align, and a path suddenly becomes apparent.** The tricky part is in understanding that even though you're walking a path, it isn't a straight line from here to there. The destination is ever changing. And more important, just because we may have identified our North Star, following it is never easy. What we must foster is the ability to face our fears and take risks. If we don't, we might end up secretly wondering, What if?

It was getting late, and as I was preparing to leave, Tracey took my hand and said, "When I was at my lowest, you told me this simple truth: **Life is for living, and living requires risk taking.** So, Hill, follow your own advice and *live*!

Life is for living, and living requires risk taking.

"You've got to take yourself back to the beginning," she said, referring to her own Wealth Cure that she'd taken to move from despair and pessimism to prosperity and optimism. "You've got to go to the very core of your faith, past the time you began to feel insecure and doubt yourself, all the way to the time before you even knew what doubt was. **True wealth is a balance of financial health and the spiritual aspects of life.**"

Like many of the men in my family, I've never been good at admitting my fears and insecurities, let alone searching for when and how those doubts started. My self-protective reaction was "Come on, I'm fine." Yet inside I knew Tracey was right. I needed to give myself permission to be vulnerable and engage in self-exploration that would be uncomfortable to me. Taking an honest look in the mirror is a much more courageous way to live than with the barricades and false bravado that I had become used to presenting.

Tracey and I discussed the fact that at the core of true wealth is spiritual wealth. **You can't have or be able to appreciate and benefit from physical wealth, emotional wealth, or financial wealth if you are spiritually bankrupt.**

> ❧
> You can't have or be able to appreciate and benefit from physical wealth, emotional wealth, or financial wealth if you are spiritually bankrupt.
> ❧

Despite being the recipient of Jarrett's large life insurance policy, Tracey felt bankrupt after he died. "I'd lost my faith, Hill. It didn't matter how much money I had. I didn't have true wealth, even if there was a lot of money in the bank, because I was devastated over losing him."

Tracey told me she realized that whenever there is a crisis, we have to start at zero. In crisis, we have strip our life to its barest essentials in every way possible, and the lessons learned in that process of removal will guide us when we begin to reassemble our lives.

"So what you're saying is that when you rebuild your—," I started to say, and then she cut me off.

"Reassemble," she corrected, "not rebuild. They are two different words. 'Rebuild' sounds too much like external work. Perhaps, even, like building a façade. Maybe it's just all in my mind, but 'reassemble' sounds much more real. As though you're internally shifting things around to suit you better for this time in your life's journey. And you have to take time away from your normal routine to give yourself adequate space to reassemble."

It has been said that **divine timing is the best**, and I have to agree, because the news in my pathology report was given to me at the most opportune time. Tracey thought that I should take time away from my normal routine, and she was right. Since I had just finished shooting *For Colored Girls* . . . , I was in a position to clear my schedule, to cancel whatever needed to be canceled, and to take some time off. I had nowhere to be, nothing specific to do. My time was my own, which was new to me.

What would I do? I could travel, but where to? I'd just been down South. . . . I could go see Sean in Chicago.

I had spoken to him again recently, and he had explained why he and Lorraine were splitting up—largely due to irresolvable conflicts over money. The last straw was when he discovered that she had been hiding purchases from him and trying to intercept the credit card bills so he didn't see them when they arrived.

Before Sean, Lorraine, and their kids were displaced by Hurricane Katrina, Sean's job kept him so busy that they didn't really spend a lot of day-to-day time together as a family. To make up for that, they'd take two big vacations every year. Sometimes he and Lorraine would even pull the kids out of school for a week for those trips, because it was often the only way they could schedule them.

"That's why we were at Disney World when the storm hit," Sean had told me. "Spending time together as a family is what saved us from Katrina. But I couldn't save my marriage, Hill. I couldn't."

In the aftermath of the devastation caused by Katrina, Sean's priorities changed. He spent more time with his kids and scaled back his freelance work schedule. He wouldn't be able to buy as many games and toys for his kids or a new car every few years or support his wife's shopping habit to the same extent—but he would be able to help his children with their homework and they could dine together most nights.

Lorraine was happy to have Sean home more but not about the overall reduction in family income. Over time, she became increasingly unhappy. She had gotten used to the sizable paychecks. In L.A., where people are much more into conspicuous consumption than in New Orleans, Lorraine felt the cutbacks even more keenly. She wanted designer clothing for the kids, so they'd fit in at school. She wanted them to have private violin and horseback-riding lessons. She wanted to go to Maui, because two of her new best friends were going with their families. Lorraine allowed herself be influenced by the group of people she had started hanging with, and it caused a huge rift in their marriage. At some point they simply stopped communicating. To be sure, two people make up a relationship, and Sean was equally responsible for their communication breakdown. He refused to see a marriage counselor, and anger, egos, and old, unresolved baggage drove a wedge between them.

There was no doubt Sean and Lorraine had some serious decisions to make, and so did I. Oftentimes it's easier to focus on other people's problems when you are reluctant to face your own. My medical condition was weighing heavy on my mind. And there wasn't really a decision to be made. I had to have my thyroid removed. I did some research and found a great surgeon to do the procedure, and my surgery was scheduled. All I had to do now was wait for two weeks.

I can't stand hospitals. And I was dreading that day, which would be the first time I would go under the knife and spend even a night in a hospital. Ironically, I had performed plenty of surgeries *playing* a doctor, but this was real. I shook my head and thought, Cancer . . . really? I'm not going anywhere. I'm just gonna hole up in my place and wait for my surgery day.

And then, like some sort of sign, the words from *On the Road*, a book I hadn't even thought about since college, popped into my head.

"Why think about that," Jack Kerouac wrote, "when all the golden land's ahead of you and all the kinds of unforeseen events wait lurking to surprise you and make you glad you're alive to see?"

Taking a road trip through the heartland of our great country had always been a dream of mine. One problem, I didn't feel like driving thousands of miles, by myself. But what if, instead, I took a train from Los Angeles to Chicago? That might be just what I needed.

I immediately called Amtrak, checked the schedule, and booked my trip. Maybe it would give me time to sort out my own priorities. Certainly I needed to get some things straight in my own life. I needed my own Wealth Cure.

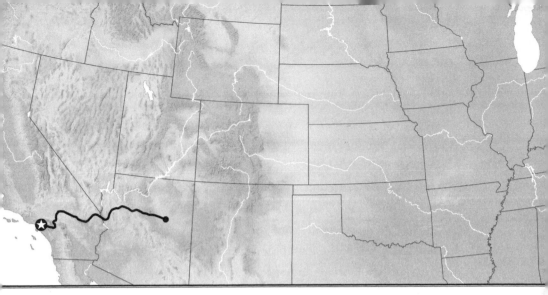

BEGINNING THE JOURNEY

"It has never been, and never will be easy work! But the road that is built in hope is more pleasant to the traveler than the road built in despair, even though they both lead to the same destination."

—Marion Zimmer Bradley, American author

"**M**ind if I join you there in Chicago?" I asked when Sean picked up. "Man, are you kidding? I'd love the company. When does your flight get in?" Sean seemed confused when I explained to him I was taking the train.

"Dang, how long is that gonna take?"

"I'm not sure exactly. Two nights and three days . . . I didn't really look at what time I get in."

"Is everything okay, Hill?" Sean asked.

It didn't seem right to tell somebody, especially a close friend, over the telephone that you most likely have cancer. I could tell that despite my assurances, he didn't believe that everything was all right. I'll tell him in Chicago, I thought, to justify not being completely truthful. Sean made me promise to check in with him.

When I told Tracey about my plan to take the train more than halfway across the country, she was less than impressed. "Seriously, a train . . . ?" she'd asked, "Why would you spend three days on a train when you can fly there in a little over three hours? If you really want to have a 'spiritual experience,' why not take the bus, or better yet, hitchhike?"

"Very funny. But I already got my ticket," I said, laughing. To me, the idea of riding the train from L.A. to Chicago was thrilling, but Tracey's point was well taken. Flying was certainly the fastest and easiest way to get there.

"I want to see and feel the country, take in the landscape, and not just look down on it from thirty-five thousand feet, and I can choose to spend three days of my life any way I want," I teased back, and then I got a little serious. "Plus, I have to sort some things out."

"Aww, Hill, this is so romantic . . . except you're alone." She sighed as we pulled into Union Station in downtown Los Angeles. "Maybe you'll meet somebody and fall in love, like in one of those old black-and-white movies. People always fall in love on trains."

I looked at her, shook my head, and grabbed my luggage. It was so great to have my friend back. I was glad that she'd weathered the storm.

"Oh," she said, as I was about to say good-bye. "I almost forgot." She turned around, picked up a manila envelope from the back seat and handed it to me. "This is information about Mastermind Circles. It really turned things around for me. Promise me you'll at least read through it and think about doing it."

I took the envelope from her. "Sure thing," I said. "I'll call you when I arrive."

By taking this train trip, I was hoping to implement my own Wealth Cure along the way. I wanted to return to the foundation of my spiritual wealth to figure out how best to respond to this health challenge facing me. Also, I wanted to sort out my priorities. In a way, that's exactly what Sean was doing in Chicago. He was using the apartment as a safe space, a place where he could just think and regroup after his breakup with Lorraine.

I suppose Tracey had been doing that, too, during the year after Jarrett died. It was understandable, but we were all worried when she all but stopped speaking to our circle of friends. Was it because we brought back too many difficult memories of Jarrett and their time together?

"Yes and no," she had told me in the car. "It wasn't that I couldn't move forward with you guys. It was that I couldn't move forward in the way that I wanted to. It'll make more sense to you when you read the packet."

I'd reserved a Superliner Bedroom on Amtrak's Southwest Chief, a comfortable room with a foldout couch that faced a huge window. I settled into the room, took off my shoes, and turned the couch into a bed. I put my head on the pillow, stretched out my legs, and looked out my window as Los Angeles rumbled by. As the Southwest Chief got up to speed, the ride settled into a nice, soothing sway. It was all so relaxing, exactly what I needed as I sought to examine and rearrange my life.

Although my upcoming surgery and its many possible complications concerned me, I knew that worrying or obsessing over an event that was out of my hands was pointless. As my journey began, I chose to clear my mind and focus on the task at hand . . . getting right with my own Wealth Cure.

When I woke up at dawn, my face warm from the light streaming through that huge picture window, we had already passed by the Grand Canyon and were approaching Winslow, Arizona. I'll never forget the first time I stood on the edge of the Grand Canyon and looked down. It was breathtaking—the size, the depth, the colors. The Grand Canyon is almost indescribable, as if nature were sending a message that anything is possible.

I was famished, so I got up, threw on some clothes, and walked to the dining car for breakfast. It was more like a restaurant, with tablecloths and formal seating for which reservations were recommended. Luckily, I was able to grab a table. I sat there writing in my journal. After that, I tried reading a newspaper with much difficulty. I didn't want to immerse myself in the reality of the outside world. I enjoyed the feeling of being incubated on that train, of just staring as the world floated by like a moving mural.

I was sitting there just looking around, people watching and glancing out of the windows on either side of the car, when I noticed a young man seated at one of the other tables. He seemed to do a double take when he saw me, and I wondered if he was someone I'd met through work, or if he merely recognized me from *CSI: NY*. I nodded to the young man and simply fixed my gaze on the window.

The Southwest region of the United States is the home of the four major deserts in North America—the Mojave, the Colorado, the Chihuahuan, the Sonoran.

Deserts are inhospitable areas to growth and development. They are arid, receive a negligible amount of precipitation, and can only support a limited range of vegetation and wildlife. This is what makes the communities in the Southwest both fascinating and appealing to me.

When people migrated to the Southwest, they envisioned the world they wanted to live in and created it. They found ways to irrigate places where there was no water. They transplanted trees and designed beautiful landscapes. When that was not possible, they used rocks and the vegetation native to the area, a small but impressive selection of succulents that can survive in harsh conditions.

After breakfast, I went back to my room and continued to marvel at the beauty just outside my window. We were now in New Mexico, approaching Albuquerque. **So many cities in the Southwest began as just a vision or an idea and had to be carefully and creatively designed. And with courage, discipline, and perseverance, the vision was manifested into reality. All of us have the ability to do that in our own lives,** but most of us do not take the time or apply careful thought to create the workable blueprint that we want to execute.

During my cross-country trip, I hoped to take a look in the mirror, refine my thinking, and create my own blueprint.

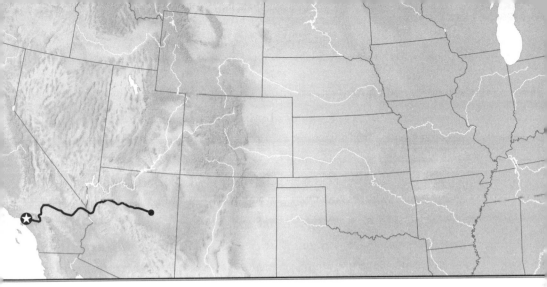

CREATE A BLUEPRINT
FOR A WEALTH CURE

"You've got to start with a plan. When I was in
school, I took architectural drafting and that
taught me that everything starts with a plan.
The biggest buildings in the world start with
a plan."

—Ice Cube, American rapper, actor,
screenwriter, film director, and producer

We all have our own ideas about what it is to be wealthy. For some
people, it means being able to send their kids to Ivy League colleges. For others, it's owning a large residence and a vacation home or
having a million dollars in the bank on the day they retire. For some, it
could be paying off a car loan or a mortgage.

I want to shake up our ideas about external wealth and help create a
blueprint for true wealth—which has nothing to do with which restaurants

we dine in or whether we take our vacation in Vienna or Orlando. **True wealth is having our life balanced and organized so we are free to pursue any dream or happiness.**

A while back, I was invited to the premiere of a fascinating documentary by Tom Shadyac, *I Am*. Shadyac was the director of many films, including *Evan Almighty* and *Ace Ventura*. Then, at the height of his career, he had a horrific cycling accident. He recovered physically but suffered from persistent concussion syndrome, which caused him to feel a wish for death. Shadyac fell into a deep depression and isolated himself from friends and family. He stopped working. Eventually he gave up his mansions and private plane and moved into a trailer park. It was an upscale trailer park by the beach, but it was still a far cry from the gated mansion he'd been living in to that point (only in Hollywood can a trailer be worth more than a million dollars).

His documentary examined his realization that his immense wealth and possessions had not made him happy. Now living a much simpler existence he has a renewed interest in work and in life. Of course, most of us don't have a private plane to give up, but we can still learn from Shadyac's journey. It's obvious he is more content without all the material trappings. Tom Shadyac created his own Wealth Cure by reprioritizing his life.

My grandmother taught me to live within my means. But certainly, at times, buying a piece of property or a nice car has its appeal. Yet I found that there is nothing like cancer to help you sort out your priorities. The love of family and good friends, peace of mind, and time to relax and unwind were way at the top of the list. My possessions were near the bottom. It's not that I was going to stop striving to be successful in my career, but maybe I needed to focus more on what I wanted out of life, as opposed to how I wanted to spend my paychecks.

You don't have to experience a horrible accident or be diagnosed with cancer to undergo the Wealth Cure. Initially, all it takes is self-examination. If you're someone who has always had to have the latest technology, from iPhone to iPad to seventy-three-inch flat-screen HDTV, think about why you need to run out and buy the newest model. Does it really make a difference? If you spot a Birkin handbag in *Vogue*, do you have to blow most of your take-home pay on a pricey knockoff? If so, what does that say about your priorities?

Money can be the source of a lot of worry. Not having enough money to meet basic needs is incredibly stressful. Once we do have enough to meet our basic needs—food, shelter, clothing—then how much more do we need in order to be happy? Is it the three million that a third of Americans said they needed to feel rich? How much is enough? Are money and happiness truly entwined, or do they exist outside of each other?

People are happier if they *earn* their own money.

Studies have shown that earning their own money makes people happier than winning the lottery. I was fascinated to see a recent report from Princeton's Woodrow Wilson School that put a monetary benchmark on happiness. The study concluded that at annual earnings of $75,000, people were generally happy with their situation. The farther below that income people went on the monetary scale, the less happy they were. For instance, if you earned $35,000, you were supposedly only about half as happy as those at the $75,000 level.

The findings didn't stop there. The study, by economist Angus Deaton and psychologist Daniel Kahneman, polled 450,000 Americans. The results showed two different types of happiness: mood or emotional well-being and a sense that life on the whole was going well. Those who earned $75,000 or more did not see any improvement in overall mood, but the more a person earned over the baseline, the more he or she felt that life was going as planned and was on target.

The study also reported that 85 percent of Americans felt happy, while 40 percent felt stressed. Apparently, stress and happiness are not mutually exclusive. The $75,000 salary came into play most when other extenuating factors were present, such as being divorced or having a chronic health issue like asthma. People earning less than the baseline felt these problems more acutely than did adults who earned more.

Does this mean that if you are earning less than $75,000 a year, you should forget about trying to be happy? Absolutely not. Happiness is an individual choice, and studies do not take into account individual differences. You are not defined by your salary. You might earn less than $75,000 per year, but if you're adept at saving, you could eventually wind up with more in the bank than someone making twice that amount.

Americans today are less satisfied with life than their counterparts in the 1950s, even though we earn two times more when incomes are adjusted for inflation. I believe that much of this dissatisfaction comes from being constantly told what we should look like, own, and desire.

Daniel Gilbert, a Harvard psychology professor and the author of *Stumbling on Happiness*, says "Research reveals that memory is less like a collection of photographs than it is like a collection of impressionist paintings rendered by an artist who takes considerable license with his subject." In other words, the feeling of newness of a fancy watch wears off in a few weeks, and the high from purchasing a top-of-the-line computer quickly evaporates as soon as the first virus invades it.

I have heard several friends who are parents comment that girls in the 1960s grew up owning one Barbie, if they were lucky. Nowadays, even three-year-olds have multiple Barbies, not to mention all of the accoutrements. When I go to the home of one of my friends with daughters, you would swear the dolls were multiplying overnight, like rabbits. So were the little girls of the '60s miserable because they only owned one with limited accessories? Not at all. That was the norm, just as it became the norm in the 2000s to own five, ten, fifteen dolls complete with pink plastic cars and dream townhouses. It's all a matter of expectation and, of course, keeping up with the Jones'.

Another study, reported by *The Washington Post*, was conducted by Gallop in 2005 and 2006 and included 136,000 people in 132 countries. People all over the world, in rural areas as well as huge cities, were asked about the sources of their happiness. Overall, people felt good if they compared positively with their neighbors in terms of wealth. Feeling that they were doing just about as well economically as people who lived in their communities was a big indicator of happiness. Yet positive emotions were affected much more by social interactions and job fulfillment than by how much actual money a person had—which demonstrates that the Wealth Cure is backed up by real science.

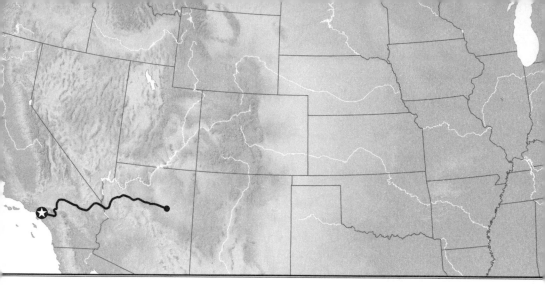

How High Is the Cost
of Being You?

"Don't tell me where your priorities are. Show
me where you spend your money and I'll tell
you what they are."

—James W. Frick

M oney is the biggest stress inducer in the lives of Americans. We
worry more about money than our marriages, our health,
and our kids. When we are trapped in a vicious cycle of spending and
debt, our cortisol and stress levels build to unimaginable proportions,
which in turn can lead to patterns of
overindulgence—with food, alcohol, and other substances—that increase our stress and harm our
health even more. Debt induces the
same hormone response we have

when we are physically trapped. **You can't be free if the cost of being you is too high.**

Being in debt is like being physically unhealthy—they both exact a toll on us. They both excise a cost on our lives. I had my own experience with stressful debt a while back. A few years ago, I bought a $350,000 lottery ticket in the form of an investment in a high-tech start-up. Keep in mind that at the time of this investment I was not debt free. I had mortgage debt for my home as well as a great deal of debt in noncommercial real estate investments. The business I invested in was supposed to become the equivalent in online advertising to what Google is to search engines. With this investment, I was going to hit it big! As Dave Chappelle says, "I was gonna be rich, B****!" Within one year, it tanked—not because of the technology or the patent; I had done my research, and they were solid. Actually it tanked because the CEO fell out with the COO, the founder left, and subsequently, people didn't want to work with them any more. The company declared bankruptcy, and within one year, my "sure thing" investment was entirely gone. Three hundred and fifty thousand dollars—gone! "Poof." "Up in smoke." I felt like an idiot. How many times had I been taught to not get sucked into a get-rich-quick scheme? I could have paid off my house—I can feel my cortisol levels rising just writing about it now! I'm still recovering financially from that setback, and I learned my lesson about making risky investments. I remember my grandmother always telling me, "If it seems too good to be true, then it probably is!" Instead of freeing myself from debts I already had, I made the mistake of chasing more.

Certainly, it is possible to feel free, even when it may seem that you are physically stuck. Nelson Mandela stated that even though he was in Robben Island Prison for twenty-seven years, he felt free spiritually. If an incarcerated man can feel free, then why can't we? How can we begin to dismantle the web that has us stuck?

First and foremost, our lifestyles cost too much! In order to become unstuck, we must cure ourselves of this crushing cycle of spending and debt. A sense of freedom is inextricably linked to happiness. Being stuck in an unrewarding job and afraid to make a move because of crushing debt can be soul destroying. Feeling trapped by a never-ending cycle of debt, making only the minimum payments every month, and seeing the balance rack up higher and higher through accruing interest, are other crushing stresses. A recent poll revealed almost a third of Americans say they would need $3 million in the bank to feel as if they were rich. That's a huge sum of cash and nearly impossible for most of us to attain.

So many of us want to be "rich" by having a lot of money—yet there is a much easier way to have true and lasting wealth. Simply shift our value system. **If the cost of being you is too high—if the spending has you feeling trapped so that you can't see a way out—then you aren't free, and you can't lead a fulfilled existence.** You need to implement your own Wealth Cure in order to be free and fulfilled—what I call being "unreasonably happy."

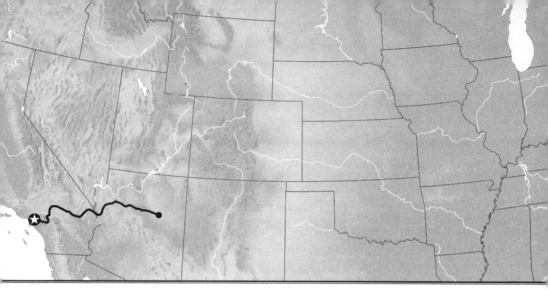

Achieving Unreasonable Happiness

"It isn't what you have, or who you are, or where
you are, or what you are doing that makes you
happy or unhappy. It is what you think about."
—Dale Carnegie, American lecturer, author

I'm a wordmonger. I love learning about the etymology of words. As I began unpacking the clothes I needed for the next two days on the train, I wasn't in a very good mood, but I started thinking about two words that at first glance seem very similar. "Happening" and "happiness" have similar roots and spellings. In many ways, the words are twins separated at birth. Our challenge as individuals is to bring them back together: What's *happening* in our lives right now that can bring us *happiness*?

We decide what attitude we bring to any situation. Will we decide to be happy right now? Or will we continue being vaguely dissatisfied, without doing anything about it? Buddha said, "All that we are is the result of what we have thought." I certainly wasn't happy at that moment, and I didn't think any amount of positive thinking was going to change that. I needed an attitude adjustment.

I strive to be unreasonably happy because I feel that it's every person's right to aim for that high level of personal fulfillment. I want you to be more than happy. I want you to be *unreasonably* happy—satisfied and fulfilled beyond reasonable expectations. We *all* can obtain happiness. The questions each of us must answer are, What does unreasonable happiness look like for me? And how do I get there?

One of the ways to create a Wealth Cure is to examine our lives and list our *Wealth Factors*—those elements of life that make us happy. I'm not talking about things that produce an ephemeral good feeling, like a pair of shoes or a nice glass of wine in a restaurant. Instead, we need to identify what provides us with a deep, enduring sense of well-being. Which aspects of our existence that are essential to our self-worth and pursuit of happiness? Writing out a Wealth Factor list can be helpful:

1. **Define happiness for you and you alone.** Make sure that these are things that truly make you happy—not things that you think you *should* like. The ideas embraced by society, your parents, children, spouse or partner, friends, minister, teacher, or boss about what you *should* want do not come into play here. Do not write "spending more time with Jake" if you don't enjoy being around your brother-in-law Jake. Instead, your Wealth Factors have to be your private list of what *you* need to be happy. Include only those things *you* want as a focal point of your life.

2. **Don't make judgments about anything on your list.** Quite often we judge the things we find pleasing as "not acceptable" or "not possible." Even though we know we do like or admire something, we are not willing to admit it to anyone, not even ourselves. How you came to like the things that you do

doesn't matter. It's where you are, and who you are. Be honest with yourself in making this list.

A sample Wealth Factor list might include:

1. Time to take my kids to watch football games
2. More family time at home with TVs, computers, and video games turned off
3. A date night with my partner once a month
4. Fulfilling sex with my partner
5. A girls' or fellas' night out once a month
6. Recognition and/or a promotion at work
7. Time to do creative activities such as painting, writing, or playing guitar
8. Volunteer work
9. Publication of my novel

And so on. The point is that the list is entirely personal; there is no magic number, only you can create your list of Wealth Factors.

Now, how do we go about incorporating and achieving these Wealth Factors in our daily lives? This might involve some negotiation with a partner, spouse, coworker, or boss. The important thing right now is to identify your Wealth Factors and realize that you can have true wealth with or without money. **True wealth isn't the value of your bank account but the value of the items you have in your life account.** Those are the things worth spending on, investing in, and putting your energy toward.

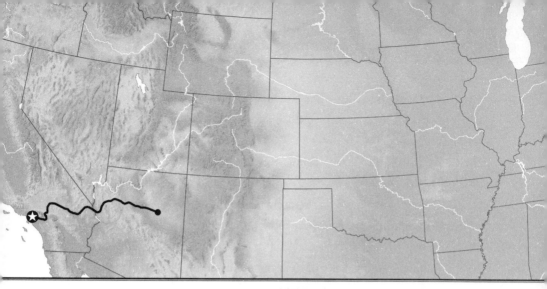

MONEY IS ENERGY

"Whoever desires, is always poor."
—Claudius Claudianus, Roman poet

Money, simply put, is energy. If we shift our perspective to view money as energy, then we will be able to keep money in its proper place. If we truly relate to money as energy, then we will see it as neither good nor bad. In that way money is just like light. In our homes, we *want* light. Light is extremely useful. But when we want to sleep, it is not useful to us at all, so we don't use it. Yet there is comfort in knowing that, in an emergency, we can flick a switch and have light again. We can view money as a source to be used when we *want* or *need* it. It is not something that is inherently good and needs to be pursued in and of itself. Like light energy. Sometimes money is useful, and knowing the resource is at our disposal reduces stress in our lives.

There was a time in my life when I would walk with a little more spring in my step if I had a few crisp C-notes in my pocket. Is that a very spiritual or enlightened way of being? No, but I'm being honest. Somehow those dead presidents can imbue a life force to those who hold them. With plenty of cash in our wallets, we feel more confident, stronger, more virile. When I was in the cast of the film *He Got Game*, director Spike Lee challenged some of the actors to ad-lib on camera how our characters would feel on a basketball court. One of my favorite improvised lines of my entire career came to me in that moment. I had my character Booger say, "I feel handsome when I'm on the court playing ball."

Many of us feel more handsome when we have money, too. Give any man a stack of hundreds, regardless of how wealthy he is, and that knot will make *him* feel more attractive and confident. Some guys say they even like the smell of new bills. **But it isn't about the money itself; it's about the energy that money represents.**

Wouldn't it be incredible to experience that same energy without needing a fat wallet or a money-filled purse? The truth is, it is possible. First we have to redefine wealth. True wealth is not a list of material assets. It's not having a Rolex, Bentley, or Louis Vuitton bags. True wealth is being able to meet the criteria for most of our personal Wealth Factors as well as feeling that our other life goals are within reach. Being healthy is definitely way up there on my list of Wealth Factors. That concept was driven home to me when I was confronted with the possibility of having thyroid cancer. Without health, all the money in the world doesn't do us a bit of good or make us happy.

Having a positive self-image is another factor in true wealth. Often we waste an enormous amount of energy dealing with baggage from the past—energy that could be put to use in building our future. There is simply no way to be happy if an internal voice is always running us down. Or if we rely on having money in our pockets to lift us up.

My friend Janice, a superbly intelligent and attractive media consultant, had to address this issue in her life. Her mother had been a very critical person, and as a little girl Janice didn't escape her barbs. Every time that she looked in the mirror, she heard her mother's voice carping at her for her unruly curls or her "stupid" decisions. Only after some years in therapy and realizing her own self-worth was Janice able to overcome her negative mental image and accept that she was extremely accomplished and interesting. By working through these issues, she increased her own true wealth exponentially. As a side benefit, her career took off once she became more self-confident.

You may not have a hypercritical mom like Janice's, but you still might get down on yourself from time to time, unnecessarily. An honest evaluation of your strengths and weaknesses is fine, but habitual self-criticism does not lead to true wealth. You need all of your positive energy focused upon creating real wealth in your life.

My accountant has an interesting take on money as a driver of income. A few years ago, I told her that I had found a home that I wanted to buy. It was in a great neighborhood and school district, was a lovely piece of property, and a fantastic value, but the price was a little bit higher than what I had expected to spend. She listened carefully and then told me that the *value* of the property was more important than the price of the house, because it wasn't ludicrously overpriced or out of my budget range. She encouraged me to buy the house because it had so many positive attributes that it could only increase in value over time. This wasn't a house I was planning to flip. I wanted to stay in it for a number of years. I wound up buying the property and have never regretted it. Not only is it a comfortable and lovely residence, but it has steadily increased in value as well.

My accountant said that in her experience individuals who pushed themselves to strive to afford legitimate expenses—real worth in a home, education, or saving for their children—wound up finding that their own income increased to meet the new demand. In my case, this turned out to be absolutely true.

The demand for value drives income.

While I sat in my cabin writing about the abstract idea of money as energy, I remembered an e-mail from my cousin Reverend Michael Bernard Beckwith. I pulled it up on my laptop. Not so coincidentally, he had sent it the day before tax day.

April 14, 2010

Dear Hill,

I've been hearing a lot of fear thoughts on the news lately about the "M" word. You guessed it. Money. I'd like to address this.

Generally speaking, when people use words like "prosperity" and "affluence" they are polite substitutes for "money." Somehow in American society it is considered indelicate, impolite, to discuss money in a direct way with anyone other than your banker, broker, accountant, or employer!

Such is the CHARGE we have around money.

What I want to remind you of is that money represents ENERGY. When we give money to someone for a service, or product, it is an exchange of energy. Money is a promissory note in that it is an agreement that money has been, or will be exchanged.

Isn't this a far more expansive view than "spending" money? When we spend something, it eventually runs out. It becomes spent.

Conversely, when we circulate energy it keeps coming back to us, as in the truism, "What goes around comes around." This is a simple, accurate description of the Law of Circulation.

Money itself is neither good nor bad; it is neutral. Money has the meaning that we invest in it.

For example, in what state of mind do you pay your bills? When bills arrive in your mailbox, do you say, "Oh, no! How am I going to pay all these bills?" How different it would be if you said instead: **"These bills represent an ABUNDANCE of the goods and services I have received to enhance my life. Now I have the BLESS-ING of circulating the energy of money in exchange for them."**

That was a lot of words, but you get the idea that when you respond in such a feeling-tone, you shift your relationship to money.

Through skillful means, we can come into a spiritual, mental, and emotional comfort zone about true abundance. I wanted to remind you today, that it is possible. **Remember to practice gratitude.** Life is good!

Peace & Blessings,
Michael Bernard Beckwith
Founder & Spiritual Director,
Agape International Spiritual Center

Wow. Having received that e-mail the day before tax day, how powerful would it have been for me to shift my relationship with money by viewing it a blessing to be able to write a big tax check to the IRS? So much around us tells us to resent paying property taxes. But Rev. Beckwith suggests that we can circulate and empower our use of money by being grateful for being able to circulate it. Sitting and re-reading this email reminded me of a lesson my grandmother taught me when we were in church and the collection plate passed. "A closed hand isn't open to receive," she would say. Yet another wise take on money in circulation as energy. So this is going to be hard, but the next time I write a check to the IRS, I will do it with gratitude. Perhaps having to pay a lot of taxes really is a blessing because that means I earned a lot. I need an attitude of gratitude when any bill arrives. That will be one of the challenges for me in my journey toward a Wealth Cure.

Building true wealth is an individual journey. Much like embarking on a train trip, we all start where we are right now, and we have a desired destination. The more clarity we have about where we're starting from, and where we want to go, the higher the likelihood that we will arrive at our desired end point.

Sadly, around issues of money, most of us board the train without really knowing where it is headed. We *hope* that it will get us to where we want to go and, moreover, that the conductor will wake us up and let us know when we've arrived. Some of us stay on the train too long, way past our stop. We often stay in relationships, jobs, debt, and fear for far too long.

We need a plan—we need to know where we are starting from, where we are headed, and the resources we will need for the journey. We also need to be willing to learn new information and make creative, courageous new choices while we are on the train. Sometimes we may realize that we want to get off the train for a while and explore a new place. Or choose a new destination based on new input, ideas, and information that came into the mainframe that is our brain. But even taking into account shifts in the journey, we must start out with a very clear idea of where we want to wind up, and a well-designed plan to get there.

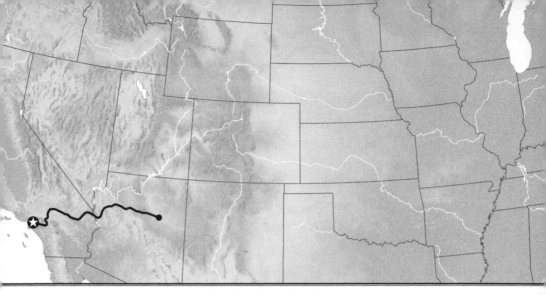

BUILDING A VALUABLE
FINANCIAL FRAMEWORK

"Faber est suae quisque fortunae." (Every man
is the artisan of his own fortune.)
—Appius Claudius Caecus,
Ancient Roman politician

H ave you ever toured the Bureau of Printing and Engraving in Washington, D.C., or in Fort Worth, Texas? It's a fascinating place.
After seeing how money is made, I am always impressed by the fact that
it's all just paper. On the tour, you view millions of dollars literally rolling off the presses. There are about $405 billion total in circulation. **It's
ironic that people often associate money with power, because the
more money a country prints, the more its value decreases. Real power
rests in things that *increase* in value as more is created—such as happiness, good health, a deepening relationship with God, laughter, and
a divine view of ourselves.** There is, however, one extremely valuable

resource that we can't make more of—time. So, how we spend our time and what we spend our time pursuing is critical. Money, that thing most of us spend time chasing, that we die for, that some of us go to prison over—is really just paper.

Who gives this paper its value? We do. Just as European traders valued salt in the 1600s, Native Americans valued beads in the 1400s, and ancient Egyptians used weights and measures to signify the value of goods, today, we give paper notes their value. **Perhaps in today's world we are finding that money isn't able to hold the value we are giving it.** What if we decided to value something else—something more valueable? What if we decided to value the items on our Wealth Factor list? By doing this, we take control of our lives, and we increase our chances of being unreasonably happy right now—not at some distant point in the future.

When we decide to live by our own Wealth Factors, we become the active architects of our own lives. We can actually use the tools and resources at our disposal to build whatever life we want.

One of the most important things we can do to take control of our own financial situation and put money in

> When we decide to live by our own Wealth Factors, we become the active architects of our own lives.

its proper place is to create a personal budget. I'll admit that at first the idea of keeping track of every cent you spend may seem like as much fun as a trip to the dentist's office. But once you get the swing of it, it's not as onerous as it seems. In fact, after you start keeping a detailed record of what you spend, you might find it very empowering to know exactly where your hard-earned green is going.

First of all, it's a good idea to make a chart. I suggest using the one below; you can personalize it any way you like, but this is a starting point:

Monthly Bills												
	Jan	Feb	Mar	Apr	May	Jun	Jul	Aug	Sept	Oct	Nov	Dec
Rent/Mortgage												
Car Payment												
Car Insurance												
Life insurance												
Health Insurance												
Student Loans												
Heating Fuel												
Gas												
Electricity												
Water												
Trash Removal												
Telephone												
Cell Phone												
Tuition												
Vacations/ Travel												
Childcare												
Cable												
Gym												
Credit Cards: Fees, Interest, and Non-duplicate Expenses												
American Express												
Visa												
MasterCard												
Discover												

Credit Cards:												
	Jan	Feb	Mar	Apr	May	Jun	Jul	Aug	Sept	Oct	Nov	Dec
Store Cards												
Other:												
Other:												
Other:												
Other:												
Other:												
Other:												

Daily Expenditures							
	Mon	Tues	Wed	Thurs	Fri	Sat	Sun
Groceries							
Gasoline							
Car Maintenance							
Public Transportation							
Cabs							
Medical not covered by insurance (Doctors, CoPay, Pharmacy)							
Clothing / Shoes							
Toiletries and Make-up							
Haircuts							
Mani/pedis							
Entertainment							
Class Fees (yoga, Pilates, etc)							

Daily Expenditures							
	Mon	Tues	Wed	Thurs	Fri	Sat	Sun
Books/magazines/ music downloads/ CDs							
Gifts							
Charity							
Other (housekeeping, babysitting, etc):							
Other:							
Other:							
Other:							

Write down everything you spend per day, week, and month using exact amounts. When you get your credit card bills, go through them, categorize your new spending, and enter it into your chart. If you are paying down an existing balance on a credit card, enter that amount under "Monthly Expenses." Within a few weeks, you should have a pretty precise account of how much you're spending on what types of bills and items. The value of keeping a spending record is that it automatically makes us more conscious of how we spend our money.

After a month of keeping track of your spending, sit with your chart and figure out what expenses you could cut. Do you really need to order takeout three times a week? Could you cook two more nights and reduce takeout to once weekly?

After tracking your expenses for one month, plan a budget for the year, estimating what you will need to spend month by month. "Need to spend" is the operative phrase here. Include only the basic costs, without frills. Then add in a few extras, perhaps a weekly meal in a restaurant, but pare back on what you were spending prior to focusing on your budget. Now take the difference, and, as the experts say, pay yourself first. One of the best ways to do that is by keeping a certain amount of cash in the bank, available for emergencies and unforeseen expenses.

Jordan, one of my best friends, relies on this simple budgeting plan, and he's been doing it for years. Sometimes it annoys his wife that he keeps such careful records of what they spend, but he swears by it. "How else do you know where it's going?" he asks. "I feel much more secure knowing what I've spent month by month. If I know I have a vacation coming up, I can spend a bit less in the previous months anticipating the extra expense of the trip." His wife accuses him of being obsessive about it, but they have a comfortable savings and have paid off their mortgage. Not bad for a family of four living on his full-time and her part-time income.

How do we make a budget and stick to it when the cost of living continues to rise? One small way to cut unnecessary expenditures is by paying special attention to those fads we start to follow mindlessly just because everyone else is doing it. Take something as simple as water, for example. Back in the 1980s, a marketing genius decided that it would be a good thing to bottle drinking water and market it to consumers. Until that point, everyone just drank water from the tap without a second thought. Suddenly it became unfashionable to drink tap water—you had to have it in a bottle, preferably sporting a fancy label. Restaurants jumped on the bandwagon and stopped offering free tap water—why give water away when people will pay three dollars or more per container? In fact, bottles of Aquafina and Dasani, made by Pepsi and Coca-Cola respectively, are more expensive than a can of Pepsi or Coke—which are made *with* water!

After more than twenty years of guzzling water from plastic bottles, many people are now reverting to tap water. Concerns about the environment, landfills piling up with non-recycled plastic, as well as the economic downturn have made people reconsider what comes out of the faucet. And if you are really concerned about the quality of your tap water, you can buy a fairly inexpensive filter that quickly earns back its price in bottled waters. Millions of dollars have gone into purchasing water in little plastic bottles, and this trend has been horrendous for the environment and a real drain on our pocketbooks.

And coffee! How many of us have grown accustomed to pulling three dollars or more from our wallet for our daily caffeine fix? Some of you might be feeling right now, "Hill Harper really is a killjoy. He's taking away my morning Venti iced cappuccino."

I'm not saying we shouldn't *ever* go out for coffee drinks, but we need to stop mindlessly spending on frivolous things that don't add value to our lives. By cutting back on a few luxuries, we can cut calories, lose weight, and reduce further medical expenses. Being conscious about how we spend and stick with a budget can create wins in multiple areas of our lives.

PART THREE

Compliance: Sticking with a Treatment Plan

comply \kəm- plī\: adherence to a recommended course of treatment

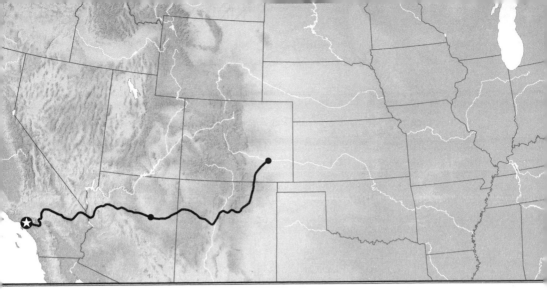

COURAGE IS A MUSCLE

"Courage doesn't always roar. Sometimes
courage is the quiet voice at the end of the day
saying, 'I will try again tomorrow.'"
—Mary Anne Radmacher,
American author and artist

Courage is a muscle. We have to exercise that muscle in the same way
we would work any muscle we want to strengthen. In order to build
courage, we need to follow our hearts and not allow fear, doubt, or the
negative projections of others to deter us from taking any action we want
to take. For instance, there is an incredible amount of societal pressure
to have the newest car, clothing, and so on. We can use our courage to
maintain our self-esteem and choose to use our money more effectively
and efficiently. To cure anything or solve any problem, it takes courage
to stick with our plan.

Saving money is similar to losing weight. The method for accom-

plishing both is deceptively simple: **Spend less than you earn; burn off more calories than you take in.** Accomplishing either is not necessarily easy, particularly at first. This is why we have an obesity epidemic in this country and also a debt epidemic—which I call "indebtgestion." I keep wondering why that term hasn't caught on.

While working in my cabin, I wanted to print out some of the notes that I had been taking and was surprised to find out that there was a small business center in one of the train cars. I guess I had figured that people on business trips would never take the time to ride the train, so why would there be the need?

As I walked into the business center cabin, there was a middle-aged gentleman working in one of the cubicles. I connected my laptop to a printer and just as I hit "PRINT," he looked up at me and said, "How's it going?"

I said, "Great." Which was really just an automatic response and not altogether true.

"I'm Josh."

"Hill."

"What are you working on?" Josh asked.

"A book I'm writing on money and financial literacy."

Hearing that, Josh began to chuckle.

"What's so funny?" I asked.

He shook his head and responded, "I can never get away from money."

I looked at him curiously. "I'm a wealth manager," he said. "I manage the assets and family estates of people whose net worth range between 10 million and several billion dollars. "

"Wow," I said. "Can I pick your brain?"

"Sure."

We proceeded to have a conversation lasting three hours about all things money. His perspective was brilliant yet quite simple. Which made me appreciate the truth that sometimes there's brilliance in simplicity.

Joshua Rothstein is a private wealth adviser and one of the top money managers in the country. Josh told me of the time he took his two daughters to the nail salon, and the manicurist asked him what he did for a living.

When he told her he was an investment adviser, the inevitable question followed: "How should I begin to save money and what should I buy?"

She had thought about buying stock, but had no expertise in that area. He advised her to consult with an investment adviser recommended by family or friends. I recommend meeting with more than one adviser and seeking out a second opinion to gain as much information as possible. For people who don't know a lot about the stock market or who don't have a time to monitor the market, Josh thinks mutual funds are a great way to go. I personally invest in "no load" (low commission) index mutual funds like funds offered by Vanguard and Fidelity. For instance, the Vanguard 500 fund indexes 500 stocks so you are invested in the market as opposed to individual stocks. I also recommend dollar cost average, which is an investment strategy where I automatically invest a set amount every month directly from my bank account. If the market happened to be lower, my auto investment purchases more shares; if the market is higher, I get fewer shares, but my account value is higher. Automatic electronic investment ensures that I am investing and saving monthly.

Josh made a point of telling the manicurist that the only way to have enough money to retire is to stop spending so much and start saving more. There really is a powerful but often overlooked way to increase one's net worth: **Stop spending what you don't have on what you don't need.** He reminded her that it's okay not to buy that new TV or PlayStation. Those things are only there to entice you. **It's actually an exercise in courage to save money,** build wealth, and not allow ourselves to be pulled to spend.

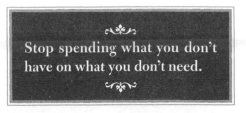

Stop spending what you don't have on what you don't need.

How do you become financially wealthy? As of the last Census, the mean yearly income in the U.S. was approximately $50,000, which equates to about $4,000 per month. To build your finances, you have to find a way to save more of your paycheck than you are saving now.

Josh explained to the young woman that most people don't realize that every dollar they spend today has the potential to be $10 in value at retirement if it is put into a mutual fund with a good return, for example. If a person deposited $4,000 per year, 10 percent of her earnings in a tax-deferred retirement plan or a mutual fund that reflected an average annual total return of around 7 percent, by retirement, in thirty years, that original investment has the potential to grow to nearly $500,000. **The first step to having enough money is to start saving more.**

Many people are gradually returning to their core values. They are simplifying their lives by choice, and wisely so. Unemployment numbers don't even count those who have given up on trying to find work. A great number of people have, of their own accord, begun streamlining their households, getting rid of what they don't need by selling it or donating it and then not filling up the empty closet space with more junk. Streamlining and simplifying our lives also requires courage and the knowledge that *you* are already enough.

Dave Bruno wrote a fascinating book called *The 100 Thing Challenge*, about how he got rid of all but one hundred items that he owned and how the mind-set of clearing things out changed his life. He had the courage to let go of sports equipment and toy train collections that had been lingering in his home for years. As Bruno puts it, "We say that we have 'arrived at the American dream.' We announce that we are 'living the good life.' And yet it has been my experience that, at least in our times, the good life and the American dream are more obsolescent than obtainable. . . . We buy things year after year, over and over again, in our pursuit of contentment . . . replacement is emblematic of our dreams more than ownership."

Are you replacing things, instead of owning them?

Our mentality should be to acquire for the long term and not continually replace our belongings with bigger and "better." For those who have worked long and hard to rise up the ranks at the office, the idea of maintaining the status quo or even downsizing might be a bitter pill to swallow. Suddenly you've arrived at a hard-won point of success in your career, whether it's as CEO, middle manager, or union leader, and you're told to scale down? Doesn't the victor have the right to the spoils? Perhaps, but lasting victory only comes with smart decision-making. And we have the power to be smart about money.

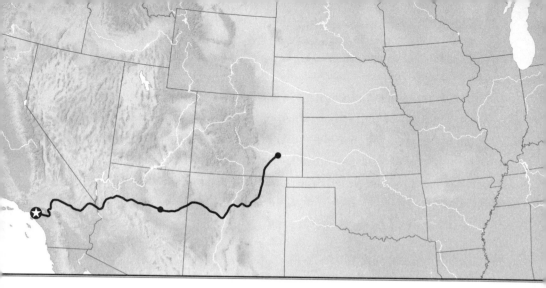

SMART MONEY VERSUS
DUMB MONEY

"If we command our wealth, we shall be rich
and free. If our wealth commands us, we are
poor indeed."

—Edmund Burke, British statesman
and philosopher

M ost people have been taught to believe that all money is the same:
A dollar is a dollar. But that is clearly far from the truth. Some
money is smart money, and some money is dumb money. **The smartest
dollar is a dollar that works for you to earn more without having
to use the most precious resource
any of us have—time.** In other
words, money that grows without
your having to use your own sweat
equity to make it grow is the smartest money of all.

> Smart Money works for you
> while you sleep.

Smart Money works for you while you sleep.

Investing in the stock market can be a smart use of money, or it can be a form of gambling. I gambled big time a couple of years ago. Normally I am pretty cautious with my money, having lived through periods of working as a waiter and driving an ancient car until I could afford better. But I did get sucked into a risky mentality with one investment. GM stock was low at the time, and the company was solid. I wanted to bet on a great American business and thought I could make a killing when the stock price rose. And "bet" I did—it truly was a gamble. I lost heavily when the stock sank even lower than the price I paid. If I had held on to it for a decade or more, it might have come back, but I basically panicked and wound up losing money. I learned an important lesson: **When investing in the stock market, think long-term.**

Only put in money that you can afford to leave in the stock for a very long time. Think at least ten years, if not longer. This is not money that you want to stick somewhere for six months, planning to take it out at some point in the near future and make a sure killing. Though the stock market is a good place to put your money—as long as you can leave it in for a long time—it is never a sure bet. You have to have the intestinal fortitude to put the money in and basically forget about it. If you are constantly checking your portfolio online or your stomach ties up in knots when you get the statement showing that your investment is now worth less than what you put in initially, the stock market might not be for you. You have to have the mentality that you are in it for the long haul, and ride out the bumps. **As Warren Buffett says, "Only buy something that you'd be perfectly happy to hold if the market shut down for ten years."**

INVEST WITH CAUTION

As mentioned earlier, one way to hedge your bets when investing in stocks is to put some of your savings into a mutual fund, for which talented money managers invest in a large number of diverse stocks to spread the risk. A good guide for finding the type of fund you want to invest in is www.morningstar.com, which rates the performance of the top funds. Morningstar shows you past performance, how many years the fund has been in existence, and all kinds of statistics, including turnover in management. And there are various types of funds: international, large cap, small cap, and so on. Use your Smart Money skills and ask a financial adviser or do research in order to invest in a fund that will work for you.

Another way to turn your savings into Smart Money is to put it into a general index fund. Index funds cover the entire stock market and follow its performance. You want to be in a no-load fund, meaning that you don't have to pay a sales or redemption charge. And you want your dividends—money that the company gives to shareholders out of its earnings, usually quarterly—to be reinvested automatically, so that in addition to the savings you add each month, the dividends also increase the investment's growth. Again, in that way, your money works for you.

On the other side of the spectrum, the dumbest dollar of all is one that is spent on things that provide no value. **Credit card interest payments are the dumbest money of all.** When we purchase something with a credit card, it's good that the card allowed us to gain access to the item or service we bought with it—if we really needed it and can afford to pay for it. If we are only paying the minimum and allowing interest to accrue, the item may wind up costing us from three to five times its original price for every dollar spent. That's a dumb use of money.

> Credit card interest payments are the dumbest money of all.

Our money should work for us, yet unfortunately that's not what happens for so many of us. The big myth is that you have to be a multimillionaire to have Smart Money. The truth is that it doesn't matter how little you start with—a single dollar can be working for you. Both the rich and not-so-rich can have dumb money, which causes you to spend more money for past purchases than their original price. Getting in over your head in debt is obviously dumb money, but so is purchasing things that decrease in value over time instead of things that appreciate. Automobiles, flat-screen televisions, cell phones, and computers all depreciate. If you limit what you spend on such items and replace them as seldom as possible, you are well on your way to minimizing your use of dumb money.

The average credit card debt per household is more than $15,000, and the average APR on new credit cards is 14.35 percent—highway robbery, in my opinion. And penalty fees from credits cards added up to about $20.5 billion in 2009, according to Robert K. Hammer, a credit card consultant cited in *The New York Times*. Think what could have been done with that $20.5 billion that went to the credit card companies. The UN Food and Agricultural Organization estimates that with $30 billion, global food insecurity could be solved through agricultural programs. So $20 billion would take care of feeding two-thirds of all hungry people, worldwide. (And by the way, Americans throw away $75 billion in food per year, according to a USDA study.) In order to visualize how much money we are talking about, one billion dollars is equal to the annual income of 25,000 people, so as a country, **we are spending the incomes of half a million people on credit card debt alone.**

Smart Money is using your money to leverage your position and expand your options. Money put into savings is Smart Money. By saving, you are showing that you control your cash, as opposed to the other way around. You are in control of your finances, and are actively decreasing your debt so that you will eventually reach a point at which you are debt free.

SMART MONEY RULE

The Smart Money Rule is: The purpose of money (contrary to what most people think) is not to spend it. Rather, the true purpose of money is to collect it in order to gain access to build a financial wealth base to gain access to less expensive money—money that costs us less of our time and sweat equity to produce. In other words, if we grow a solid financial foundation, we become free to use our money in smarter and smarter ways. In some ways, this idea is complex, but in other ways, it's pretty simple. What do I mean by "The purpose of money is not to spend it"? Well, when most people think about money, they think about what they can buy with their money. But people who truly understand the Smart Money Rule view their money as a part of a continuum of wealth building that they use to create more money, influence, or a legacy in the world. This is how the saying, "It takes money to make money" originated.

Money is a tool. A lot of times, when people are asked what they want in life, it amazes me that they'll say they want money, or they'll name a thing they would buy if they had money. Rather than saying that they want happiness or health. Or even saying they want the wisdom and foresight to create the things that would manifest enduring wealth for them and their family. No, they go straight to m-o-n-e-y. Why? Because they have been taught to think about the purpose of money completely wrong. Most of us have been taught that money is a result rather than what it is, a tool.

The more money we spend on goods and services that we don't need, the less we are saving our money and, thereby, not using it as a tool to acquire more access to less expensive money. Greater and greater access to less expensive money is the Smart Money goal.

Smart Money Contract

- Never accumulate credit card debt.
- If you currently have credit card debt, you should be paying more than the minimum payments. Negotiate lower interest rates directly with the credit card company. (Yes, this actually works. Try it! And no, a debt consolidation company is not required.)
- Research the type of investments that are appropriate for your goals.
- Make investing part of your monthly budget.
- Don't ever make rash decisions regarding your investments. Remember, investments are cyclical in nature and go up and down in value.
- Start now. No matter where you are in terms of age or income, you can and should seek to invest in ways that are appropriate for you.
- Reinvest your investment income and dividends. Many investment accounts, mutual funds, and stocks pay interest or dividends. Your investments can grow exponentially if you reinvest the income they generate. I have all my accounts on automatic reinvestment so I'm not tempted to spend my interest income or dividends.
- Think long term, not get rich quick.
- Be patient and don't ever panic.
- You can do it! You can become a Smart Money Master.

Credit card debt weighs you down, causes unnecessary angst, creates fights with your spouse, and undermines your potential for true wealth. Did you know that, according to *The New York Times*, in 2006 there were 1.5 billion credit cards in use in America? We only have about 2.3 million adults in this country. What could we be doing with 1.5 million credit cards? If those cards were stacked up, they would reach over seventy miles into space, and be as tall as thirteen Mount Everests. I found this fact shocking: According to the FINRA Investor Education Foundation, almost a third of all poll respondents did not know the interest rate on their own most-used credit card. Here's another eye-opener. Add up the interest that you paid on all of your credit cards in the past calendar year. Now think of what you could have used that money for—preferably paying off the entire debt and then socking the rest of the money away so that it works for your future.

Instead of handing our money over to the credit card companies and banks, let's begin to take steps to get out of the pit of credit card debt. Let's commit to implementing our Smart Money Contract.

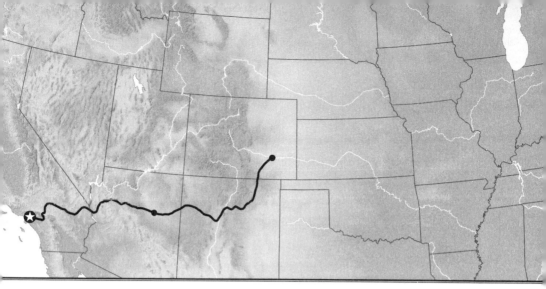

PURCHASED IN A
BLUR OF ENDORPHINS

"The only reason a great many American families don't own an elephant is that they have
never been offered an elephant for a dollar
down and easy weekly payments."

—*Mad* magazine

Now that you have seen how much interest you've been paying on
your credit cards, take the past six months' bills and itemize the
types of expenses that you charged. Make two columns: "Necessities" and
"Unnecessary Expenditures." If you're like most people, the "Unnecessary" column will total far higher than the "Necessities" column. Look at
individual items that you bought, and try to recall the exact moment that
you decided to purchase them.

Money is legal tender, but it can also be emotional tender. How you use
it or spend it can elicit feelings. The problem is the positive feelings that

come with buying something you value can sometimes be confused with the exchange of money in general. You can become addicted to the feeling you get from spending the money and not just what it buys you.

Let's say you bought three new shirts. You went into a store thinking you could use another good button-down shirt for work. The salesman flattered you when you tried it on and showed you a couple other colors that would look good on you. Suddenly you found yourself at the cash register shelling out close to two hundred bucks for what you thought was going to be a single shirt, maybe a sixty-dollar purchase. And what did you do with those shirts? Did one of them sit there in your closet because your girlfriend told you it wasn't a good look for you? Did you really need to buy all three?

This is a trap. **We have to recognize the "rush of the spend," so that we don't get "spent from the rush."**

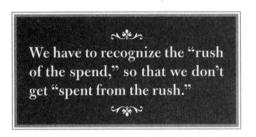

We have to recognize the "rush of the spend," so that we don't get "spent from the rush."

Go through your bills and try to recall the exact circumstances in which you made some of these purchases. Make notes next to the entry: Did the purchase make a difference in your daily life? Did it turn out to be disappointing or, at the very least, so unremarkable that you can't recall why you bought it? So many of our purchases are done in a blur of shopping endorphins: "I'm feeling good today, so I want to treat myself to something fun." Or "I'm feeling down tonight, so I want to pick up my mood with a quick mini-spree." Or, "I'm bored and don't have any plans for the weekend, so I'll blow some cash to give myself something to look forward to." This kind of spending is not using our money in a smart way.

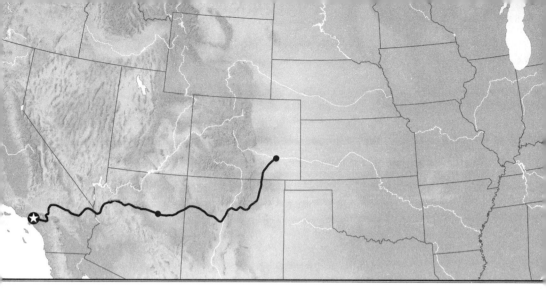

SERVANT TO THE
CREDIT CARD

"Money is a good servant but a bad master."
—Francis Bacon Sr., English lawyer
and philosopher

I n the dining car, as I continued scribbling notes in my journal about what we have to do to repair our relationship with money, I got an e-mail from Sean. As I pulled out my credit card to pay for my meal, I read Sean's message:

Hill,
I know you've been on the train and couldn't make it to church today, so I wanted to send you this word I heard today. It's divinity at work, my friend, that I happened to

go to this church and hear this man. Especially since we were talking about credit card debt in our last conversation. Pastor Soaries was a visiting pastor at House of Hope this morning, so I went to hear his sermon. He's incredible! He really hits the spot with this message. Let me know what you think. Enjoy.

Talk soon,
Sean

Pastor DeForest Soaries Jr., senior pastor of the First Baptist Church of Lincoln Gardens in Somerset, New Jersey, preaches a gospel of personal financial responsibility. In his book *dFree: Breaking Free from Financial Slavery*, he describes three types of spending that can enslave us: compensatory consumption is spending to gain significance; conspicuous consumption is spending to gain status; and confused consumption is impulsive and just plain stupid.

Have you ever noticed that when you are intently focused on something you attract exactly what you need? I settled in to read Pastor Soaries' sermon.

PROVERBS 22:7,
"THE BORROWER IS SERVANT TO THE LENDER."

In Proverbs 22:7, I want to replace the word *servant* with the word *slave*. The word *slave* just really rubs us the wrong way. The idea that we would be voluntary slaves is offensive to all of our sensibilities. But the Bible says "The borrower is servant to the lender." Then Peter said anything that can control you more than you can control you has you in slavery, in bondage (2 Peter 2:19).

Imagine if Visa and MasterCard were to send me a letter that says, "Dear Mr. Soaries, we're going to send you a brand-new card. It's still going to be platinum, but we're going to change the name from 'Platinum' to 'Slave.' We're going to send you a slave card. That's the best card you can have. *Slave*." See, you don't even have to know the rest of the story, right? But they don't send me a slave card. They send me a "platinum card" or a "gold card"—a preapproved credit card with a large credit limit. They don't use the word "slave." And so I carry it with pride, whip it out on the counter at the store. "I'm paying with my gold card."

The first step of getting out of slavery is *identifying the reality of our condition*. And the reality of our condition is that we are servants or slaves to the lenders. That is where we start.

Let's look at Luke, chapter 14, starting with verse 28. Jesus is telling a series of parables. "Suppose one of you wants to build a tower." You can replace the word "tower" with "house." Suppose one of you wants to build a house, or suppose one of you wants to send your child to college, or one of you wants to buy a suit or start a business or lead a church. In other words, Jesus is using this tower simply as a symbol for anything that costs money.

Suppose one of you wants to build a tower. Will he not first sit down [stop everything] and estimate the cost . . . ? The King James Version says "count the cost." Yes, what we normally call *counting the cost* is *preparing a spending plan or a budget*.

If you're going to build a house, if you're going to buy a tie, if you're going to go on a trip, why don't you first sit down and prepare a budget or a spending plan? . . . Estimate the cost to see if he [or she] has enough money to complete it? You can't get any more practical than this. Jesus says, in effect, **"If you're my disciple, there shouldn't be anything so weird about you that exempts you from the need to have a budget."**

Here is a four-step plan for getting out of financial slavery: *Admit, Attitude, Action, Adhere.*

Step 1: *Admit.* The only way a sick person can get well is to first admit he or she is sick. You'll notice in the Gospels when Jesus would encounter people who were sick or lame, Jesus would often say, "What do you want? Do you recognize your situation?" (See John 5:2–15.)

You have to admit that you are a slave to debt. If you have mail that you know contains bills and it's three months old and you refuse to open it because you know what is inside and there is no need to open up a letter asking you for money that you don't have, you have a problem. If you're using a credit card to pay off a credit card even though they've said you'll pay no interest for now, you have a problem. If you find yourself shopping and waiting until your spouse is not home to sneak in what you bought—first because you don't want them to know you're spending money and secondly, because if he or she finds out, they're going to go spend some more money—then you *both* have a problem.

If you're paying off last month's bills with next month's check—in other words, you've spent the money before you make it, you have a problem. If you don't mind paying late fees and say, "Well, I'll just have to pay the fee," then you have a problem. So many people live lives of fantasy. They get bills, but don't read the bills. They get bank statements, but don't read the statements. And once you realize you have a problem, you need an attitude shift.

Step 2: *Attitude.* In *How to Get Out of Debt, Stay Out of Debt, and Live Prosperously,* Jerrold Mundis makes the very important point that **"You are not your bank account."** That's an attitude shift. The attitude shift is that I am separate from what I have and what I own because once I can separate my identity from the things I have, when my bank account gets low or when my possessions get old or when I can't keep up with the proverbial Joneses, I still feel good about myself because I am *me* in spite of what I have.

Step 3: *Action.* We have to get up and leave slavery ourselves. Sometimes taking action simply means buying a book and reading the book. Sometimes taking action means joining a group. Promise yourself, I'm going to contact Debtors Anonymous.

Action often involves connecting with people who are honest. They've admitted and their attitude has changed. And now we're going to help each other. If I'm married and have a family, the first connection I have to make is with my family. My wife and I have to agree on a budget and spending. **We have to track our finances.** Taking action requires tracking our finances, writing down what we spend and what we spend it on every time we spend it. Do something.

Step 4: *Adhere.* The fourth *A* is *Adhere.* One of the great challenges we have in helping people with debt is that they'll rip up their credit cards. But three months later, they have the cards again. They pay off their bills, and three months later, they go through the cycle again.

In our foreclosure prevention work, we discovered nationally that when we work out a new mortgage, what we call a loan modification with lenders, within six months, 50 percent of the people who got loan modifications in 2008 were back in default.

In many instances, the person who got the loan modification never got out of slavery. **Even if you give them the house, they'd lose the house.**

So let's be very serious about the nature of the problem. Yes, the banks have been guilty of mishandling their end of the process. The bond agencies and the rating agencies have been guilty, too, but they were able to take advantage of our mentality because many of us fell into the trap. Paul said in Romans 12:2, **"Be not conformed to this world, but be transformed by the renewing of your mind."**

Figure it out. Ask yourself, Can I afford this? And if I can, why can I? And suppose something happens? Do I have a Plan B? Do I have *a contingency plan? Do I have an emergency fund?* If you have that plan, you need to adhere to the plan. This simply means once you put your plan in place, you'll stick to it.

The truth is, you don't get in trouble by yourselves. You're surrounded by all of these forces. We are the victims of all-out attack. **Somebody wants us in slavery.** This is not neutral. This is not coincidental. This is not just, "Well, things happen."

You need to stop acting like you can do this by yourselves. "I'm going to rip up my credit cards." No, you better rip up your credit card in the name of Jesus. We didn't get in this wreck by ourselves and we can't get out by ourselves.

Prosperity is when we live according to God's plan and God's Word. The Bible says, "He that the Son sets free is free indeed" (John 8:36).

So there is power in his name. Let's get out of slavery.

Pastor Soaries' words really hit home and reinforced everything I had been thinking about the Wealth Cure. The train continued to rumble on as I contemplated his powerful message about connecting our relationship with money to both individual freedom and spirituality. It certainly resonated with me. I suspected it was more than just a "coincidence" that Sean had sent me this particular sermon.

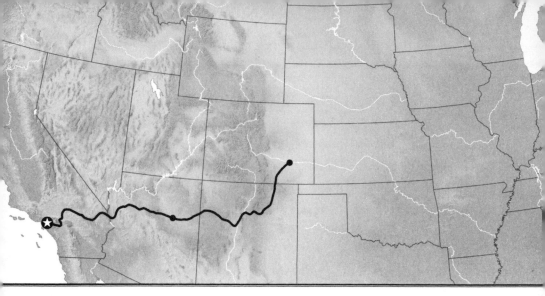

CREDIT FIX-UP

"Today, there are three kinds of people: the
have's, the have-not's, and the have-not-paid-
for-what-they-have's.

—Earl Wilson,
American newspaper columnist

If you're badly in debt like millions of Americans, one of the first things
you need to do is fix your credit score. First, you should get a copy of
your credit report from each of the three agencies: Experian, Equifax,
and Transunion. Do *not* pay for this report. By law, you are entitled to a
free copy.

> ## CREDIT SCORE
>
> Also known as a **credit rating**. Many lenders use this numeric calculation of your **credit report** to obtain a fast, objective measure of your **credit risk** and consider your **score** when deciding whether or not to approve a loan. (Source: Wells Fargo) Your credit score is also known as a "FICO score," named after the company that invented it.

Once you have received all three reports, read each one very carefully. Check to see that all of the information is correct, and be sure to look out for possible listings that you could dispute. You might find a typographical error, out-of-date information, or information that is not complete. Each of these is a reason to dispute the veracity of the report. You may see that an item shows up on one report but not on another. Be sure to consider every distinct item on the three reports.

If you do find any incorrect amounts or any other inaccuracies in the reports, you can file a credit dispute online or by mail. Be sure to include as much documentation as you have: sales slips, copies of cleared checks, credit card bills, and so on. If you have paid off a debt, but it is still showing up as unpaid, send the proof that you have paid in full to the reporting agency to have it cleared.

If you have accounts that you aren't using, close them out. If you have quite a lot of credit cards, you should definitely close some of those accounts. Your FICO score is calculated with a debt ratio formula. A bunch of maxed-out limits can drastically bring down your score. **Many experts recommend that you maintain your revolving credit accounts at less than half of your available limit.** Of course, going forward, once you get your debts in control, you will not be using your credit limits.

If you're late in paying a bill, it can stay on your report for seven years. Make all future payments on time. Be sure to work out an agreement for any outstanding debts. Often, and especially during a recession, companies are used to being paid late or not at all and are likely to work out a plan with you.

Most people don't realize that creditors are often willing to negotiate—particularly in uncertain economic times. You may be able to get your monthly payments lessened or get your interest rate reduced in order to eliminate debt and/or loan payments. You may even get an extension on a due date that you've been dreading. Be assertive. A debt settlement is better for your record than a charge-off. Be certain to get the agreement in writing so that you have proof of the deal in case any questions ever come up.

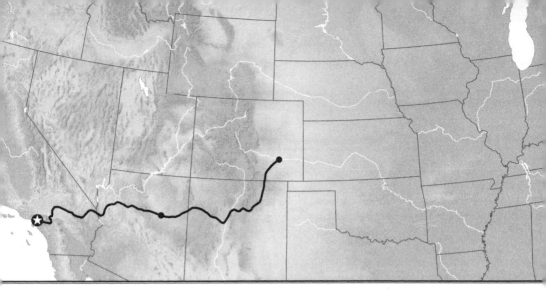

The Biggest Purchases You Are Likely to Make

"A bank is a place that will lend you money if
you can prove that you don't need it."
—Bob Hope, British-born American
comedian and actor

O ne of the benefits of saving is that when your savings have eventually reached a certain point and you have a good down payment
saved up, you can begin to look for a home. One of the first things you'll
discover is that your excellent credit rating and the amount of money that
you have put away will get you a lower interest rate on your mortgage.
Banks like to give loans to someone who seems like a solid bet, so if you
have been diligent in paying your bills and have a nice down payment
ready to go, you will get a better rate on your mortgage. Now, that's
Smart Money at work.

According to Bankrate.com, here is what a borrower could expect to be charged in interest for a $300,000 thirty-year fixed-rate mortgage, based on her credit score (using 2011 rates):

Credit Score	Rate
760 to 850 tier	4.557%
700-759 tier	4.779%
660-699 tier	5.063%
620-659 tier	5.873%
580-619 tier	7.360%
500-579 tier	8.271%

The way Smart Money works for you is clear from this example. Smart Money allows you to leverage your money to save even more on purchases, especially what it costs to borrow money to buy a home. That lower rate is going to hold for fifteen to thirty years, depending on the terms of your mortgage.

Another way to use Smart Money, once you do have a mortgage, is to make extra payments on the principal amount above the monthly mortgage payment, which includes the interest. My friend Tom got a thirty-year mortgage, but decided that he didn't want to be paying the bank when he was in his sixties. Every other month, he sent in an extra thousand dollars toward the principal. He wound up taking eight years off of his mortgage, paid it all off at age fifty-one. Since then, he has enjoyed putting big chunks of money into his savings and retirement accounts. He has the comfort of knowing that he owns his own home outright—something that not many of us can say.

In fact, in the last ten years, there's been a 7 percent decline in people who own their own homes free and clear of debt, leaving only about 30 percent of homeowners who have paid off their mortgage. These people tend to be older couples who are now in their sixties, seventies, or eighties, and who were averse to debt.

Josh talked to me about paying off a mortgage. He said, "My definition of wealth is the freedom to do what you want and to live without fear. My grandfather is ninety-one, and my father-in-law is eighty-eight. The number one goal of that generation was to pay off their mortgages. Those values got thrown out the window with "C credit" and interest-only mortgages. Banks really don't want you to pay off your home loan, because then they aren't making money from you any longer. But nowadays most people don't even think about paying off their mortgage. One reason that we are seeing an uptick in spending is that so many people have walked away from their mortgages, or else have short sold, and now they have extra cash, since they're renting.

"One of my clients who is close to forty and very wealthy asked me if he should pay off his house or invest. I suggested that he pay off his house. He liked the idea and did just that. Later he told me he didn't know how good it would feel to own his own home. That can be a goal for almost anyone, if you are living within your means. At the end of the day, if you're paying 6 percent interest on your house and could be earning 7 to 8 percent in the stock market, why not pay off your house? You won't get the tax deduction on the interest, but you will have huge peace of mind knowing that you own your own house. In fact, the wealth that our grandparents' generation accumulated is mostly in their homes.

"If you told most people that at retirement age they could own their own home, and have enough money to pay for food, utilities, and medical insurance, they would feel wealthy. So why not begin to save now for something that would mean you were truly wealthy by the time you're ready to retire?

"When America was created, how did our forefathers define wealth? Until the Buttonwood Agreement in 1792, which created paper securities, land or local businesses were the only investments available. You could get land just by claiming it, and you could chop down trees and build your own home. Freedom was true wealth to those Founding Fathers: liberation, religious freedom, and property rights. That is my definition of true wealth. Our grandparents know that. They lived through World War One and Two, and knew not to take our freedoms for granted. If you take away freedom, then wealth isn't worth anything."

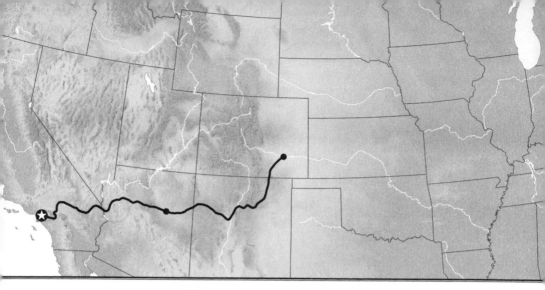

DEALS ON WHEELS

"If you think nobody cares if you are alive, try missing a couple of car payments."

—Earl Wilson,
American newspaper columnist

"Cars are where many people rack up way too much debt," Josh, the private wealth investor, told me. "Some people feel that they have to have a new car every three years, whether they really can afford it or not. My car, which I bought in 1999, has a hundred thousand miles on it. My other car is ten years old. I could afford to pay cash for a Bentley, but why would I waste my money on something like that?

"I believe that the average commercial airplane is somewhere between ten to twenty years old, has traveled hundreds of thousands of miles, and it runs every single day," he continues. "Yet we think nothing of flying. We don't ask why the planes we fly aren't brand-new. Of course the airlines maintain them well and rebuild the engines, but we can maintain our cars well, too. If a fifteen-year-old airplane is good enough for us, then a ten-year-old car ought to be all right, too."

What makes much more monetary sense is to *buy* the kind of car that you can *afford*. It might be a used Hyundai, but if that's what you can afford to buy at that time, then that's what you're going to be driving. My debt rule says that if you can't afford to pay cash for the car, then you shouldn't buy it. Some people like Josh didn't go that far and think that affordable car payments are okay. But we both agree that leasing a car is like throwing money to the wind; it's truly dumb money. You have no ownership in the car, but you are paying a monthly chunk, and after a couple years of leasing, you still don't own anything. Better to pay a monthly amount that works toward your owning the car. The day will come when you can afford a car more to your liking. But leasing is for fools—as in "A fool and his money are soon parted."

On the train, Josh told me, "Leasing a car is one of the easiest ways to burn money that I know. You pay a hefty chunk of change in order to drive a car that you don't own. In the end, you have the privilege of purchasing a depreciated asset for a higher–than–*Blue Book* price."

Josh offers this heads–up. "The biggest scam is when people put down money to reduce their payment on a car lease—never do this! The car dealer might offer, 'Give me three thousand dollars now, and I will reduce your car payment from five hundred dollars per month to four hundred.' If you have three years to go on your lease, you have just given the bank use of your three thousand dollars over the next three years in order to save six hundred during that time. This makes no sense at all. That's three thousand dollars that can be used for retirement. The greater question is, Why are you buying a car with payments so high that you'd be willing to give up three thousand dollars of your savings?"

If you are paying more than 10 percent of your total income on your wheels, you might consider selling, unless you're nearing the end of your car loan and almost own it free and clear. You can determine whether or not it makes sense to sell your car by getting the value of it from the *Kelley Blue Book,* the bible for valuing used vehicles. If you have a long-term loan ahead of you and you can sell the car for an amount that makes sense in terms of what you've already paid out, you might do better by selling it. People sell cars through Autotrader.com, Craigslist.com, used-car dealers, ads in papers, and other resources. Again, use the *Blue Book* to find out the real value of your used car, and then check out local and online ads to see how other people are pricing similar cars. After you have sold your car, be sure to buy a pre-owned vehicle that is far less costly. Taking these steps to reduce your fixed costs is a great way to invest in your future.

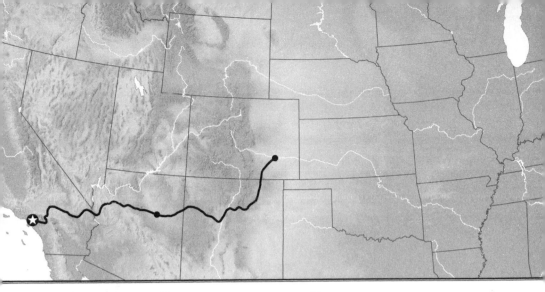

LEARNING TO SURF

"Surfing is such an amazing concept. You're taking on Nature with a little stick and saying, 'I'm gonna ride you!' And a lot of times Nature says, 'No you're not!' and crashes you to the bottom."

—Jolene Blalock, American actress

The train ride from Los Angeles to Chicago was giving me the luxury of uninterrupted time to think about the Wealth Cure. Convinced I was onto something very important, I decided to take a break and walk down to the lounge car. I was getting a little stir crazy and in the mood for company and conversation. As soon as I walked in, the first face I saw was that of the young man from the dining car at breakfast. I sat in one of the empty seats across from him and introduced myself. He laughed.

"I know who you are, man," he said, taking hold of the hand I'd offered him for a shake. "I watch you on TV. I'm Scott."

"You going to Chicago?"

He nodded. "All the way."

"You from there?" I asked.

He shook his head. "I've been living in L.A. for the past five years. I'm going to Chicago to meet up with my brother." Scott told me that he'd been recently laid off from his job and that he was going to move in with his brother for a while. He also told me that he'd moved to Los Angeles to pursue his dream of becoming an actor.

"That's great," I told him. I always try to encourage young actors, because what they usually hear from most people is "It's hard." And it is, but so is everything else. I'd never want to discourage anyone's dreams and one would hope that what drives a lot of people to their career of choice is a passion for doing what they love to do. Someone who can't stand the sight of blood would not try to become a surgeon. And someone who doesn't like to write would not become an author. And if the idea of being rejected over and over again at humiliating auditions makes you nauseated, you may not want to become an actor. But if you love what it is that you're doing, that generally makes it seem pleasurable rather than burdensome.

I asked Scott if he'd been able to find an agent and go out on auditions during his time acting.

"Yeah, I even got cast in stuff. Nothing big, but it was looking up."

"Then why are you stopping?" I was prepared to share with him some of the words of wisdom and encouragement that people have shared with me over the years.

Scott shook his head. "I got a great job. I worked as a delivery person for this company, and it was the perfect job for acting because my hours were flexible, so I could go on auditions. But then they gave me a promotion."

"And that's a bad thing?" I asked.

"Nah." He sighed, leaning forward in his chair and resting his elbows on his knees. "I thought it was one of the best things that had ever happened to me." Scott went on to explain that before he knew it, he'd become a full-time business executive, something he'd never imagined doing. But there he was, spending his days in an office. "At first I loved it. I couldn't believe it . . . an executive. I moved into a nice apartment and bought a car that wasn't made before I was born. I could afford to pay for dinner at a nice restaurant with my girlfriend."

"I'm really sorry you got laid off," I said.

"Oh, I'm not sorry," he said emphatically. "I'd been looking for an out for the past couple of years, but I didn't know how to do it. I wasn't twenty-one anymore. I didn't know how to make it work. I didn't want to go back to living with a roommate and driving a hooptie."

I chuckled, remembering my own hooptie-driving days (a $350 sixteen-year-old green crusty Toyota Corolla (that I paid cash for ☺) my roommate nicknamed "the Rusty Green Hornet"). When you start, most new actors have to figure out how to do what feels next to impossible—find a job that pays you enough to live and finance your career aspirations while leaving you enough time and flexibility to go on auditions and call-backs and take acting classes.

"Then I lost my job, so I had all the time in the world to act, but I couldn't afford to support myself out in L.A. It's just not practical, so I'm going home. Who knows? Maybe I'll even start acting again. Do some local theater or something."

Sometimes it's amazing how much people reveal to complete strangers. We begin what we believe to be nothing more than polite conversation but end up engaging in an intimate and in-depth discussion, often baring our souls. It's as though the moment we leave home, we also leave behind some of the defenses that we've put up, as if we leave behind our definitions of privacy. It may present a time of healing, a type of confessional. For some, it is the spontaneous opportunity to share their secrets with someone anonymous, someone they might never see again.

Maybe that's how I felt. After Scott finished telling me all about what was going on in his life, I started to reveal what I was going through. He didn't even have to ask. I told him about my diagnosis and the upcoming surgery. I told him about my father and all the men in my family who'd succumbed to cancer.

"Are you scared?" he asked. His voice was hesitant and soft, as though he was afraid he might say something to offend me.

"I'm trying not to think about it too much," I said. I also told him about my grandparents and the time I'd spent in Iowa.

"Iowa?" he asked incredulously. "Really?"

I nodded. "Yup. Really!"

That got us talking about the Great Migration, the movements of African Americans from Southern states to the North in search of a better life.

"Are you married?" Scott wanted to know.

I told him I wasn't.

"Do you have any kids?"

"Not yet," I said, shaking my head.

"So it's just you," Scott added.

I didn't expect that comment, and it kind of threw me. I took a second to let his statement sink in before I replied.

"Yup," I said, a lump forming in my throat, adding not so conveniently to the other five that needed to be surgically removed. "I guess so."

Scott's comment stung. It touched on one of my greatest fears. Family is extremely important to me. I didn't like thinking of myself as being alone, as having no one. Suddenly, I felt I wanted to explain myself. I told Scott that my last relationship had recently ended. That she was a terrific woman named Nichole, who lived in Washington, D.C., with her daughter. I told him about her penchant for stargazing, and I described some of the wonderful times we'd spent together.

"Once, on a trip to Costa Rica, Nichole and I decided to try to learn to surf," I said. "We got up early in the morning and met our instructor. He began by putting two long boards on the sand and said first we should become accustomed to what it feels like to stand on a board on land. He then took us out into the water and began 'the real lesson.'"

Scott smiled. "I never did learn to surf in all those years in California," he admitted.

"Don't feel bad, neither did I. Nichole and I spent what seemed to be an entire day getting up, falling off, and climbing back onto our boards. Though neither of us ever caught a wave that day, truth be told, she was a lot better than I was. Even as we fell, we laughed. The more we tried, the more we enjoyed and respected the art of surfing. We would laugh and fall, fall and laugh. It was an amazing time. At the end of our lesson our instructor said, 'The next time you go, you will be just that much better. No one else will be able to really tell, but you'll know on the inside.'" And then he said something I'll never forget. "You see, the joy of surfing is actually in the learning, being out there on the water, trying your best. Whether you ever catch a wave or not really doesn't matter. **Just keep learning**." I shook my head, smiling at the memory.

"So what happened?" Scott wanted to know.

"To what?" I said.

"Between you and Nichole," Scott shot back.

"I don't really know. We became distanced somehow. It was a challenge to spend consistent quality time together with our hectic schedules. Since she also worked and had her daughter in D.C., she couldn't just pick up and fly to L.A. anytime she wanted. I guess we just became frustrated in the process and eventually grew apart."

Scott shook his head and said, "Too bad, you seem like you really cared for her."

"I did. I mean, I do," I said. "I really do."

With my head and heart spinning, I told Scott that I was going to go back to my cabin to make some calls, and he suggested we hook up for dinner. I gladly agreed and walked back to my sleeper car. I took out my Black-Berry and hit Sean's number. I wanted to hear a familiar voice right about then.

"How's the road?" he wanted to know. "Where are you?"

We were now in La Junta, Colorado, right in the middle of prairie land, on the south banks of the Arkansas River. I could see the mountains to my west.

"Ah, the Centennial State," Sean said. "Great place. My favorite place there is the Mile High City."

"I don't think we're going through Denver," I told him, trying to remember all the stops on our route to Chicago. I gave Sean an update on my trip. I described my cabin, the huge window, and all the places we'd passed through, at least the ones I'd seen.

"Have you fallen in love with any beautiful women yet?" he asked.

"No. Where'd that come from?"

"Isn't that what people do on trains?" he teased. "They fall in love. Don't you watch the movies?"

"You sound like Tracey. I'm not DeNiro, and I highly doubt that Meryl Streep is on this train. My Lena Horne is probably in a plane flying across country, not on a train anyway. But speaking of love, what's going on between you and Lorraine? Have you heard from her?"

Sean's voice suddenly changed. It was as if I'd pulled him back into a reality he'd been desperately trying to escape.

"No, we agreed that it would be better to take some time so we can each figure out what the next step will be."

"How long is the break gonna be?"

"It's starting to feel permanent . . . look, Hill, I've gotta roll," he said.

"Man, I'm sorry to hear that," I said. Sean didn't respond. I knew we would talk more about this in person, so I told Sean that I'd call him the next day, and we hung up.

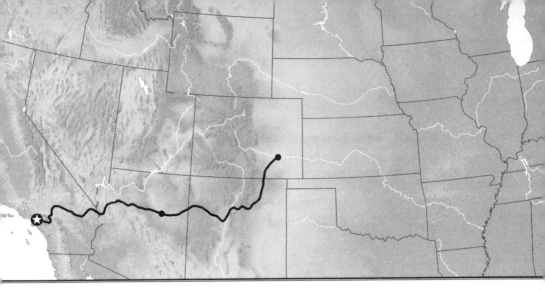

YOU'RE IN THIS TOGETHER— RESOLVING OPPOSITIONAL MONEY STYLES

"Money is akin to having a third party in your relationship that showed up on the first date, never went away, and is constant and absolutely necessary . . . It also amplifies what is working in your relationship as well as what needs to be worked on."

—Jacquette M. Timmons,
American investment expert,
financial coach, and author

I sat in my cabin thinking about the wedge that had formed between Sean and Lorraine because of their disagreement over money. Issues surrounding money top the list of things that couples argue about. Ideally, money should be one of the primary areas they support and partner each other about.

Enlisting your spouse or partner to support you in your war on debt is critical. As Chip Heath and Dan Heath say in *Switch*, their groundbreaking book about how people manage to make real and lasting changes in their lives: "We can say this much with confidence: When change works, it tends to follow a pattern. **The people who change have clear direction, ample motivation, and a supportive environment.**"

This made me think about how supremely important it is for our significant others to be on board with our goals, wishes, and dreams. This is the person closest to you, in whom you can confide your innermost desires. You should be able to express freely where you envision yourself in the next five, ten, fifteen years; what you would like to accomplish in your career and personal life, and how you hope to reach your goals. In turn, you need to be a receptive listener when your partner is ready to discuss his or her own aspirations.

Often, couples have completely opposite personality traits, for example: shyness versus sociability, bookishness versus athleticism, or optimism versus pessimism. Couples tend to vary widely in money styles as well. I have frequently observed that people who tend to be savers often hook up with those who aren't happy unless the money is flowing freely. And such conflicting viewpoints can cause real heartache unless they are resolved to the satisfaction of both parties.

Arguments over money can poison a relationship—as it had with Sean and Lorraine. If you're a budgeter, but your husband never enters a check in the checkbook, much less balances it, then the two of you have a real challenge on your hands in terms of finding common ground. One of the ways to resolve conflicting money styles is for both people to put a specified portion of their paycheck into a mutual checking account, from which the monthly bills and other agreed-upon expenses are paid. A certain amount from each check should also go into savings, and then what is left remains in each individual's personal checking account to be spent at his or her discretion.

By keeping the personal money separate, the couple agrees not to engage in arguments about how it is spent. If the woman wants to save most of her leftover cash, she has the option to do so. If the guy wants to spend his on golf equipment or whatever strikes his fancy, then he can do that, too. I've seen many couples benefit from this peacemaking setup.

If you don't want to go as far as using separate bank accounts, at least try to sit down and come to some agreement over how your money will be spent. Create a savings goal together, and agree on what you are working toward: college funds for the kids, a nest egg for retirement, and so on. If you can hammer out the basics now, you will save yourself years of nagging, bickering, and outright fighting over what can be a source of contention for even the closest couples.

Jeanette Perez, an outstanding business manager and financial coach, gave me a glimpse of how she works with couples with different attitudes toward money:

"You have to address the emotional side of money. A few years ago, I worked with a couple that was experiencing problems because their beliefs about money were very different. They had to examine why they felt the way they did about money. He felt as if he was the only saver in the family. She felt as if she worked hard in the home, and should be able to spend as she wished.

"I got them to think about their attitudes, and get to a place where they could work together. Once you understand what is driving you, then it's easier to come together. I often use a guided meditation to help people recall what their first experience with money was. Often, you can connect the dots to your childhood.

"How did your parents handle money? My own dad was a great money manager. On the other hand, my mom was not. My mom never got a paycheck. She was a homemaker and mother. I watched their contrasting money styles and respected how they came together, despite their differences. My dad didn't allow us to feel 'I need it right now.' His attitude was 'It's only money.' There wasn't an urgency about money or an environment where money was everything. It was a very healthy attitude to pass on to one's children. That is the kind of attitude I try to instill in my clients, to help them address their differences about money."

This gifted financial coach was helping couples settle their conflicts about money so that they could achieve a Wealth Cure together. Remembering her words made me reflect on how destructive our spending habits can be if we don't understand why we want to spend in the ways we do.

PART FOUR

Maintaining Your Health and Wealth

maintain \mān-tān\: to keep in an existing state; preserve from failure or decline

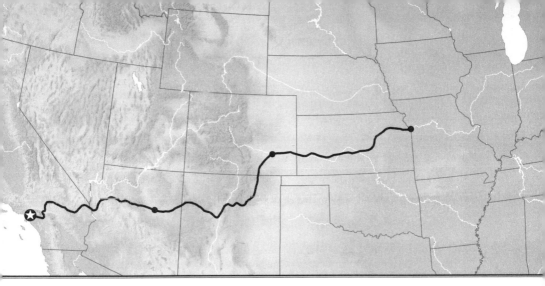

Put Your Money Where
Your Mouth Is

"When we're working solely for money, our
motivation is getting rather than giving."
—Marianne Williamson,
American author and lecturer

Why is it always quiet when it rains? It's as though everything has decided either to shut up or shut down and let the rain take center stage.

When I got back to my sleeping quarters on the train, I kicked off my shoes and slid under the covers in the lower berth. It began to rain. I stared out the window and tried to listen to the rain. I could hear the rhythmic sound of my own breathing, but because of the train's insulation and the sound of the wheels on the track I couldn't hear the rain at all. I could see it, of course, raindrops crashing against the glass and then sliding down in crooked little rivers. I felt as if I were in a vacuum-sealed capsule. Time was at a standstill, and something about that idea warmed my room the way my grandfather's voice used to when I was afraid as a child. I closed my eyes and tried to conjure my grandfather's comforting presence and the tenor and timbre of his voice. I really needed to hear his voice, and I needed to hear his soothing words.

"Why is this happening to me?" I asked aloud.

My fear was palpable. I've always valued my health and treated my body with respect and care. One saying that I love and have shared often with people is from the feminist author and activist Gloria Steinem: "We can tell our values by looking at our checkbook stubs." It's such a profound and true statement. Our words are not always in sync with our deeds, and sometimes we don't even realize it. Not consciously, anyway. We think we believe in certain ideals and principals and values, but sometimes when it comes down to it, few of those beliefs are reflected in our actions. I guess that's where the saying "Put your money where your mouth is" comes from—the need to prove the worth of our words.

Albert Einstein once said, "Try not to become a man of success but rather try to become a man of value." Which was I? A man of success or a man of value? Is it possible to be both?

I know people who swear up and down that they're not materialistic yet will be the first to own whatever new electronic "toy" is placed on the market or invest huge amounts of money in designer clothing. It always amazes me to hear these same people say "I can't afford it" when responding to a request for a donation or when discussing sending their children to a particular camp or program or taking a trip someplace. You can't afford it? I'd think, looking at their Louis Vuitton handbag or touch-screen cell phone.

My reaction caused me to reevaluate the way I use the word "afford." Sometimes I'd catch myself saying that I couldn't afford something that I could have managed to do financially. The truth was that I wasn't prioritizing it. What are the things we prioritize in our lives? How do those things affect our financial health?

My ex-girlfriend Nichole is one of the most nutrition-conscious people I know. She spends a significant amount of her income on food because she's extremely particular about what she puts into her body and into her daughter's body. While we were dating, I must have heard her say that "you are what you eat" one hundred times. She buys entirely organically grown produce. She only eats foods that are seasonal and grown locally, and she mostly shops at a farmer's market.

Not only did Nichole know all of the farmers at her local farmer's market, she'd taken the time to drive out to their farms to see the conditions in which the food she was eating was grown. I thought I was a healthy eater, but Nichole took it to a whole new level. At first I thought it was a little obsessive and that she was going overboard.

One night while we were preparing dinner, she started telling me a story about one of her colleagues, an English teacher, who owned a Carrera. "Poet in a Porsche" is what people called him. Nichole talked about how meticulous the man was with his car, how he only used premium gas, the best oil, top-of-the-line everything.

"He gave me a ride in the Porsche once," Nichole told me. "I sat down, and the first thing I saw was a diet soda. And there was also a package of some sort of convenience store pastry, the kind that always has an expiration date that's like five years away. Why would you put something into your body that can sit on a shelf in a 7-Eleven for that long? And how can someone care more about what he puts into his car than what he puts into his body?"

That story Nichole told me really changed my perspective. Whenever she mentioned that she couldn't afford something, I was not tempted to suggest that perhaps she should consider adjusting her budget so that she didn't spend as much on groceries. I understood that she budgeted her money the way she did because it was a reflection of her priorities. She would much rather spend money on organic kale than on a bracelet.

"And think of all the money I end up saving on medical bills," she used to say, only half joking.

Going to the doctor is admittedly expensive. I'm sure that a lot of people would readily say that they value their good health and would do anything to maintain it, but a large percentage of those very same people would probably balk at the thought of spending $300 on a preventative medical visit or lab tests. Yet they would not blink an eye if told they'd have to cough up the same amount for an appliance, designer shoes, or car maintenance.

I know quite a few people who never go to the doctor, even when they suspect that something is wrong with them. My friend Jennifer is a classic example of this. She had been complaining of a pain in her lower abdomen for months. It had, in fact, been bothering her for a year. Her friends would plead with her to see a doctor. Whenever I would talk to her on the phone, she'd tell me how much worse it had gotten. "Jen," I told her pretty firmly, "stop playing with your health."

"I don't have any insurance. I can't afford it," she'd said on more than one occasion. Jennifer's a freelance writer. She works temp jobs to make ends meet and teaches a class at a local college as an adjunct professor. I felt heartbroken that someone who worked so hard couldn't afford something as basic as a doctor visit. The reality is that a large number of people in this country find themselves in the same situation as Jennifer. I had this conversation with her when the national debate on health care had reached a fevered pitch—and I was speaking as loudly as anyone in favor of improving our health care system. That's probably one of the primary reasons I wanted to put my money where my mouth was.

One day I called Jennifer and made a lunch date with her. It was my intention to offer to pay the bill for her doctor visit and any lab tests that needed to be done, up to a specified amount. I was slowly working my way to the subject with small talk, questions about her writing and anecdotes from my recent travels. We'd barely been sitting at the table for five minutes when Jennifer showed me her new Gucci purse. "Huh?" I thought. How could someone choose a purse over the resolution of her physical pain?

"What about going to the doctor?" I asked her. I couldn't tell through the blank expression on her face whether she was offended, embarrassed, or a combination of both. What I did know, though, was that I sounded horribly judgmental. I could hear it in my voice, but right then, in that moment, I didn't care.

"I'm saving toward that," Jennifer announced hesitantly. "I'll go just as soon as I get enough money." Her eyes were lowered, and her tone was apologetic, like a child who'd been chastised. My judgment had prompted her to feel ashamed. Even though I was embarrassed to have brought that on, I felt it was absolutely appropriate. She *should* be ashamed of herself, I thought. I didn't really know what to say after that, and clearly neither did she. The rest of our lunch was awkward, full of long silences and cautiously spoken statements.

It wasn't until the bill came that I started to soften my stance. When the waiter brought the check, Jennifer immediately picked up her brand-new purse, opened her wallet, and started counting her bills.

"What are you doing?" I asked, grabbing the bill. "I invited you. This is my treat." She didn't pay me any mind. She continued counting her money. I realized then that I hadn't just made her ashamed of her actions; I had also unintentionally wounded her pride. Jennifer had every right to buy herself a purse. She didn't need my approval, and I had no right to make her feel bad about herself. But as a friend I have an obligation to let my friends know my perspective when I think a choice that they're making is potentially harmful. In friendship, silence is not always golden.

When I first started seeing Nichole, she would tell me about how guarded she'd become when it came to revealing information about anything she'd done or intended to do for herself. This included things that might bring her pleasure or joy, for fear that people would judge her and make her feel bad about herself. She was a single mother, and people had their specific ideas and perspectives on how she should behave and what was appropriate or inappropriate to do. If people spotted her out at night, they'd ask her who was watching her daughter. If she bought herself something new, people would make her feel as though she'd sacrificed her daughter's needs for her own selfish desires. They never took into account the possibility that they might not have all the information, that there might be circumstances of which they were unaware and, most important, that it wasn't their place or right to judge her. And now here I was doing something similar to one of my friends.

Isn't it funny how we can so easily use a possession as a way to make ourselves feel superior to others, as though our lives, our wishes, our opinions, matter more? Money is one of those possessions that illicits this sort of warped sense of entitlement. I hear people talking all the time about what "poor" people should and shouldn't do, what they have and don't have, and why their behavior is a problem. I didn't want to be one of those people. And in my own way, here I was treating *my friend* as though she were a "poor" person and judging her actions.

At that moment, I realized that if I decided to help someone I shouldn't do it with conditions. It isn't my place to judge her; it's my place to either help or not. I needed to put my money where my mouth was and not put any conditions or judgment on it. "Actually," I told her as I slid my credit card into the leather check holder. "I invited you to lunch for a reason." I went on to tell her about my offer to cover the expense of her doctor visit and lab tests. I did something else that I hadn't intended to do when I'd set the lunch appointment. I told her that I would go with her to the doctor, if she wanted me to.

It had taken me no time at all to recognize Jennifer's shame and wounded pride. What it had taken me longer to see was the fear. Once I did see it, I realized it was her fear that had kept her from going to the doctor. Fear prevented her from making her pain a priority—timewise and money-wise. Her complaints about the pain in her abdomen might have been her way of asking for help—not financially but in another way that is worth even more than money between friends. She'd wanted someone to walk with her through the experience. I became absolutely sure after I'd volunteered to help her. **She was much more moved by the offer of my presence than the offer of my money.**

Our financial actions and our decisions about what we can and can't afford can so easily be guided—and misguided—by fear. Only we know what we're afraid of and why we sabotage ourselves. **Sometimes the "good" life we create for ourselves is only an elaborate and oftentimes**

expensive way to avoid the "true" life that we're intended to live, the one that revolves around authentic joy.

The only way to afford the life we were meant to live is to release ourselves from those fears. I was determined to find out what those fears were in my life and why this illness was giving rise to them. Yes, I was afraid of death, but why? Death is inevitable. It is the one thing we can be certain of in this life. I've met and witnessed lots of people who were at peace with the news of their impending death. Jarrett was one of them. During that brief span of time between when he'd learned of his cancer and when he'd passed away, he was filled with gratitude.

"I'm so grateful that I got a chance to know this kind of love with Tracey," Jarrett had told me. "I always felt like it was something that happened to other people."

He'd seen his experience of love, of building a life with his soul mate, as a precious gift he had been fortunate enough to receive during his time on earth, but from my point of view, he was robbed of the ability to fully enjoy that precious gift. Jarrett was walking his journey from a perspective of blessings, not loss. He was not afraid, he was grateful. He had an attitude of gratitude. And then it clicked. Part of my Wealth Cure had to include a shift in perspective and attitude. Away from fear and toward gratitude no matter what God put in front of me. Could I be so courageous to not even judge the challenges that come my way and be able to say, "Thank you for this obstacle; with it, you're allowing me to get stronger." Obstacles in life are just like weights in a weight room. You push the weight, and your muscles strengthen. With an attitude shift, we can strengthen in just the same way.

I believed that the deaths of my father, uncle, and even grandfather were premature. I felt I'd been robbed of the gift of having them in my life. I felt that they'd been robbed of gifts that they'd been unable to fully enjoy. And here I was, afraid of the cancer that had taken up residence in my thyroid and possibly spread to other parts of my body.

Though I wasn't as much of a purist as Nichole, I had been quite vigilant about my health. My father was a psychiatrist, and although his specialty was the mind, he was a medical doctor. My mother is also a physician, an anesthesiologist. Doctors don't scare me quite as much as they do other people. I've spent my life surrounded by them, so I am consistent with my routine checkups, and I don't hesitate to make a medical appointment if something out of the ordinary happens. Still I wound up with cancer. Did I have it in me to shift my perspective, not judge it, and approach my diagnosis with gratitude? I'm not sure I'm that evolved yet, but I could certainly do my best.

I was lying there in the sleeping cabin, suspended somewhere in the midst of a surreal, dream-like state. I thought about Nichole, about the beautiful rainy afternoons we'd shared in Washington, D.C., watching a seemingly endless stream of old movies as the three of us—Nichole, her daughter, Jade, and I—put together an elaborate five-thousand-piece jigsaw puzzle. We played board games like Monopoly and Scrabble.

Just as suddenly as those memories had popped into my head, my grandfather's voice rang through my mind. I could hear it as clearly as if he was standing beside me. Don't be afraid, nothing bad is going to happen to you. And I knew that he wasn't talking about the rain. He was talking about what I'd allowed to slip through my hands. That was one of the things that scared me about being diagnosed with cancer. All my life I'd said that I wanted to be with my soul mate. I'd wanted to have children, to be in a family unit. Yet everything I'd done, every choice I'd made, had taken me in the direction of being alone.

I'd allowed my fears—fears I'd had been harboring about relationships since the breakup of my parents' marriage—to keep me from fully committing to the life that I knew deep down would bring me my most authentic joy. I'd held that joy, ever so briefly, but I'd let go, and now I was frightened that I might not have enough time to get it back. Whenever I thought about living whatever amount of time I had left of my life—whether it was one hour, one day, one year, or fifty years—without that specific type of joy, the more afraid I became. I wasn't like Jarrett. I wasn't satisfied with having been given the gift of the experience, however briefly. Maybe he'd been able to feel that way because he'd accepted the gift; he'd committed to it in his life and allowed himself to afford it in every way. I hadn't—so I wanted another chance. I wanted more. And with that thought, the train's rolling motion rocked me to sleep.

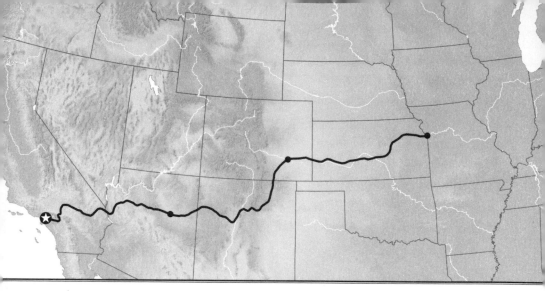

I Am George

"Follow your honest convictions and be strong."

—William Makepeace Thackeray,
Indian-born English author and novelist

S omewhere on my train ride, in that interim space during travel that isn't quite afternoon or evening, I awoke from a good nap. Half a second later, while I was still in a semiconscious state, the laughter of an older African American man stirred me to attention.

"Next stop, Trinidad! Trinidad, Colorado, next stop!" he bellowed.

Trinidad? Am I still dreaming? I thought. He was taking tickets and chatting up some passengers who were laughing at his jokes. My reaction was not up to speed with the levity. And there really is a Trinidad in Colorado. But I was still half asleep, and, in a way, I resented the chorus of laughter but couldn't source why. The passengers were content, the ticket man was happy, and yet a deep well of hurt built up inside of me. Where's this coming from? I asked myself in that kind of alert slumber that seems so real when you are awakened by surprise.

Then I remembered "George." I put him out of my mind for a moment and fumbled to get one of my phone chargers out, but George drifted back to me. I considered checking my e-mails, and while searching through my bag, I felt George grip me so tightly it was as if I couldn't move. I realized where my spirit was going, my whole response to the laughter. I wasn't just reacting on George's behalf; I was reacting as George must have done a thousand times to laughter that, unlike what I had just heard, was more at the expense of his dignity than alongside it. Except in George's case, he couldn't show his dissatisfaction. I was free to scowl and express my discomfort while reaching for any number of my expensive gadgets, whereas George, in his day, had to repress all of it—his resentment, his degradation— with a smile on his face and as much laughter as possible.

Of course it's fair for you to wonder at this point, *Who is George?* Around the end of the nineteenth century, railroad travel in America became more luxurious, and like boats, trains began to have sleeping compartments. A genius businessman and entrepreneur by the name of George Pullman created sleeping cars that could attach themselves to any company's trains (think a dedicated first-class cabin on different airlines but all owned by a single company). These were called Pullman cars, and with each Pullman car came a Pullman porter to attend to the passengers' every need.

Pullman porters had to dress impeccably and speak perfect English. They had to be willing to work for low wages and earn most of their money off of tips from passengers. They had to pay for their own food and perform cleaning duties. They had to help the conductor with his work, though they themselves could never hope to be promoted to conductor, a job reserved for white men only. See, above all, Pullman porters had to be black.

Given the limited job opportunities afforded black men during that time, a Pullman porter become one of the best jobs to which a black man in America could aspire. If you were a Pullman porter, you were doing well. The sons and daughters of Pullman porters were often the first in their family to attend college, usually because the porters themselves would save as much money as possible from their tips and earnings toward their children's tutoring and education.

Oh yes, one more thing, all Pullman porters could be referred to by any passenger merely as "George" (as in the first name of the company's owner) and would have to answer and respond accordingly, just as if their own first name had been called.

I remember hearing a story once from a Pullman porter who said he always hoped to be on the same train when the great comic Jackie Gleason was traveling. He said that Gleason would often tip each porter upward of a hundred dollars (a huge sum in the 1940s and 1950s). But more important than that, Gleason would always insist on knowing each porter's actual name and never called him "George."

A white man's first name universally given to black men was in the tradition of slaves having the last name of the slave master forced upon them. The irony and injustice of this was not lost even in those times.

Yet the Pullman porters themselves had no problem with perception and respect within their own community. They were often its pillars. They had a special devotion to education and at the same time were among the first builders of the African American middle class. In addition to a track record of economic independence and civic leadership, the Pullman porters left a legacy of conviction. Three generations of Pullman porters thrived during the heyday of American train travel. It should come as no surprise that not only was Malcolm X once a Pullman porter, but so were Gordon Parks and Thurgood Marshall.

Can you imagine a Pullman porter training young Thurgood in the 1930s and thirty years later witnessing him serve on the U.S. Supreme Court? The Pullman porters made sacrifices for the betterment of their families, community, and country. That type of effort must be a part of my Wealth Cure as well. So to answer the question *Who is George?* Me. I am George. And with that thought I plugged my BlackBerry into the charger, put my earbuds in, looked out the window and proudly stared at our country's beautiful landscape rushing by, feeling empowered by all of the Georges that had ridden these same railways before me.

Those men called George believed in dignity, conviction, and the power to elevate the means of their family through financial discipline and education. How did we stray so far away from those values? How is it that we have arrived at a place where bragging about conspicuous spending has more clout than fiscal responsibility?

So riding on that train, I finally remembered George again, and realized I am part of him, and I need to be. That we all are, as Americans, no matter what race, a part of George. When I have children, if I tell them the story of George, and they don't believe me because in their world it's impossible to conceive of, that might be a sign of real progress. But if I fail to tell them the story, or fail to remember it myself, then that is my shame. And if my lack of remembering means I forget to tell my children the story, and they make mistakes in life, that would be a sad regression from all the hard work and sacrifices that Pullman porters made for all of us.

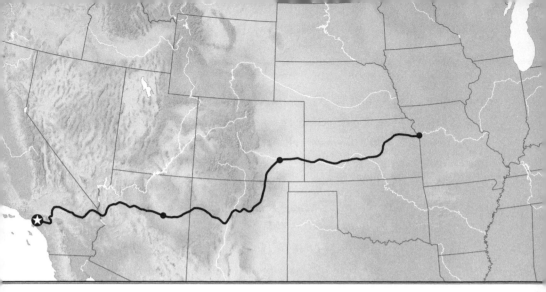

FOLLOW YOUR HEART

"You can only become truly accomplished at
something you love. Don't make money your
goal. Instead, pursue the things you love doing,
and then do them so well that people can't take
their eyes off you."

—Maya Angelou, poet

I'm not sure that my dreams for my life have ever been clear in a visual
way. I think it has always been emotional. I feel a sense of completeness
when I am where I am supposed to be, doing what I am supposed to be
doing, or with the person I'm supposed to be around. Even if, at the time,
it doesn't seem to make sense, it might feel like the right place, the right
person, the right decision.

"Right" is not synonymous with "easy," though. **The right place is not
always the easy place; the right person is not always the person who is
easiest to be with; the right decision is not always the one that's easiest**

to carry out. Learning to tell the difference was, for me, an important milestone toward understanding as well as achieving both value and success.

When I graduated with a law degree from Harvard Law School and a master's from the Kennedy School of Government at Harvard, I was offered a number of high-paying jobs. The job offers were from prestigious New York City law firms where I'd interned during my summers in law school. Since I had two graduate degrees, they said I would actually begin as a second-year attorney and that I would be earning a second-year salary. For a twenty-five year-old with student loans to repay, six figures was a lot of money. So you can imagine the look on my father's face when I explained to him that I was turning down all of the offers and acting on stage and screen.

I thought the cliché that all actors were waiters was a myth until I became both an actor *and* a waiter. The overnight eleven-to-seven shift waiting tables in a ketchup-stained apron at the twenty-four-hour diner was a world apart from the tailored suit, office-with-an-assistant position I'd declined. The pay was drastically different, too. As my Uncle Frank, who'd succumbed to cancer the year before, had told me, **"If you are making any decision solely based on money, then it is the wrong decision."**

He continued, "Money can be a factor in your decision making, but if it is the primary reason, it's the incorrect decision." Those words would become my daily scripture while scrubbing the diner floors at five in the morning after the club-goer rush. Although I was certainly an overeducated waiter, the flexible schedule allowed me to pursue my North Star. That waitering job turned out to be more valuable than any job I've had to date.

I was also really good at it. While in that apron, I was the best waiter I could be, and I strived to give customers great service. Even if the order was for eggs and toast, if they were seated in my section, they got five-star service! **Success is habit-forming, no matter what the arena.** I don't view success and value as opposing entities, although I do think it's possible to have one without the other. Success, as defined by money and fame,

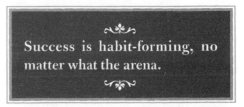

Success is habit-forming, no matter what the arena.

can be acquired and maintained without value. There is a saying that a house without love is not a home. That is because love is what gives the word "home" its meaning. If a person's success has no meaning, then all of the fame and money that person has is without value.

I've always enjoyed stepping into the lives of others, either as a silent observer or as an active participant. That passion existed long before I fell in love with acting. The same passion guided me toward a law degree and mentoring youth. An investment does not always have to be in the form of money. You can make investments in yourself—through education, for example—but investment in others offers the greatest returns.

Mentoring has undoubtedly helped me stay grounded. When you make an investment in the life of another person, there is an emotional connection, and you are forever impacted by that experience.

In many ways, I feel as though our society is drifting farther away from that method of connection. Making a positive impact in another person's life is an instant portal through which we can experience our own lives anew. **We seem to be moving away from investing in others.** The very fact that our public school system, once the greatest in the world, struggles to educate our youth is one indication of our unwillingness to invest in others. I often hear people say, "If it doesn't involve me or mine, why should I care?"

This is not to say that we're not engaging with other people. We are, in a big way. People spend an inordinate amount of time interacting with countless others on social-networking sites like Facebook and Twitter. That's not the same as connecting with people in person and baring witness to the inner landscape of their lives, which gives us a certain perspective on our own lives.

I looked out the train window and saw that we were passing by a large farm. I was suddenly back in Iowa, standing at the threshold of my grandmother's kitchen. I could almost smell her freshly baked bread. It made me smile to remember her.

There were neatly organized rows of crops flanking both sides of the highway and extending as far as I could see in all directions. I noticed there were people in between all those rows. It took me a moment to realize that they were weary-faced migrant workers assigned the arduous task of harvesting all of those crops.

Looking at the workers from the train window, I had an urge to speak with them. But what would I say? Would I tell them that I thought of them every time I paid an exorbitant price for a piece of organic fruit? (I always wondered how much of that money found its way into their pockets.) Or would I tell them that I included them in the grace I spoke before every meal? *And the hands that planted, nurtured the growth, and then picked this food. . . .* This made me think about the millions of *hands* throughout time that have cultivated the food that has allowed all of us to be alive.

I imagined they would laugh at the very idea that they got any additional money for the high-priced organic produce that some of my friends spend their whole paychecks on. I also guessed that a good number of them were probably undocumented workers, foreigners doing work that many Americans wouldn't.

So many of the young people who write to me and talk to me after my lectures tell me how hard it is for them to find work. I'll often offer suggestions, hoping to set off a light bulb. "Have you tried waitressing?" I might ask. Or "Theaters are usually always looking for good ushers." A lot of times these suggestions are met with laughter.

"Hill, I would never work at McDonald's" is a statement I've heard so much that I've lost count. I find myself trying to find the words to explain that working hard at a job, any job, that allows you to earn an honest wage so you can begin building a foundation to support yourself and your dreams should never be considered beneath you. Of course, employers have a reciprocal responsibility to offer their employees a living wage.

"Those kinda jobs don't even pay you nothin'," I've heard again and again. "You can't even buy a nice ride." And I'm amazed at the sorts of things we prioritize or feel are important to own. Meanwhile, here was this group of men and women picking crops in a field. Are they even thinking about a "North Star"? Or was their North Star simply making sure their family had food and shelter? They were doing whatever it took to help their families make it each day. **And without question, I believe the ultimate**

123

quiet dignity is providing for your family. Their work ethic reminded me of something Dr. King said: "Whatever your life's work, do it well."

I grabbed my journal to write some notes, then looked out the window again and saw two men who looked nothing like those doing the work, clearly authority figures, walking down the rows, inspecting the job that was being done.

My heart sank. My head flooded with images of slaves, sharecroppers, migrant workers—our nation and its economy were built on the labor of those sorts of people. People like my ancestors, people whose commitment and perseverance were far stronger than most of us can imagine, much like the men and women in that field, hoping to earn enough money to try to build a better life for their families.

One of my foundation's mentees told me that his mother used the saying "Money doesn't grow on trees." That adage came out of the sharecropping experience, because no matter how much you grew and how much you picked, you would still find yourself in debt. How difficult had life become for these migrant workers during this economic downturn? As I looked at the workers, their fingers quickly moving from plant to basket, I remembered what that young brother had said. Maybe his mother was right. I took up my pen and began writing again. I wrote for the next few hours until dinnertime.

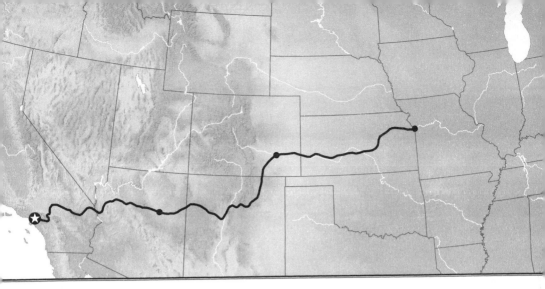

A Leap of Faith

"When you walk to the edge of all the light you
have and take that first step into the darkness of
the unknown, you must believe that one of two
things will happen: There will be something
solid for you to stand upon, or, you will be
taught how to fly."

—Patrick Overton, American author,
poet, speaker, educator

At six, I showered and dressed and went to the dining car to meet
Scott for dinner. When he arrived, he was with someone. At first I
thought it might be his mother, but we'd talked for several hours and
he'd never mentioned anything about traveling with a companion. She
was a lovely woman with a commanding presence, the sort that makes
you sit up straight and pay attention. She looked to be in her late fifties.
Her hair was in an extremely short salt-and-pepper Afro and reminded

me of the amazing Nikki Giovanni. She was wearing a stylish linen outfit, top and trousers. Her neck and wrists were adorned with the most striking necklace and bracelets I'd ever seen. I stood up as Scott began his introduction. He first told her my name.

"And Hill, this is Mabel," he finished.

"Mabel Macalaster," she added, taking the hand I'd held out to her and squeezing it between her two palms. She had a melodic voice, and she spoke as though Scott and I were the only two people who mattered. "Good to meet you."

After exchanging a few pleasantries, Scott, Mabel, and I walked over to the dining area and were seated at a table.

"Are you from Los Angeles?" I asked Mabel, trying to break the ice.

"Oh, no. I live right outside of Chicago. I went to L.A. to see my daughter. She's in her second year at USC. She found herself a job out there, so she's not coming home this summer. I thought it'd be nice to pay her a visit." Mabel told us that her daughter was studying political science and was planning to apply to law school once she graduated. I was impressed but not surprised. From the few minutes that I'd known Mabel, I couldn't imagine her raising a child who wasn't smart and interesting.

Apparently Mabel and Scott had met yesterday while I was in my room writing and napping. Waiting in line for coffee in the lounge car, they'd gotten to know each other and struck up an unlikely friendship.

"Mabel was laid off, too," Scott volunteered as though offering it up as proof that the two of them had something important in common.

I wasn't sure what to say, but Mabel didn't hesitate to speak.

"Best thing that ever happened to me," she said, smiling. "I didn't think so at the time, though. Back then, it was like the kiss of death. I mean, imagine, a single mother with a daughter who was entering her last year of high school. I was devastated. If I didn't have a job, how were we going to eat? How was I going pay for college applications? A senior prom dress? I had a list of bills as long as my arm."

"So what'd you do?" I asked, genuinely curious about how she'd gone from a place of fear to being able to sit there with Scott and me, laughing about a situation that most would consider negative but that she saw as just the opposite. I'd heard a number of very inspirational stories about how people who'd once been victims of the country's economic downturn used the difficulty as a catalyst to transform their lives for the better. I'd also heard stories that broke my heart, stories of people who'd found themselves trapped in the most horrible financial circumstances and unable to find a way out.

Mabel told me about how she started making beaded jewelry as a hobby right after her daughter was born. She used books, videos, and the process of trial and error.

"In time, it was something my daughter and I could do together," she said. "You know, spend a Sunday afternoon sitting on the carpet, stringing together a necklace while watching a movie."

She always got compliments from friends, family members, and even strangers. She and her daughter would give the jewelry as Christmas and birthday presents. Then friends who admired the pieces they were wearing would request, "Could you make me one like that, but a little longer?"

When Mabel got laid off, she had a lot of time on her hands, so to stave off depression and boredom, she spent most of her free time beading. She'd gathered quite a collection of necklaces and bracelets. One afternoon, she'd laid them out on her dining room table. She'd written her Christmas list and was trying to decide to whom she'd give what. One of her friends came over for a visit and saw all the pieces neatly displayed on the table.

"Girl," Mabel's friend said to her, "you ought to sell these." After a whole lot of convincing, Mabel agreed to let a few of her friends put together a little salon-style holiday event so she could sell her jewelry.

Each of the women invited other female friends. They bought some wine, cheese, and crudités for the guests. Nearly everyone who was invited showed up, and they all loved Mabel's jewelry.

"I sold out of pieces," she told us, laughing at the memory. "I made more income that day than I would've made in two months at my old job. It was like pennies from heaven. And now, here I am." **I found it interesting that Mabel used the word "income" and not "money," as if she realized**

what most people don't—that there is a flow to currency, either incoming or outgoing.

Mabel placed one of her business cards on the table right in front of me. It was a simple white card, probably printed on a home computer. On the card, in big navy-blue curlicue letters, it read "Made by Mabel." Sprawled in a wavy line underneath those words was the image of an unhooked beaded necklace. Mabel's contact information was listed underneath that.

"I have a website, too," she announced proudly while pointing to the web address printed on the card. "We even take PayPal."

"Isn't that an incredible story?" Scott asked.

I nodded and smiled at Mabel. "It sure is."

"It almost didn't happen," Mabel confessed. "If it wasn't for my friends, I'd probably still be reading the want ads and trying to figure out how to extend my unemployment. This happened because of them."

After that first salon, Mabel's friends suggested that she open a business. Despite the success she'd had at the salon, she wouldn't even entertain that possibility. Despite all of the compliments she'd received on her jewelry pieces over the years, Mabel didn't consider herself a professional.

"And I'm old," she added. Scott and I both assured Mabel that "old" was not an adjective that could be used to describe her.

"Oh, thanks, but you know what I mean," she continued. "I'm not some sprightly twenty- or thirty-something. I'd always believed that whatever you're doing when you get to your fifties is what you're going to keep doing until you retire. What fifty-year-old woman just ups and hangs out a shingle and says, 'Now I'm going to try to keep a roof over our heads by making jewelry?' It just felt so irresponsible. I needed to go out and act like an adult, get a real job."

Mabel's explanation felt painfully true in so many ways. **I've heard a lot of people, some even as young as their thirties, talk about all the things they'd do if they were younger.** They'd start acting, they'd travel through Europe, they'd climb Mount Everest, they'd quit work and start dancing or painting, or they'd try to write a book. But it was always something they'd do if they were *just younger.*

I knew Mabel was egging us on. She knew small businesses are the engine of our economy. And that entrepreneurs like herself control that engine. Small businesses create more jobs in the American economy than any other sector. So we, now more than ever, need more Mabels to step out, take a risk, and be entrepreneurs creating successful businesses to restart our economic engine.

What is it about getting older that convinces people that they are unable to make different choices about their lives? Why do people feel that age confines them to their circumstances, relegates them to the exact life they are living? What is most disturbing is that the choice is usually not just about the life they're living versus some fantasy life. A misguided notion of responsibility makes them believe they are bound to a certain life rather than the life to which they are attracted by a pure and simple joy.

"What made you change your mind?" I asked Mabel. I was really interested to hear what she had to say. Already I knew that I wanted to share this extraordinary woman's story. I knew that people would find it inspiring, but I also knew that they'd dismiss it as something that happened to other people, not to them. **Doubt is our biggest deterrent. It's what feeds fear—and fear is what stops so many of us from pursuing our dreams, especially those dreams that we never knew we could claim.**

"Honestly, Hill, I never completely changed my mind. There are still times when I think, Now, Mabel, you know you need to just go on and get a job." She paused. "And you know what's really funny? I was taught that it's in poor taste to talk about money with anyone other than family, but . . . I'm making so much more income operating my business than I was sitting around being somebody's executive secretary. I guess it feels funny to me because it doesn't feel like work."

Mabel went on to explain that she truly is a "diva," but not in the Patti Labelle, Bette Midler, Elizabeth Taylor way. She is a new kind of diva. Mabel said, "The best way to be a diva is to have your own ends. . . . So the money I save, I call DIVAdends!" We laughed at Mabel's pun on the word "dividend," the money that a company gives to shareholders out of its earnings, usually quarterly. What Mabel said was so profound. **We must**

pay ourselves first by saving. You can be a "diva" if you always add the "ends."

"I understand what you're saying about it not feeling like real 'work,'" I told her. "I guess what I was really trying to get at was that moment when you decided to make business cards, get a website, really turn it into a business."

She explained that after the first salon, she continued selling her jewelry because she wasn't having any success finding traditional work, and she needed the money. Her friends hosted another event, at which she again sold out of merchandise. "And I still didn't get the hint," she said. Since word had spread about her pieces, there had been more people in attendance. She was asked over and over for a business card. She didn't have any. With her daughter's help, she designed and printed out some business cards the very next day.

"After a while," Mabel said, "I was too busy with the jewelry to fool around with job-hunting anymore. You could say that's when it really became official."

"Were you afraid?" Scott asked. There was something in his voice that I recognized from when he'd asked me that very same question. I sensed that the question probably had more to do with him and with what he was going through than it did with Mabel or me.

"Well," Mabel told him, "when you're standing on a ledge, you don't look down. You just take baby steps until you get where you're trying to go."

"But what happens if you fall?" Scott added.

"Then you land on solid ground," I said, before Mabel could answer. It was the last part of a saying that my cousin Rev. Beckwith tells people all the time: "When you take a leap of faith, there are only two things that can happen. You learn to fly, or you land on solid ground."

I shared that with Scott and Mabel. When I'd finished talking, they looked at each other.

"Well, honey, it feels like I'm flying." Mabel smiled.

Scott wasn't quite as enthusiastic when he said, "I guess I'm standing on solid ground," but at least he laughed afterward.

The two of them looked at me. They were expecting me to throw down my own pronouncement. I hesitated before confessing, "Right now, I guess you could say that I'm standing on the ledge, just about to take my leap of faith."

After a pause, Mabel looked at me, gave me a big hug, and said, "You're either getting married, quitting your job, or having surgery. I pray for you either way, baby!"

And we all laughed. I was startled by her almost prescient statement. A leap of faith, indeed.

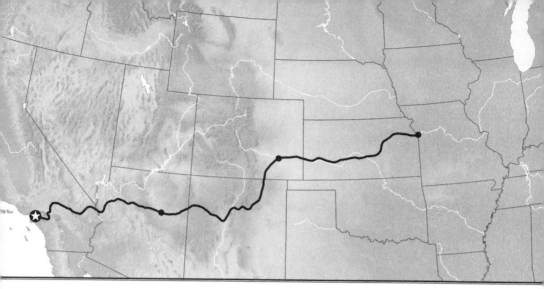

THE PATH TO BEING
UNREASONABLY HAPPY

"It is neither wealth nor splendor; but tranquil-
ity and occupation which give you happiness."
—Thomas Jefferson,
third president of the United States and
author of the Declaration of Independence

My own experience has taught me that if you follow your passion you will be successful. If your goal in life is to be unreasonably happy, shouldn't you choose a line of work that you enjoy? Let's do the math. If you work from the time you finish college until age sixty-five, then you will spend about forty-three years at your job. If you work a forty-hour workweek with two weeks of vacation per year, that amounts to eighty-six thousand hours of your life that you will spend working. And I'm not even including summer jobs before you get out of school. If you live to be eighty, you'll have lived around seven hundred thousand eight hundred hours. You will have spent almost one-eighth of your entire life working. And if you subtract out the time you spend sleeping, its even *more* of your life. Do you want to spend more than one-eighth of your life doing work that you don't find rewarding, that you don't feel you're great at, that you don't enjoy?

Margaret Roach, formerly executive vice president and editorial director at Martha Stewart Living Omnimedia, had a long and successful career in magazine publishing and media, but at a certain point, she decided that she wanted to get out of the rat race and find work that was more meaningful. As she says in her memoir, *And I Shall Have Some Peace There*, "If I was so successful . . . then why had I pushpinned a cryptic note to myself on the kitchen wall, a plaintive shorthand list called Tolerances, as in, how much can you tolerate of what for how long? Why were all my years-old diaries aching with phrases like *the hit-by-car feelings of my workday* and *where is my creativity?*" So she mustered her courage and quit her job, moved to a house in the country, began a gardening blog, and wrote an award-winning gardening book as well as an inspiring memoir about how she changed her life. She took the path to being unreasonably happy.

For many people in creative fields, their passion surfaced early in childhood. Stephen King began writing stories when he was a child, and after college, he taught high school English and wrote stories for magazines. He was either paid very little or not at all for his work, but he kept at it because he had no choice: It was his *passion*. His first novel, *Carrie*, which was discovered on a pile of unsolicited manuscripts, was published when he was twenty-seven years old. It was a runaway success, and the rest is history.

In his book *On Writing*, King describes finding work that is your passion: "Writing isn't about making money, getting famous, getting dates, getting laid, or making friends. In the end, it's about enriching the lives of those who will read your work, and enriching your own life as well. . . . When you find something at which you are talented, you do it (whatever it is) until your fingers bleed or your eyes are ready to fall out of your head."

What if you are doing perfectly fine in your field of work, yet you are not passionate about it? Do you just quit your day job and take a ground-level position in the career of your choice? What if you have obligations, a mortgage, children, the whole nine yards?

Many of us like to say, "I'll be happy when I have *that* job," "*that* house," "*that* car," "*that* amount of money." Yet what if you reversed it and realized that those things will come to you *if you decide to follow your passion and be happy first*? **When you decide to be happy, you take control of your life's direction, as opposed to waiting for the right object to fall in your path or the right job opportunity to crop up.** Using your Wealth Factors—particularly the ones that are most in your control—as stepping-stones toward happiness is the route to true satisfaction now, not in some ephemeral, undefined future time and place.

How does your life look right now, at this very second? Does it look like you want it to? If not, what are you willing to do to either transform it or change your own relationship to it? In other words, find happiness through the Wealth Factors you can control right now, or to change what is happening in your life externally? Both actions require you to be honest with yourself, to courageously face your fears, and to take risks. It can be scary to be honest with yourself and admit that this is your life, here and now—and that you must commit to being happy in it.

Let's say that your job as a retail manager is something you just fell into. You got a job on the sales floor after college, found out that you excelled at chatting up customers and selling, and eventually got a couple of promotions along the way. Now you're feeling dissatisfied, because this isn't the career path you always saw yourself following. Maybe you wanted to be a successful artist. Do you ditch your steady day job, rent a garret, and start painting self-portraits? That probably wouldn't be the best course of action for most of us, unless we're budding Rembrandts.

First, you should take a look at where you are now and how you got there. Maybe you have a particular talent for selling, and that talent is tied to your people skills. Are there aspects of your workday that you find appealing? **Is there a particular task that makes the time fly by when you do it?** Is there another division in your company where you might use your creative skills—perhaps in marketing? Are there areas of your job that do fulfill you, even though there is a nagging feeling in the back of your mind that you are just biding time?

Unless you're absolutely miserable at work, it would probably be career suicide to quit now and start being an artiste. For one thing, in the current economy, jobs are valuable, and there are many people waiting to snap up your position if you leave. If you can appreciate the good aspects of your work and determine to be happy in what you are doing, you might wind up excelling to heights that you hadn't imagined. Meanwhile, find ways to pursue your creative interests, either at work creating cutting-edge displays or advertisements or at weekend classes or other educational opportunities.

According to business manager and financial coach Jeanette Perez, "A person who isn't doing what he or she loves needs to have an 'in the meantime' plan. Even if you work in the mailroom, you can show your greatness. It is all in how you perceive your current position. Start by setting your intention to move in another direction. If you *believe* that you can accomplish something, then you will. As you work to maintain your position, you are simultaneously working to move into another place. If you wish to be creative, you can be creative in anything that you do.

More than half of all people feel stuck in their jobs. But unless you are a careful observer of your own thoughts, you are living by default. Do you believe that you can change, or that you can't?

Jeanette continues, "For many years, I wanted to leave the accounting profession. The greed and hunger for power associated with money really drove me nuts. When I moved to L.A. and started my career in business management, working with high-profile entertainers, I realized that individuals were earning thirty thousand dollars for one television episode, for doing what they loved, and activating their creativity. I wondered how I could be creative in the work that I do with finances. And it totally **changed my attitude** toward my job."

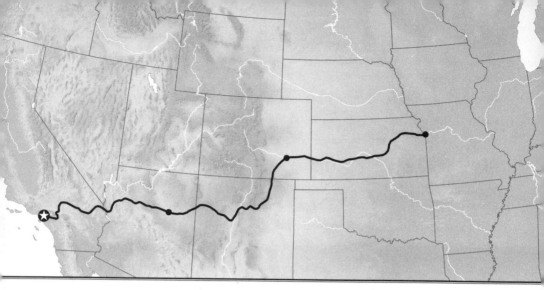

WHO TEACHES US
ABOUT MONEY?

"Often people attempt to live their lives back-
wards; they try to have more things, or more
money, in order to do more of what they want,
so they will be happier. The way it actually
works is the reverse. You must first be who you
really are, then do what you need to do, in order to have what you want."

—Margaret Young, American singer

Dinner with Mabel and Scott was fun, informative and inspiring. I
enjoyed the freedom that being on the train gave me to interact
spontaneously with people. Where would I have ever been able to bump
into and then spend that kind of time with somebody like Mabel? When

would I have been able to break bread with her and hear firsthand about one of the most significant personal and professional experiences of her life?

The story Mabel shared was a remarkable one, and there were many questions I wanted to ask. The time we were together flew by, but that's not why some of the questions remained unasked. Despite the immediate intimacy Scott, Mabel, and I all felt and displayed in our conversations, I didn't feel it was appropriate. I wanted to ask her questions that were a bit more structural. Questions about how she'd made the transition from being an employee to being self-employed, about how she'd learned to make certain decisions like what percentage of her sales income she'd use to reinvest in her company. These aren't little pieces of knowledge that you just pick up on your own or through osmosis. It's knowledge that you set out to learn, information that you go in search of. I didn't ask, because the last thing I wanted was to seem disrespectful or offensive. I just kept my curiosity to myself. But those are the types of questions you ask mentors—people who have experiences in areas where you hope to be successful, individuals from whom you can learn about their successes and missteps.

What's ironic is that the reasons I wanted to ask Mabel those questions are the same reasons I decided not to. She herself said it during the conversation: It's considered impolite and crass to talk about money. And she was right. It's just understood that you don't ask people about their salaries or how much they pay for rent or that brand-new car or that big ole rock on a finger. People are supposed to volunteer information about these things, and even then, it's a slippery slope. People who volunteer too much or the wrong type of financial information about themselves are regarded with suspicion. They are viewed as tacky, distasteful, or too showy.

Mabel said something else along the same lines that struck me. She mentioned that she had had a list of bills as long as her arm. She admitted to needing her salary in order to survive. These days, with so many people struggling financially, it's not unusual to hear people talking about the difficulties they are having, but that admission is by and large always accompanied by guilt. It's as though we're not supposed to show that we are financially vulnerable, that we need money.

"Soap opera world," is what my former girlfriend, Nichole, used to call it. "Do you ever notice how in soap operas," she told me, "nobody works a real job, but everybody lives in a big house, wears nice clothes, and knows all the rich people, even the people who've just wandered into town?"

Here's my question: If you don't talk about money, how are you supposed to learn about it? Who teaches you how to balance a checkbook or how to determine the amount to sock away for a rainy day? How do you learn about the daunting array of CDs, money markets, 401(k)s, mutual funds, mortgage rates, annuities, life insurance, tax shelters, growth stocks, dividends? Some people are fortunate enough to learn about money from their family. But if your parents don't know or don't feel comfortable discussing it, then what?

One of the best ways to put money into its proper context to avoid being overwhelmed by financial decisions is to be financially literate. You have to take the time to *learn* about your finances. Make sure you are up on the basics of financial literacy. You owe it to yourself to take an online or adult education course and read books on managing money and other aspects of personal and business finance. Especially if you plan to start a business, a small investment of your time in this arena will pay you back a thousand-fold. Also, actively seek out financial mentors. They are critical components to maximizing your success.

What I loved about Mabel's story, what made it such a great story, was that she was saved by something she loved, and her entire life was transformed. Mabel told Scott and me that several years ago, when her daughter was still in grade school, she read a book by Marsha Sinetar called *Do What You Love, the Money Will Follow*. It made sense to her when she read it, but she still found herself **believing that it could never happen to her.** She didn't think those principles of divine purpose, the expectations of unreasonable happiness, and her ability to pay bills and support a family could go together in her own life.

Often we don't associate the activities that bring us the greatest joy with money. That's why Mabel had such a hard time convincing herself that she really could have a successful jewelry business. **The truth is that the things we love can, and will, bring us the most joy and—believe it or not—the most wealth.** Happiness, like physical health, is a component of true wealth.

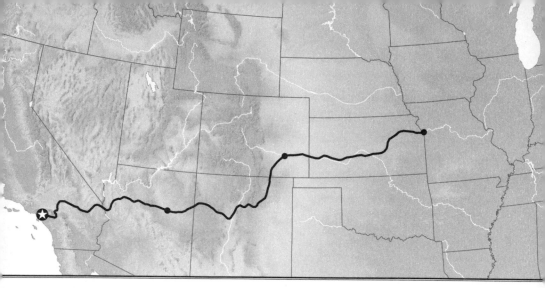

HAILING HAPPINESS

"What can be added to the happiness of a man who is in health, out of debt, and has a clear conscience?"

—Adam Smith,
Scottish philosopher and economist

I have a theory about happiness I call the "Taxicab Theory." The premise is that finding happiness in life is similar to hailing a cab. You can't just stand on the sidewalk and assume that a passing cab will know that you need a ride. You have to step out into the street and hail that cab, sticking your arm up high or waving your arm to get the driver's attention. Once you do, you've got a ride.

You can't just stand by the wayside assuming that you will miraculously become happy someday, that one day all the stars will align in your favor, that the gods of career and love will smile down on you and provide you with the perfect job that engages your passion, provides the ideal promotion, attracts the perfect matc. **You have to hail happiness actively in order to have it, and you must decide that you are going to be happy despite circumstances that are not ideal.**

And when *are* circumstances ever ideal? Rarely in life does every factor line up perfectly: love, work, kids, friendships, housing arrangements, health. There is usually a fly in the ointment. Maybe you just got the promotion that you'd been working toward for several years only to find that it involves reporting to someone you really dislike. Or you and your wife have hit a really nice groove in your relationship, and you're getting along the way you used to when you were dating, when your preteen suddenly starts acting like a total brat and there's a lot of tension in the house again. It seems that whenever one aspect of life gets worked out to a certain extent, another problem crops up in a different area. **The trick is to focus on the bright spots and seek out happiness where you can find it.** Go looking for happiness, as opposed to seeing the glass as half empty. Hey, it's been proven that optimists live longer, so there's even a health upside to being more positive.

> You have to hail happiness actively in order to have it, and you must decide that you are going to be happy despite circumstances that are not ideal.

Another way to hail happiness is to appreciate the small things in life. Most of us forget that not too long ago people had to spend an entire day washing clothes. It wasn't a matter of tossing a load into the washer and then throwing it into the dryer forty minutes later. It was called "laundry day" because it was an all-day affair, complete with icy-cold rinsing water that turned fingers red and blistered, heavy washboards against which one had to scrub dirt-encrusted clothes, and the long process of pinning clothing up to dry, then taking it all down, ironing it, and folding it. Simply appreciating modern conveniences, like access to a washer and dryer, even if it's at the local Laundromat, is one way to hail happiness.

Finding joy in the people around us can increase our happiness levels exponentially. Taking the time to say hello to the person behind the cash register at the grocery store and to inquire with sincere concern if your co-worker's daughter is over her flu are tiny gestures that can fill your day with a lot more meaning. Really listening to your spouse as he describes his meeting with his boss, as opposed to zoning out and thinking about the e-mails you still have to answer, is ultimately rewarding for both of you. He feels that he has been heard, and you focused on someone else's issues for a while as opposed to just churning things over in your own mind. Part of healing happiness is simply the ability to be present—as Eckhart Tolle describes, the ability to live in the *now*.

Another approach to hailing happiness is through affirmations, which are simply statements made today of how we see ourselves tomorrow. The theory behind affirmations is that we can affect our subconscious by repeating positive attributes or goals. Some people just repeat a word to themselves throughout the day, like "confident" or "productive." Others speak entire statements every morning or evening as they stare in the bathroom mirror. I used to tape up sticky notes on my car's dashboard that said BELIEVE and DESTINY and DREAM BIG. I even remember a part of a rhyme I wrote (when I was an aspiring rapper) in high school: "Goals and dreams are one in the same, just say you believe and both you will attain."

I understand that all this may sound way too freaky and new-agey, but many people find affirmations extremely effective. Here a few more examples of real affirmations I have used in my own life:

I am a great investor of my time and my money.

I am great at saving money and growing wealth.

I am confident that I will reach my goals.

I am a creator of joy, happiness, possibility, and inspiration; everywhere I go.

I am a true source of light, energy, and success.

The people with whom I work see that I am very good at what I do.

I am moving forward in my goal of working in a field that taps into my passion for _____.

Affirmations are all about claiming your goals and dreams. They are speaking into existence your plan for how you want to live your life. As Randy Pausch wrote in *The Last Lecture* on the importance of having specific dreams: **"You can always change your plan, but only if you have one."**

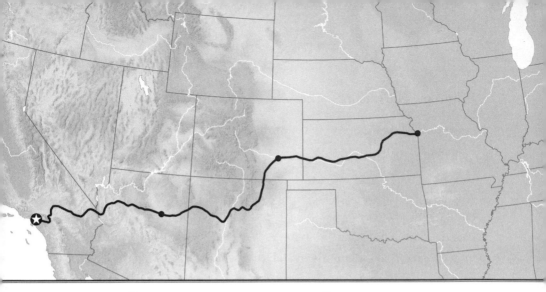

STANDING ON THE SHOULDERS
OF DRED SCOTT

"We are not human beings on a spiritual
journey. We are spiritual beings on a human
journey."

—Pierre Teilhard de Chardin,
French philosopher, Jesuit priest, paleontologist

After dinner on the train with Scott and Mabel, I decided to check in with Tracey before going to bed.

"Hey, it's Hill. Hope I'm not calling too late. I just met the most phenomenal lady. We had dinner together, the two of us, along with another young brother we met on the train."

"What's her deal?" she asked. I told Tracey a little bit about Mabel, about how she was a single mother and had lost her job, how she made the most beautiful beaded jewelry and had used her craft to turn what seemed like a setback into a prosperous venture.

"It was such an inspiring story, Tracey. Her daughter goes to school in—"

"Oh my God," Tracey said, interrupting me midsentence. "You met Mabel Macalaster? Made by Mabel? She's on the same train with you?"

I was stunned. "You know who she is?"

"Of course." Tracey laughed. "I can't believe you didn't. She's been featured in magazines, and people are always talking about her work because it's so unique. A lot of celebrities wear her jewelry. I have a few of her pieces."

"What!?" I didn't know even know what to say. "Wow," is all I could manage.

"Wow, indeed," said Tracey. "You make me want to get on the train and ride cross-country, too, if that means I get to meet and hang out with folks like that. What state are you riding through now?"

I looked out the window. It was too dark to see outside, but I was pretty sure we weren't in Kansas anymore. I reached over and grabbed the schedule. I was only half right.

"Missouri," I told her. "We're in Kansas City, Missouri. You ever been to Missouri?"

"Yes," Tracey bragged, "I've been to the top of the arch, in fact. It's pretty spectacular."

The town of St. Louis is famous for the Gateway Arch. The catenary arch, at 630 feet, is the tallest man-made monument in the nation. It is part of the Jefferson National Expansion Memorial Park, which was designed to honor the sea-to-sea expansion that took place in our country under the direction of Thomas Jefferson. There is another landmark in that park that touches me to my core every time I visit or even think about it. The Old Courthouse, located so far beneath the summit of the arch that it might seem insignificant, is where the *Scott v. Sandford* case was tried. While at Harvard Law School, we discussed it extensively. It is a case I believe every American should know. I began telling Tracey about it.

Dred Scott was a slave owned by Dr. Emerson, a military doctor, who often traveled to various military posts. Several of these military posts were in free states. Dr. Emerson treated Scott well and gave him liberties that Southern slave owners rarely provided. For instance, while he and Scott were traveling in the Wisconsin Territory, he allowed Scott to marry legally.

At the time, there was a law called the Northwest Ordinance. One provision of the ordinance prohibitioned slavery in the Northwest Territory. This territory included the area between the mountains of Appalachia and the Mississippi River, which effectively made the Ohio River a boundary that separated free states from slave-owning states. For years, there was a respect and reciprocal courtesy that the states extended to one another. Free states allowed slave owners to travel there and retain ownership of their slaves; likewise, slave-owning states allowed free black people to remain free while they traveled there.

Dred Scott moved his wife and children from Missouri to Louisiana, where Dr. Emerson was posted. While there, Dr. Emerson met and married Irene Sandford. She, along with the Scott family, moved back to Missouri with Dr. Emerson. The Scotts worked for him until his death. His widow then rented out the Scotts to other families as slaves and kept the money. **Dred Scott tried to buy his freedom from her, but she refused. It was more profitable for her to maintain ownership of Scott and his family.**

Dred Scott sued Irene Emerson. He maintained that because Dr. Emerson had taken him not simply to visit but to reside in free territories, he was in effect a free man. Three years after the suit had been filed, a jury agreed with him. By that time, Irene Emerson had moved to Boston and was remarried to Calvin C. Chafee, a well-known abolitionist who was later elected to the U.S. Congress.

Money can be a strong motivator for wrongdoing. During the trial, the Scotts were still being rented out, and the money was placed in an escrow account. Not willing to lose what was a significant amount of money, Irene Emerson Chafee never revealed to her new husband that she was a slave owner. Instead, she allowed the legal system, which did not favor women owning property, to work in her favor. She persuaded her brother, John Sandford, to take over guardianship of her assets, namely the Dred Scott's family, and to appeal the case. Sandford won the appeal. The Missouri Supreme Court struck down the earlier jury decision and stated that "Times now are not as they were when the previous decisions on this subject were made." The Scotts and the money in escrow that had been earned from their labor were turned over to the Sandfords.

Dred Scott was determined to be free. He moved his case to the federal courts, where he was able to claim jurisdiction and file a lawsuit based on the grounds that John Sandford was not a resident of Missouri. Scott lost the suit. His prominent lawyers were granted an appeal and took the case to the Supreme Court.

The Supreme Court ruling, which is now famously referred to as the Dred Scott Decision, came as a tremendous blow to black people throughout America. The Supreme Court ruled that according to the Constitution, "Any person descended from Africans, whether slave or free, is not a citizen of the United States." It also stated that the Northwest Ordinance "could not confer either freedom or citizenship within the Northwest Territory to non-white individuals." On top of that, the Supreme Court also ruled that certain parts of the Missouri Compromise, namely those that excluded slavery and gave freedom to non-white people in the northern territories of the Louisiana Purchase, were not legal because they exceeded the powers of Congress.

"I never knew all of that," Tracey admitted. "I mean, I'd heard about the case, and I knew it had something to do with a slave suing for his freedom, but I just assumed that he'd won it. I never knew all the details."

"Yeah, what really got me," I told Tracey, "was the boundless greed. It was all for money."

"So how did the Supreme Court ruling get overturned?" she wanted to know.

I informed her that it has never been formally overturned, though the Fourteenth Amendment does, obviously, nullify most aspects of the ruling. In the end, Dred Scott was given his freedom. Apparently, Calvin C. Chafee had no idea until a month before the Supreme Court decision that his wife was the owner of the most famous slave in the country. Since that contradicted every principle to which he'd devoted his life and career, Chafee made his wife relinquish ownership of the Scotts to the Blow family. They were Dred Scott's original owners and the family who had sold him to Dr. Emerson.

The Blow family had recently become abolitionists and were vehemently against slavery. Since they lived in Missouri, it was within their right and power to give Dred Scott and his family their freedom once ownership was transferred to them. In fewer than three months from the date of the Supreme Court ruling, Dred Scott and his family were free.

All that and not so long ago. "We certainly have come a long way, haven't we?" Tracey said.

And with a quiet smile, remembering my Harvard law classmate who was sitting in the Oval Office, I responded, "Yes, we certainly have."

Tracey and I remained silent for a while. I sat through the silence, thinking about America's journey, thinking about how easy it is for me to take my liberty for granted and how hard people in the past had to fight for the most basic freedoms.

"By the way," Tracey interjected, "speaking of freedom, did you get a chance to look at the papers in the envelope yet?"

I told her I hadn't but planned to soon.

"At least read the first two pages about the Native American parable. I think it will really resonate with you."

I promised her that I would. After we hung up, I fell asleep listening to the train wheels rumbling over the tracks.

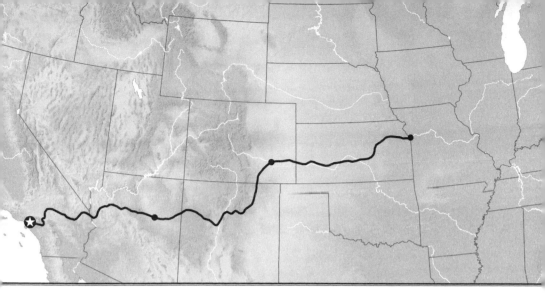

WHICH WOLF
ARE YOU FEEDING?

"I am a great believer in the power of perspective."
— Suze Orman, personal finance expert

Before going to breakfast the next morning, I got on my knees, said
my morning prayers, and then sat down in the seat by the window
to read my journal.

The pages flipped open to an old entry. I caught a glimpse of a sentence,
and that was enough to draw me in. I spent the next several minutes reading
what I had written on that day, July 2, 2010.

*The doctors said that I should receive the results of my biopsy in about a
week. Somehow I thought it would happen faster than that. Have I just gotten
too used to speed, to having everything happen instantly? I suppose that's the
world we live in now. Even technology, as advanced as it gets, becomes disap-*

pointing as it never seems fast enough compared to the expectations the newest model creates in us. We want more and we want it quicker.

I've also been thinking a lot about John Wooden. [If you don't know Wooden, he was one of the greatest basketball coaches of all time. While at UCLA, he led the Bruins to an unprecedented ten NCAA championships over twelve years. But ironically, it wasn't basketball, which became his greatest legacy. It was a life philosophy outlined in what become known as his Pyramid of Success.] *When I heard that Coach Wooden had passed, I knew right away that it was a loss that would be felt far and wide. I guess I didn't realize just how strongly it would impact me. To say he was inspirational would be an enormous understatement. I realized just how often I repeated his positive messages or mentioned him in my everyday conversations.*

Coach Wooden once said, "You can't live a perfect day without doing something for someone who will never be able to repay you." I truly believe that if I try to focus on living each day in that way, then it won't matter how many more days I have remaining on this earth, or what the result of the biopsies are, or what the battles ahead of me might be. If I give, I will have lived a perfect life. It seems oddly counterintuitive, but giving is perhaps the most perfect way to invest in yourself.

I read the entry a couple of times, then closed the journal. I thought about an observation that my friend Paula, a single mother of two, had made a while back. It was right at the beginning of the American public's awareness of the national economic downturn. Almost overnight, the suicide rate spiked. Paula read to me several snippets from various articles about men, primarily, who had ended their lives because they'd lost significant amounts of money that they'd invested.

"Hill, some of these people lost almost all of their savings and fortunes," she said, "but a lot of them were still worth at least six figures. If someone told me today that I was worth a hundred thousand dollars, I'd jump for joy, not out of a window."

"Yeah," I said, "perspective is definitely an individual thing."

Paula told me that she'd always considered herself blessed and fortunate. She attended a top-notch school and had a great job as a psychotherapist. "You know, I'd never tried to see my life through somebody else's eyes. But the idea that somebody would rather be dead than live at the financial level that I live—well, I'm not sure whether I should laugh or cry about it. I mean, should I feel sorry for that person or should I feel sorry for myself?"

Paula explained to me that sometimes when she drove through Skid Row, she'd have an overwhelming sense of pity for the people she saw. "I'd think, 'How can anybody survive sleeping in the street like that?' I wonder if it's what those rich people were thinking when they saw me going about my life. I wonder if they asked themselves, 'How could anybody live like that?'"

Paula's observation has stayed with me. It continues to make me think. We all have our ideas about what constitutes a good life. Sometimes, it takes a major crisis to gauge our sense of a good life. I wondered if my own illness was directing me toward new measuring sticks for my own life—directing me toward my Wealth Cure. Pondering this, I headed out of my cabin to have breakfast.

When I got to the dining car, there was a short line waiting to be seated. The familiar and delicious smell of eggs and sausage filled the car. I overheard a man behind me say to his wife, "Boy, those eggs smell good. I wonder if they use powdered eggs or the real thing on the train."

I turned around and smiled. "I had them yesterday. They're the real McCoy."

The man smiled back and said, "Thanks for letting me know! By the way, do you know the origin of that expression? It's apropos for being on a train."

Intrigued, I replied, "No, I've never heard it. What's the origin of 'the real McCoy?'"

"I was just reading about it in a history book. I'm a real history buff," the man said. His wife nodded, rolling her eyes a bit, but in an affectionate way. "Elijah McCoy, who was the son of slaves, had escaped from Kentucky to Canada," the man continued. "His father had served in the British army and was rewarded with farmland. He and his wife raised Elijah and his eleven siblings there. At age sixteen, Elijah was sent to Scotland for an apprenticeship in mechanical engineering. He became a master mechanic and engineer. After the Civil War ended, the family returned to the U.S. and settled outside of Detroit."

"Now, Harry, don't bore this young man with one of your history lessons. You're not in class, you know." His wife turned to me and added, "He's a teacher."

"Oh no, I'm definitely interested. What happened next?" I asked.

"Because he was African American, Elijah couldn't get hired as an engineer. He worked instead as a coal fireman on the railroad, shoveling coal into the firebox of the train and oiling its moving parts. Trains ran on steam then. The pressure of the vapor pushed oil away from the parts that required lubrication. Being an educated engineer, Elijah realized that he could keep the engine running more efficiently by using steam pressure to pump the oil to where it was required.

"In a workshop at his house, Elijah invented a lubricating cup with a piston inside an oil-filled container. In 1872, he got a patent for it. He took it to the Michigan railroad officials, and the cup became a standard part of locomotive machinery. Then he left the railroad company and moved to Detroit. In 1915, he received a patent for an even better lubricator."

"What a great story," I interjected. "I hope he made a lot of money from of his inventions."

"Well, actually Elijah didn't have the capital to manufacture his products, so he sold many of his patents to investors and thus received very little money. Many people also did inferior knock-offs of his inventions and he couldn't afford to sue them to make them stop." Harry added, "By the end of his life, he had a bunch of patents but had kept ownership of only a handful. When people bought parts for railroads, they would say they wanted *'the real McCoy'* to distinguish Elijah's inventions from the knock-offs. Ever since, the phrase has meant 'the genuine thing.'" Harry smiled. I could see that he was great at his job. He was obviously passionate about teaching.

"That's a fascinating story," I replied. "Thanks so much for telling it to me." When the waiter came to seat me at a table, I added, "Have a good breakfast." As I placed my napkin on my lap, I thought about Elijah McCoy and felt inspired. **We all have the capacity to be the real McCoy.** We can lead genuine, authentic, and happy lives. If you are genuine, your word holds more value than any possession. But to be genuine, we first have to be willing to be completely honest with ourselves and then with others.

Just then, Scott entered the dining room, and I motioned him over. I asked about Mabel. He said he hadn't seen her yet that morning.

"Did you know that she's kinda famous?" I asked.

Scott's eyes lit up and he laughed. "You didn't know that? My ex-girlfriend read about her a few months ago in some magazine, *Essence* or *O*, I damn near put myself in bankruptcy buying those necklaces for her birthday. But I gotta say her stuff's pretty special. If my mom was still alive, she'd have gone nuts for it."

I felt I was the last person on earth to find out about Mabel's jewelry.

The waiter came by to take our orders. While we waited for our meals, I started going through the packet Tracey had given me.

"It's some information that a friend gave me," I said in response to the quizzical look Scott shot me. I found the pages with the Native American parable Tracey mentioned.

"Read it," Scott said as he munched on toast and jam.

I shot him a look.

"Come on," he said.

"All right. . . ." The passage was about a conversation between a Cherokee elder and his grandson.

"A fight is going on inside me," the elder tells his grandson. "It is a terrible fight, and it is between two wolves. One wolf represents fear, anger, envy, sorrow, regret, greed, arrogance, self-pity, guilt, resentment, inferiority, lies, false pride, superiority, and ego. The other wolf stands for joy, peace, love, hope, sharing, serenity, humility, kindness, benevolence, friendship, empathy, generosity, truth, compassion, and faith. This same fight is going on inside you and inside every other person, too."

The grandson thought about it for a minute and then asked his grandfather, "Which wolf will win?"

The old Cherokee smiled at his grandson and simply replied, "The one you feed."

Printed below the parable was a quote attributed to Henry Ford: **"Whether you think you can or you think you can't, you are right."**

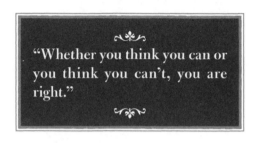

"Whether you think you can or you think you can't, you are right."

Both the story and the quote struck a chord in Scott and me. I stared out of the train's window. The sun was beaming, and the colors of the landscape were crisp and bright. The rural landscape looked like the place where such a conversation between the elder and grandson could have taken place. "Which wolf will win?" I kept asking myself. I returned my attention to Scott.

"Which of your wolves is going to win?" I asked him. "Are you afraid you're gonna fail?"

He nodded. "I'm afraid I've already failed," he said softly. "I blew it, man. I was doing it. I was going out on auditions, and I was booking jobs. It was happening. It was really happening. Then I took that job, and next thing you know I'm wearing a suit and tie, and people are calling me Mister. I can't go on auditions anymore because my calendar is clogged up with business meetings. That's the wolf I fed. I let the wolf win."

"But the money was good?" I asked.

"Yes."

"Too good to walk away from?"

He nodded again, avoiding eye contact.

"Did you save any of it?"

"A little bit," he said, "but that's what I'm using to move to Chicago. I don't have a cent, or anything else, to show for the time I spent working that job. I had to get rid of my car and most of my stuff, because it won't fit in my brother's place."

"You got caught in the golden handcuffs," I responded.

Golden handcuffs can happen to any of us. We do something for money at the expense of passion. It's not what we love so we start expanding our lifestyle and spending that money. It's as if we are trying to fill the void. And since we have accrued larger bills, we become stuck in a vicious cycle. *Gotta keep earning to pay for the stuff I bought because I took a job I shouldn't have taken in the first place.* I then turned to Scott and admitted to him something I had never admitted to anyone before. "To be completely genuine, sometimes I feel that way about the role I accepted on *CSI: NY.* Sure, I've gotten paid well, but I truly believe that I got overextended in real estate and made too many risky investments because I was disappointed that I was no longer able to do artistic films and theater, what I loved most about acting."

Scott looked at me like I had horns growing out of my head. "But you get to act every day, Hill!"

"It's all perspective, Scott. Anyone can feel like they are caught in golden or not so golden handcuffs." And it was right then that I realized how millionaires can get so depressed that they choose to commit suicide. It's truly an individual journey, and no one really knows what anyone else is going through, and that's the real McCoy. **To figure out which wolf you are feeding, you have to be willing to be** *real* **and** *genuine* **with yourself.** I then told Scott that there is a great lesson in this: "So now you know that you're not the type of person who can be happy doing something solely for the sake of money. Lesson learned. That's good!"

"But what if it's too late? What if I can never go back to L.A., or move to New York and start acting again? What if I really blew it? What will I do? I don't know how to make jewelry or fix cars or any other type of hobby that I can turn into a business. All I ever wanted to do was be an actor."

"Scott, you can only start from where you are," I reminded him. People often feel as though they have to be right in the thick of things to get noticed, but that's not true. When we are in our element, we attract things and people to us and into our sphere. "Throughout history, talent has been recognized and found, no matter where it is. You could be in a town of five hundred people, but if you're that special, people far away will hear about you. And now with all this technology, the world is only getting smaller.

You can reach the whole world right from your living room. Just look at somebody like . . . ahhhh . . . Justin Bieber. He did it."

Scott thought about that.

"But what if I'm not good enough or special enough to be noticed?" he asked. "What if I fail?" Before I could speak, Scott interjected, "I know what you're gonna say." I gestured, palms facing the ceiling, as if offering him a platter. "You're gonna say, 'What if you don't fail?'"

"Close," I confessed. "I was going to tell you—I am telling you—that **when you're doing something you love, there is no such thing as failure. Every victory and every disappointment is an arrow pointing you in the direction of your next move and leading you toward greater joy and fulfillment."**

So when your failures feel just as motivating (not debilitating) as your victories, that's when you know you are doing something you love. Example: Thomas Edison's assistant, exasperated from the one thousandth failed experiment to discover the filament for the light bulb, said to Edison, "Sir, this experiment is an utter failure!" Edison responded, "Nonsense! It's victory. Now we know one thousand ways it *doesn't* work." What others may deem as failure may be exactly what is getting us closer to our own personal goals.

A lot of actors I know make a clear distinction between the work they do because it pays their rent and the work they do because it feeds their spirit. Many actors will even take jobs that are essentially disposable, something that they can quit at a moment's notice if they need to. That's why many actors wait tables, work for catering companies, do freelance bartending, or take temp jobs.

It is important to remember that a job is not necessarily the same thing as a career. When Scott first started working at the company that had just laid him off, it was a job, something that could pay his bills while he directed his efforts, attention, and time toward acting. Once he accepted the promotion, he placed himself on a career track at the company. They were paying him more because they wanted more from him. They wanted Scott to direct his efforts, attention, and time to their company. For somebody else, somebody whose passion fell in line with the company's objectives, a promotion like that would have been the best thing in the world, an achievement they might still be boasting about. For Scott, it felt suffocating.

The potential problem with confusing a job with a career is that it can distract you from your goals. Listening to Scott, I assumed that's what happened to him. He made a lot more money than he'd been earning previously, and he was able to afford a certain lifestyle. He became comfortable in that lifestyle, too comfortable to walk away voluntarily, even though it required that he sacrifice the one thing he wanted most.

Scott had pulled out his train schedule and scanned the pamphlet. "We're going to pass through your old haunts in a little while." I must have looked confused because he added, "Iowa. You said your people were from Iowa, right?" I nodded. "That's where we're headed. It says here it's the first stop after Missouri."

Of course it was. I'd almost forgotten that the Southwest Chief route cut through a little corner of Iowa before moving into Illinois, on the way to its final destination, Chicago.

Scott left to make some calls, and I went back to my cabin. I checked my e-mails before starting to write and found a message from Andre. "Where ya been, bro? Partying is not the same without you!" He had attached a picture of himself with a gorgeous woman on each arm. He looked like he was living large—the envy of ambitious, young men everywhere.

Since our last night out in L.A., I wondered how long he would keep enjoying the high life. Mindless blowouts and picking up the tab for instant friends had to get old at some point. Andre wasn't a bad guy. I just couldn't understand how he could waste so much time and money and continue to enjoy that lifestyle. But I guess, like everything else, that's just a matter of perspective, too. Like Arnold, Willis, and Mr. C: *"Diff'rent Strokes* for different folks . . ."

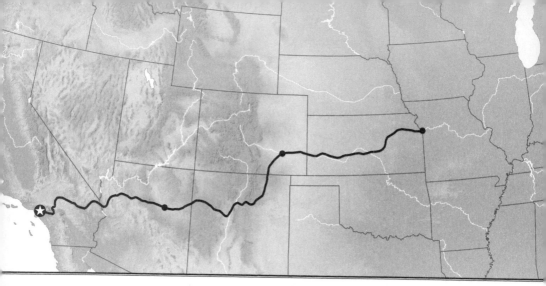

You Are Your Own
Lottery Ticket

"Forget the lottery. Bet on yourself instead."
—Brian Koslow,
American author and entrepreneur

One out of four Americans believes the best chance of getting rich is by playing the lottery. Five percent of lottery-ticket buyers purchase 51 percent of all tickets sold—that means that those people are probably spending an inordinate amount of their paychecks on tickets. You see them lined up on payday, carefully giving the person behind the counter their lucky numbers. Did you know that the chances of winning a single-state lottery are eighteen million to one, and the chances of winning a multistate lottery are as high as one hundred twenty million to one? You are literally more likely to be struck by lightning than to win the lottery.

In addition, studies of lottery winners have shown that 75 percent of the "lucky" winners have blown through their entire earnings within five years, and many winners state that they are no happier. Many report they are often much less happy. Studies of past winners show that happiness levels typically return to where they were beforehand. So why this obsessive focus on winning the lottery? I think it comes from the quick-fix mentality that pervades our society. We have become accustomed to having everything fast, and the idea of slow, progressive saving up over time is unfathomable for many. But smart saving is the path to real financial wealth—not throwing away large portions of expendable income on fly-by-night items like lottery tickets or ultra-risky investments. Money used to buy lottery tickets or on other get-rich-quick schemes could have added up in meaningful ways over the years.

Increasingly, the notion of "winning" is becoming a prevalent part of our culture, especially with the increasing popularity of contests and reality shows. People believe they can skip over all the other steps to success and still to arrive at fame and/or financial wealth. The importance of education, of practice and preparation, are either underestimated, overlooked, or ignored.

Many people in our country have fallen victim to the lottery mentality. It's as if we all want to be rich, but we want it the easy way. Malcolm Gladwell, in his book *Outliers,* estimates that ten thousand hours of hard work are required to master a craft. Instead of putting in our ten thousand hours and growing in skill and stature, we want to get lucky, be discovered, be on *American Idol,* and the rest is history, right?

I understand this tendency. We have become more and more reliant on speed, particularly the speed of technology. We've gone from postal mail to telegrams, from faxes to e-mails and text messages, from instant messaging to Skype. In my grandmother's time, you couldn't place a telephone call without an operator and a landline. Now no matter where we are in the world, we can receive calls on the phone in our pockets or purses. These advances enable us to do more and see more—and they create an appetite for more. The more technology we consume, the more insatiable we become. We are willing to take ridiculous gambles in hopes of making a fast buck.

We are all hoping to win the lotto. But it simply doesn't work that way. This mentality reminds me of the old joke about a man's first trip to Las Vegas: "I love Vegas. I arrived in a thirty-thousand-dollar car and left in a six-hundred-thousand-dollar bus!"

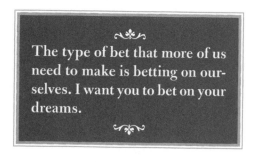

The type of bet that more of us need to make is betting on ourselves. I want you to bet on your dreams.

I strongly support one type of betting that is not only fine but needs to be encouraged. You see, the word "courage" is part of "encouraged." **The type of bet that more of us need to make is betting on ourselves. I want you to bet on your dreams. Bet on your goals. Bet on the vision you have for your life. Bet on your new ideas. Bet on your passion.** When you place those types of bets by putting money toward the pursuit of what is in your heart, it is not only a good bet, it is an investment.

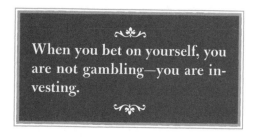

When you bet on yourself, you are not gambling—you are investing.

When you bet on yourself, you are not gambling—you are investing.

By investing in yourself, I do not mean going out and buying a lot of new stuff. I'm talking about something much more meaningful. I'm talking about appreciating your best qualities and making sure you are in a position to **shine**, by highlighting your most impressive talents. As William Blake said, "He whose face gives no light, shall never become a star."

In my speeches, I often talk about approaching life with a "warrior light." By this, I mean the ability to exude a powerful and positive energy in all arenas. We are all familiar with the experience of seeing a person who "lights up the room," or who is a "star." I'm not talking about a celebrity. I'm talking about someone who seems to radiate from the inside. You've probably known one or two people like this. It's all about the energy they give off. When someone is a "star," they emanate light and energy, and they do this wherever they go.

Some people don't believe that they are capable of *producing* this sort of energy. They feel they need props, a knot of cash in their pocket, or something they buy and adorn themselves with. This is where the terms "bling" or "shine" came from. People feel that if they could dangle the most brightly shining jewels from their cars or necks, then the glow from the jewelry would convince others of their exaggerated worth. A guy might think that driving a flashy car will give him that kind of aura or, like my friend Andre, that making it rain in a club, possibly the most ignorant use of money ever, will elevate him in others' eyes.

What these people don't realize is that they have been seduced by the energy of money. **They don't realize that every person has the power to be a warrior of light with energy derived from themselves, not from an outside source.** The bling that anyone purchases—jewelry, cars—and audacious displays of cash are ephemeral sources of shine that vanish the moment the person steps out of the Porsche or takes off the diamonds.

From the cars we drive to the clothes we wear, all reveal something about us; they reflect our priorities. Most of us are not entirely aware of or comfortable with the entirety of the messages we are sending.

One of the first big purchases that Tracey made after she'd resurfaced from her grieving was a car. She bought a fancy pearl white BMW. "I've always wanted to be the woman with the nice car. I used to park blocks and blocks away from where I was going sometimes, just so people wouldn't see my old car. I wanted a car that I could give the parking valet my keys to without feeling as if others were laughing behind my back."

Within a couple months of owning the BMW, she traded it in for a small hybrid. When I asked her why, she said, "I didn't like the way people looked at me, the things they were assuming, all because of the car I owned. It made me uncomfortable. I don't like being profiled."

I laughed, because that's precisely what she thought she wanted when she bought the car. Now that she had a possession speaking for her, she didn't like what it announced, because it wasn't the whole truth of who she was.

People sometimes consciously acquire material possessions with the hope that it will tell a specific story about them, knowing full well that story is not true. My friend Meri, who is a writer, once told me that her cousin called her up to ask if she'd help her figure out what books she should buy to put on her bookshelves.

"The ones you've read or are going to read," Meri told her. The woman persisted. She told Meri that when she'd come to Meri's house, she'd enjoyed scanning all the books and that it made her want to get to know Meri better.

"When I asked her what her favorite books were, she told me she didn't really like to read, she thought it was boring," Meri said. "I was speechless for a moment. Then I asked her, 'Why would you even spend money buying books, then, if you're never going to read them?'"

Obviously, Meri's cousin wanted people who came over to her house to believe a certain fiction about her, one that would make her come across a certain way in their eyes. And she was willing to invest in that fiction. There is nothing wrong with Meri's cousin wanting to be perceived a certain way, but why not go the extra step by investing to make it authentic and genuine? Meri's cousin could invest in herself by reading and filling her shelves and her mind at the same time.

For other people it's not a fiction but a truth they want people to know about them, and so they make an investment in it. My older brother and I were raised by my divorced father. My father, an entrepreneur as well as a psychiatrist, was a hard worker, a driven man who wanted nothing but the best for his family. He took a lot of risks with different careers and projects in an effort to achieve his definition of success. A number of those ventures worked, but a fair number also turned out to be disastrous economic failures.

Success was extremely important to my father, like many parents. It was something he desperately wanted. Everything about him revolved around attaining and announcing his success—even his wardrobe. *Especially* his wardrobe. He was a somewhat flashy guy. He wore a good amount of jewelry and drove showy cars. He wore a tie every day, but he had jewelry underneath. When his shirt was open, you could see lots of chains. He was consistently impeccably dressed in the finest Italian suits, the finest everything, actually. He sought the best of the best.

My father used to order Omaha Steaks every year for Christmas. I thought this was weird because we lived in Iowa, which was cow territory. Why not just buy a fresh steak from down the street? Apparently, the Omaha Steaks brand was considered the best of the best. There was a quality and prestige attached to an "Omaha Steak." To my father, there was no such thing as flying under the radar. He wanted people to know he was there; he was present; he was successful. That was the story my father wanted told.

My father truly *lived* his life on his own terms. He was energetic and dynamic. So in many ways, as flashy as my father was, it was his truth. Internally, he shined as brightly as his jewelry and fancy suits. He was not presenting a façade. All this to say that nice cars, fancy jewelry, and fancy clothes are not bad if they are truly who you are and not some fake image you are attempting to portray to cover an insecurity. My father was truly his own man. And his possessions told that story. What are the stories you want your possessions to tell about you? Are those stories based in fact and authenticity, or are they fiction?

If you need outer accoutrements like a fine car or designer clothes to feel like a star, you are denying your own potential and your own warrior light. Each person is unique and has his or her talents, special qualities, beauty, and grace. Instead of grasping things, focus instead on what only you can bring to the picture. Ask your boyfriend or spouse what he sees in you that is unique. Ask your girlfriend what she likes best about your personality. You may be surprised at some of the answers. My favorite way to discover what's special about you is to ask a child who's in your life what they enjoy most about spending time with you. Many of us don't realize the myriad of ways we impact others around us.

A great example of someone who glows with warrior light is Tyler Perry. He believed in his own star, and he placed huge bets on himself when no one else would. While I was shooting the film *For Colored Girls,* Tyler decided to have a dinner party at his home in Atlanta. He invited the cast, and he also had surprise guests—Oprah Winfrey and Gayle King. Sitting around the dinner table discussing life, politics, entertainment, and legacy were Whoopi Goldberg, Phylicia Rashad, Janet Jackson, Oprah Winfrey, Tyler Perry, Kerry Washington, Kimberly Elise, Gayle King, Anika Noni Rose, and me. There was laughter, tears, and plenty of wine. After dinner, Tyler offered a tour of the grounds. To say that his home is magnificent is an understatement.

Tyler is certainly someone who bet on himself. Yet he grew up in an abusive home. He did not complete high school but did go on to earn his GED. As a young man, he endured several severe setbacks and difficult years. In his early twenties, he saw someone on *Oprah* describe how writing can be therapeutic. He began writing letters to himself, which became his musical *I Know I've Been Changed*. At twenty-two, he used his twelve-thousand-dollar life savings—an enormous amount of money for someone that age and in his circumstances—to produce a performance of his play at a community theater.

That first production led Tyler to write and produce many other plays that eventually sold more than $100 million in tickets and another $20 million in merchandise, according to *Forbes*. Tyler's first movie, *Diary of a Mad Black Woman*, grossed $50 million in the United States, and he has gone on to film and television stardom and fame as a producer. All this happened because a young man had enough faith and belief in his own ideas and abilities to bet on himself.

Investing in yourself is supremely important and one way to do this is to get a good education. Some people feel that the financial expense of college isn't worth it. I disagree. I believe that at *any* age, investing in your education is always valuable. Sandy Baum, an emeritus professor of economics at Skidmore College, wrote a report on the difference in lifetime earnings between a high school grad and a college grad. He came up with an average figure of $450,000—almost a half million dollars—for four extra years in school.

The earnings gap doesn't even tell the whole story. Education buys options. The more options you have, the higher the likelihood that you will be able to choose a career that makes you happy. The difference between the type of career you can have if you obtain a college degree or higher, as opposed to not having your B.A., B.S., or a graduate degree, can be significant. It may mean the difference between rote clerical tasks and information technology, between working with your hands, which is wonderful if that is what you are talented at and desire, or creating designs that will be carried out by skilled artisans. Not only will you have larger lifetime net earnings, but you will also have a better chance of spending your life working at something you are highly engaged in, rather than just holding down a job and bringing in a paycheck. Education buys us the options to find a career as opposed to simply having a job. And it is never too late to seek more education. I just signed up for a language class at a local community college and I have two graduate degrees. Continually educating ourselves should be a lifelong endeavor. There are many professions, like medicine, where continuing education is required to maintain certification. Many businesses require this as well.

We can manage our lives as if we are our own business.

One element that has created so much success at Microsoft is the commitment the company asks its employees to make. Microsoft asks each employee to set goals by making commitments in their performance evaluations. These commitments "are the primary means of determining the work that individuals do and what the company accomplishes," according to a technical paper published in 2006.

What about commitments to ourselves? We should devote at least this much time to thinking about our specific commitments to ourselves. This includes personal goals, monetary and otherwise. When we make a specific commitment, we are that much closer to creating a plan for how we will reach those goals.

Let's say that you want to save 15 percent of your salary this year. You may be saving for your children's college fund, for your emergency fund in case of job disruption, a home purchase, or for your retirement. It's easy to do the math and calculate 15 percent of your salary, but how do you actually go about saving?

First, you must make a commitment to yourself that you will do just that. Write this statement down and put the note in a place where you will see it often, a desk drawer that you use frequently, for example, **"I will save 15 percent of my salary this year."** That represents a conscious commitment that you are making to yourself.

Next, look at your monthly budget to see where your money goes and what you might cut out in order to save the amount you've committed to. How much is flowing out for things such as movies, restaurant meals and takeout, lattes, clothes, and so on? Make a real commitment to yourself to cut down spending on those items. Challenge yourself to see how much you can save in order to reach your goal. **Don't view it as skimping; view it as an investment in your future.** Those constant small daily expenditures can really add up. Is it cheaper for you to use public transportation than to drive, given the cost of gas? What about the lost art of carpooling? Can your kids take the school bus instead of being dropped off by car?

Once you train yourself to look for ways to limit spending, it becomes a habit. As Stephen J. Dubner and Steven D. Levitt say in *Super Freakonomics,* "A good set of data can go a long way toward describing human behavior as long as the proper questions are asked of it." Think not only about what you are spending, but *why* you think you must spend it.

Many of us feel like, Hey, I'm working so hard, don't I deserve a little reward every week for all my efforts? I'm working long hours, doing everything I can to hold on to my job. What could it hurt if I want to take in a movie on Saturday night, treat my girlfriend to a nice dinner out, or buy theater tickets?

Yes, you *are* working hard, and you *do* deserve a break—a break from that awful feeling when you rip open the credit card bills and realize that, yet again, you barely have enough to pay the minimums and barely enough left over to meet the monthly rent or mortgage. That is one pressure you don't need to live with. I can promise you that the relief of not seeing the amounts on the credit cards inching up every month due to exorbitant interest rates is worth the little pang you might feel at giving up a weekly movie and other unnecessary expenses. Besides, that's what Netflix was invented for!

Financially wealthy people always pay themselves first. You've heard this phrase before, but what does it really mean? This means that you take out a chunk of your paycheck and put it into some form of interest-bearing savings—a savings account, CD, money market, 401(k), mutual fund, or other form of savings. Do this every month. That way, you are guaranteed to meet your savings goals.

Does your company offer to match or partially match your 401(k) savings? If so, take full advantage of this offer. This is a real perk that many people overlook, and not only are you saving pretax dollars, you are getting free money! Many companies are getting rid of their matching plans, so if you're lucky enough to work for a business that does offer it, max out your contribution. And don't ever borrow against your 401(k)—the interest and penalties make borrowing truly not worth it.

You can't get out of debt if you are living in fear.

Jeanette Perez, the financial coach I mentioned earlier who has helped many clients get out of debt, says you have to begin by understanding your relationship with money. She says, **"There is far too much fear in our relationships with money.** When I work with clients, I start by examining what is driving their financial experience. More fear shows up around debt than with anything else. When you move out of fear, then your perception of debt begins to change. Once you have overcome your fear of the debt, then you can address practical methods to reduce it." One of her clients couldn't even begin to look at how much she owed. Her life was stagnating because of debt. Once she realized that it really wasn't as bad as she thought, she was ready to work on an action plan.

"Together, we looked at her debt. The interest rate on her credit cards was 30 to 35 percent—triple what she should have been paying. My client believed she would be paying her debts for the rest of her life. When you get your credit card statement, it tells you that if you only pay the minimum, it will take you a certain number of years to pay it off—sometimes as many as twenty years!

"First, we called the various credit card companies and said that she was closing the accounts. The interest rate immediately drops to about half when you do that. We asked what programs for renegotiating the debt were available. My client had been deeply in debt for ten years, but after eight months, she is now 50 percent paid off, and she feels so much better about her financial situation.

"You need discipline, a budget, and a plan, and you need to address both emotional and monetary issues. Reduce the interest on all your cards, and you will feel better immediately. I don't recommend debt consolidation, because if you don't do it yourself, then you aren't addressing your fear, and you're handing your debt off to someone else. It's better to deal with each individual credit card company yourself and negotiate the best deal."

Jeanette's approach to debt is eye-opening and effective. She has had incredible success in getting a wide range of clients out from under crushing debt.

Are you a satisfied customer in your own life?

You can continue to apply a business model to your own personal goals by thinking in terms of customer satisfaction. Who are the customers in your personal life? Well, there's you, first and foremost. Are you a satisfied customer? Go back to your Wealth Factors and identify those goals you feel are out of reach at the moment. What incremental steps can you begin to take in order to reach one or two of those goals in the near future?

A young friend of mine, Katie, graduated from a good school a couple years ago, but was still living with her parents as she worked two part-time jobs. She had earned a degree in social work and also studied marketing, but her degree in social work hadn't yet translated into a full-time job. So she was babysitting for her cousin's young children by day and freelancing for an Internet site at night. Both jobs paid fairly well, but Katie longed to find work in her chosen profession and to get a place of her own. She had combed the newspapers and viewed apartments, but couldn't find a space in her price range.

"Am I doomed to be living with my parents when I'm thirty?" she complained to me over coffee one day. "I can't take this much longer. I know I could do a great job as a social worker, but the city isn't hiring. How will I ever find work in my field?"

"Have you checked into volunteering?" I asked her.

She gave me a blank look. "I'm already working two jobs, when would I have time to volunteer? And how would that help me?" she retorted.

"Katie, you know you will be great at social work, and I know it. But the people who could potentially hire you haven't seen what you can do. What about volunteering for an outfit that might not have an opening right now but could in the future? Then since they know you and realize how terrific you are, they would think of you first whenever an opening does come up."

Katie thought about that. "Actually there is a place downtown that I've thought of volunteering for, but I just haven't gotten around to it yet. I know I could do a great job with the children. I tutored kids during college, and they loved me."

"There you go. I would go in this weekend and see how you can help. Who knows what it could lead to? At least you'll feel you're being proactive, instead of just being stuck."

Katie started volunteering at the community center that very weekend. Although they didn't hire her, several months later an older woman who volunteered there with Katie noticed her commitment and energy and told her about an opening at the nonprofit where she was employed. Eventually, Katie was hired in the marketing department and has managed to move from her parents' place into a share with one of her college friends. She has a tiny room in a small apartment, but she says it feels great to be out on her own. She upped her own customer satisfaction, and even her parents are more satisfied now that she's flown the coop.

CREATIVE WAYS TO PAY FOR YOUR EDUCATION

Though I cannot stand debt, I think of education as an investment, and I believe that in most cases, it's okay to go into debt for your education. Zac Bissonnette, an enterprising senior at the University of Massachusetts, makes a persuasive case for not relying on student loans in his book, *Debt-Free U*. In these

---

cash-strapped times, the average student debt load is $23,000 for an undergraduate degree. Bissonnette contends that such a debt can be hazardous to the financial health of parents and/or graduates. Starting out in the hole can be constraining when it comes to career choice. There are some jobs indebted graduates cannot afford to take.

He says, **"Relax! You will be able to get a champagne education on a beer budget."** He advises kids to work during high school, at college, over breaks, and to save that money to put toward tuition. Rather than applying to private colleges that now run between $40,000 to $60,000 a year, he recommends that students go to a state school which costs $15,500 annually on average with a tax credit. He suggests going to a community college for the first two years, then transferring to a more prestigious school to cut costs even more. Your degree will be the same as that of students who spent four years at the school.

If you're worried about graduate school, he reminds you that elite graduate programs accept lots of students with nonelite bachelor's degrees. The same is true of most selective employers. You can do it!

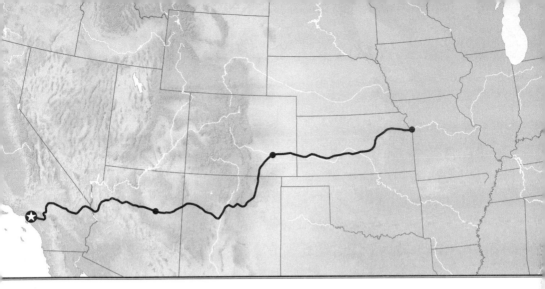

YOUR PERSONAL
BOARD OF DIRECTORS

"No young man starting in life could have better capital than plenty of friends. They will
strengthen his credit, support him in every
great effort, and make him what, unaided, he
could never be. Friends of the right sort will
help him more—to be happy and successful—
than much money."
—Orison Swett Marden, American writer

Another way that we can treat our life like a business is to use outside
consultants. Who are the people in your life that you look up to?
Who has spent time mentoring you or giving you advice in the past?
Come up with a list of those people who are influential to you. The list
might look something like this:

1. My parents
2. The CFO at my job who always stops by to say hello and see how I'm doing
3. My high school football coach
4. My friend Tom, who seems to have his act together in ways that I don't yet
5. My former college professor who was my thesis adviser
6. The minister at my church who gives such inspiring sermons

Think about ways to ask for guidance from your mentors—or, as I like to call them, your own personal board of directors. It doesn't have to be a formal request. You can just invite a mentor out for coffee, stop by his or her office, or talk by phone or Skype. You might ask your parents how they handled paying the bills when they were young marrieds. Ask if they were ever in debt and if so, how they got out of it. You might ask the CFO where she started out and how she rose in the business. You might make an appointment to stop by your minister's office for a casual check-in about the direction in which your life is going.

Most people are very flattered to be asked for advice. It's rare that someone doesn't have a little bit of time to offer help. If you are seeking direction in a humble way, your consultants will come through for you. Effective mentoring can also come from articles, biographies, and autobiographies. Paul Robeson is on my personal board of directors, even though he passed away when I was nine years old and we've never met. Learning about how someone you respect navigated choices in their own life is just like having them as a mentor. I call it mentorship on paper.

My Uncle Frank served as an important consultant to me. He gave me great advice when I was in graduate school and trying to figure out whether to be an actor or a lawyer. I had seventy thousand dollars in student loan debt. When I was looking at six-figure job offers from law firms, **Uncle Frank encouraged me to go into a line of work that I loved—even one as precarious as acting—rather than just following the money.** Ultimately this career has earned me more than I probably would have ever made as a lawyer, not to mention giving me the satisfaction of doing something I love. With my uncle's guidance, I aimed toward unreasonable happiness.

Our consultants should ask questions that will help guide us to our destination. They should ask us the same fundamental question we should ask ourselves. *What do I want my life to look like?* And then our consultants should help us mold a plan to make it happen. Whenever I go to foreign countries, I always hire tour guides to show me places of significance and teach me about the culture of the country. **Our consultants are guides in our life's journey.**

My adviser at Brown, professor and sociologist Martin Martell, committed his life to educating people. He was another consultant who really motivated me. Although I was doing very well academically, he could tell that I wasn't putting in 100 percent of my effort. Dr. Martell pulled me aside one day and said, "Hill, you're getting really good grades, but those grades don't necessarily mean you're doing your best. The grades are someone else's assessment of you. They shouldn't dictate the way you live your life. I can tell that you're not putting forth your best effort. You're skating off your abilities and doing things that fit your skill set. But if you want to achieve at your highest level, you have to develop the areas where you're not as good."

I realized immediately that I *had* been skating along and not putting in all the effort I was capable of. **A good consultant will risk his or her relationship with you in order to be completely honest.** You need this level of honesty to move forward. A consultant will tell you things that you really might not want to hear at the time; but that assessment will help you progress toward your goals.

I have had other exceptional consultants in my life who have shown me the way. I studied acting with Tony Greco, a well-known teacher who studied with the legendary actor, director, and acting teacher Lee Strasberg. What I learned from Tony about acting applied to my life as well. He taught me that acting was about being truthful. Acting is not about fake emphasis and putting on airs. You do your preparation and emotional work and feel the truth of a character in your heart. You stay present and see what happens. That's when the magic occurs and surprises in performance take place. As far as I'm concerned, that's a way to live a great life. Don't try to impress. **Live the truth from your heart and then see what happens.**

Stanley Jordan, my cousin, is a world-class jazz guitarist. He taught me that **great lives are lived like jazz.** Jazz musicians are extremely well trained. They do all the foundational work to reach a high level of expertise. And when they play together, they loosen up and let it flow in a moment of improvisation. You can't have that sort of fluidity and spontaneity without having worked long and hard at your art. It takes extreme discipline and passion to make it look cool and easy.

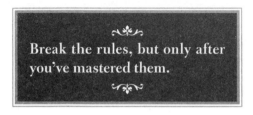

Break the rules, but only after you've mastered them.

So take a lesson from the jazz greats and **break the rules, but only after you've mastered them.**

A lot of the problems you hear about in Hollywood occur because many celebrities don't have an honest personal board of directors. Instead, they have yes-people and sycophants who are unwilling to say, "Actually, there is a problem with the way you're doing things." This reluctance leads to huge public relations disasters, careers being ruined, arrests and sometimes deaths—because no one is being honest. Celebrities as well as CEOs of companies should keep in mind that people who make money off them might not always speak with the highest level of honesty. The lesson for us is that we should seek out a personal board of directors who have no outside incentive to direct us in one way or the other.

One of my friends from Brown University found himself in this situation with his family. He had spent three years working his way up the ladder at an Internet start-up in California. His family visited and was clearly impressed with his new pad. Never mind that previously he had lived in a cramped share with three roommates, taking turns sleeping on the foldout couch, until he could comfortably afford to set up in his own place. Never mind that he had worked seven days a week without breaks for three years in order to move up within the company. The attitude of his parents and his teenage sister seemed to be, "Wow, Carl has it made. I want to participate in that!"

Carl explained to his folks that he couldn't afford to help them with a down payment on a new car—he told them he still didn't have a car himself and was using public transportation to get around or borrowing a friend's car for necessary trips. They understood his situation a bit better. His sister continued to nag him about buying her stuff. It created a rift between them that was healed only when she herself got through school, had her first job, and began paying her own bills.

Choose an activity that you can throw yourself into.

Napoleon Hill, author of the classic *Think and Grow Rich*, stressed that a person cannot "succeed in a line of endeavor which he [or she] does not like." Hill talks about the importance of finding an activity "into which you can throw yourself wholeheartedly."

I'd only known Mabel for a few hours, but it was obvious to me that she did not at all like the job she'd had before she started her business. She never said anything blatantly negative about it, but her usually melodic voice flat-lined when she spoke of that job. Yet when she spoke of her jewelry or of finding beads, an excitement in her entire demeanor was immediately evident and quite infectious. Many times during our conversations, I found myself wondering how I could have gone through my entire life without noticing beads and the breathtaking jewelry they make. Mabel's excitement introduced me to a whole new world. **Her energy made me want to buy some of her work.**

Mabel and Scott both spoke of how losing their jobs proved to be a blessing in disguise, though for entirely different reasons. So many people are stuck working jobs they don't like, but, like Mabel, they have responsibilities to a spouse or children or parents. They have bills to pay. The stress from that type of unhappiness is particularly dangerous because it's pervasive. It infects every aspect of an individual's life, from their financial well-being to their physical health, from the quality of their relationships to their emotional and psychological well-being. In other words, hating your job can lead to hating your life. Likewise, giving up in your job can lead to giving up in your life.

I would guess that's why beading played such an important role in

Mabel's life to begin with. Even though she referred to it as a hobby, I realized it was much more than that. It was a sacred space. The act of beading
took a huge investment of time, and that required a solid commitment especially for a full-time-working single mother. That Mabel liked to share the
activity with her daughter told me that beading did more than bring joy
into her life; it also provided her with the means to manifest her love for her
daughter and for the friends to whom she gave the necklaces, bracelets, and
earrings she'd made. As she beaded love, she developed skill and expertise.
Without realizing it, she was putting in her Gladwellian ten thousand hours.

I would also guess that if I'd asked Mabel whether she was happy at
her job while she was working as an executive secretary, she'd have told me
yes. Unless we absolutely hate our jobs, many of us mute our displeasure.
We try to make the best of them. We rationalize staying in our jobs, reminding ourselves that we are adults, and adults have responsibilities. From early
in our childhoods, we've been taught to think of a job as work and to think
of work as something hard—the furthest thing from fun. They don't call it
work for nothing, as the saying goes.

We've also been taught to narrow our definition of the word "reward"
to mean only money. With all these preconceived notions at play, work could
never be fun and certainly not enough fun to be its own reward. But it can
be, and it is for a lot of people. **If we don't learn to start thinking about
work as its own reward, we'll forever be stuck in less-than-satisfying
situations; we'll forever be uncertain about our life's purpose, and we'll
assign someone else the power to attract our fate and grow our fortune.**

Mabel was truly succeeding at *her* life. She was fortunate to have been
pulled into understanding that the thing she loved could fill her life with
wealth. Now what? That's what I'd wanted to ask. Listening to Mabel talk,
I understood that she hadn't been brought up knowing about money. Just
because we are able to make money doesn't always mean we learn how to
keep it. This doesn't necessarily mean that Mabel was in debt or that she
was irresponsible with money. She didn't seem to be that sort of person.
As a single parent, she'd probably learned through trial and error how to

handle her personal finances, but dealing with building and sustaining a business is another thing altogether.

I hear stories all the time about people who used their last fifty dollars to start a business or moved to Manhattan with just a hundred dollars to their name. Of course, these stories always end well, with the person becoming a huge success. Duke Ellington traveled by train from Washington, D.C. to New York with one thing in mind: making it big as a musician. While on the train, he went to the dining car and used most of the little bit of money he had to his name to buy himself a steak. Since I'm as much a pragmatist as I am a dreamer, I always wonder about the particulars whenever I hear stories like that. What were the decisions that filled the distance between what we've been told about the individual's beginnings and what we know about their later achievements?

Where does a person who has only a few dollars to his name find a place to sleep once the bus has dropped him off at Port Authority? Did the person who began her business with fifty dollars already own a printer and a computer? Was Duke Ellington confident that he'd have friends to stay with when he got to New York? Those things matter. **An understanding of the nuts and bolts allows us to find a balance between practical issues and issues of hope, faith, and joy. They help us to determine when, and how, to take our leap of faith.**

Let's say there's a man, we'll call him Ed, who is currently working as a customer service rep for a large corporation. He spends his days in a tiny, nondescript cubicle on the fourteenth floor of a large office building that looks like any other office building in the area. Ed is not satisfied with his job. He's grateful for the employment, but what his soul is yearning to do, is be a fashion designer. One day Ed decides that he has to give it a shot. If he doesn't, the question "What if?" will eat him up for the rest of his life. He has a savings account that will carry him for six months. Ed quits his job and sets out to be the next Tom Ford or Ozwald Boateng.

Is this foolhardy, or is Ed simply following his dreams by taking a leap of faith? The answer is probably a little bit of both. **A leap of faith is often**

**not one grand action but a series of smaller positive actions that move
you in the general direction of where you ultimately want to be.** Once Ed
made the decision to pursue designing, an entire universe automatically
opened itself to him. The very act of exploring that universe was enough to
start creating major shifts in his life. Ed might have even found that he was
happier at his job now, knowing that he wouldn't be consigned to it for the
indeterminate future.

Ed might end up being one of those success stories we hear about all the
time. He may very well be the person who, with ten dollars left to his name
and an eviction notice posted on his door, lands the big deal. Or not. Ed's
fate could also take a completely different turn, one that is not as immediately positive. Both of these examples are extreme. Most people's circumstances are not as severe. Most people are more methodical in their
actions, so the results are measured.

There is a third way, one that allows Ed to follow his dream and hedge
his risk. Rather than quitting his job, I would have recommended that Ed
sign up for evening or weekend classes in sewing, design, or small business
development. He could have started reading books about the fashion industry. These are the smaller leaps of faith, which would have inevitably led
him to other leaps. **Planning is key, and you are the architect.** You are
already creating your life exactly how it is now. So why not design, build,
and create the exact life you want?

As I've already written, that is being an *active architect of your own life.*
Without walls and the beams, every temple would fall apart. It takes planning to decide where those walls and the beams will go, lots and lots of
drawings, calculations, and thought. Most important, it takes a foundation
to support them. **I believe that the size and thickness of the foundation
we have to build in our lives is directly proportional to the size of our
goals and dreams. If you have big goals and dreams, then you need a
strong foundation to support them.**

The same is true of the temple that is our life's purpose; this, too, takes
planning, calculations, and thought. Mabel and her friends had to plan the
first salon. Once Mabel had decided to start her business, she had to make

specific plans and take certain actions step-by-step. For instance, she had to register a company name, open a bank account, print business cards, and, she'd told me, eventually rent out space where she could keep her office and set up a showroom, because her home could no longer contain the level of activity and foot traffic her work was generating. All of that involved calculation, thought, and planning. Each of those steps was a leap of faith for Mabel. No wonder she felt like she was flying. She had designed and built her own plane.

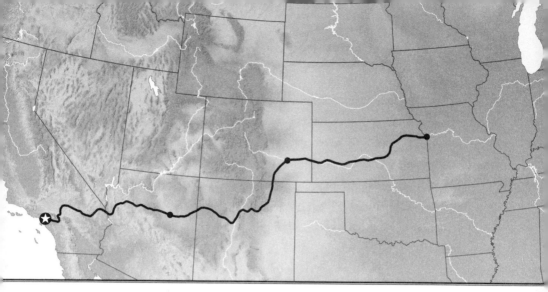

You Decide
Where to Go

"I would rather fail at my life than succeed in
someone else's."
— Andre Gide, novelist, critic, and essayist

While I was in bed my last night on the train and waiting for sleep
to arrive, I found myself thinking of *The Wizard of Oz*. Blame it
on the fact that we had recently rolled through Kansas. But that didn't
change how appropriate the movie was to everything I'd been thinking
about the entire day.

When I was little, *The Wizard of Oz* was one of those movies I always
enjoyed watching. The journey that Dorothy and her newfound friends took
was adventurous and fun. Yet stripped of its song, dance, and all the vibrant
colors, I found the journey utterly perplexing. How could they have not
known that they were already in possession of the very things they so desperately wanted? Why did no one tell them? How could nobody in all of

Oz have known that the wizard was only a scrawny, pathetic old man who sat behind a curtain pulling levers and giving orders in a disguised voice?

Even for a child, it was plain to see that the Tin Man had a heart, the Scarecrow had brains, and the Cowardly Lion had courage. Only as an adult did it occur to me that maybe it was plain to see because I was a child. I hadn't yet encountered the power of doubt. I wasn't aware that the outside world could project onto us false images of ourselves and that those images could strip us of our confidence and convince us to believe things about ourselves that aren't true. **The essence of who we are exists in our actions.** What we do says a lot about who we

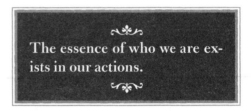

The essence of who we are exists in our actions.

are deep down. And we can do anything our heart desires. We have that power within us. *The Wizard of Oz* was all about the effect of False Evidence Appearing Real.

One of the ironies of the society we live in is that all throughout our childhood these ideas are drummed into us through literature, film, television, and music, yet by our adulthood, they are all but forgotten. Or worse, they are written off as childish. At what point does the fissure occur? At what point does "plausible" turn into "impossible"?

Several of my friends have young children, and I often find myself in the midst of family time. I had dinner once with my friends Janice and Sam in their home in Chicago. After we were done, I stayed and had a chat with Janice while Sam was giving their five-year-old son, Brandon, a bath. After bath time was story time, which was a family affair. The parents usually took turns reading a few poems and stories before tucking Brandon in and saying their prayers and good nights. They asked if I would mind reading something to Brandon, and I readily agreed.

While searching the impressively stocked bookshelf in Brandon's room for just the right poem or story to read, I was transported back to my own youth. I remembered having quite a few of those titles read to me when I was around the same age as Brandon. Books full of nursery rhymes with tales of blind mice, people living in shoes, jumping over candlesticks, or running through town in their nightgown making sure all the children are in bed. I decided on one of my all-time favorite authors, Dr. Seuss, and his book *Oh, the Places You'll Go!*

> *"You have brains in your head.*
> *You have feet in your shoes.*
> *You can steer yourself*
> *any direction you choose.*
> *You're on your own. And you know what you know.*
> *And YOU are the guy who'll decide where to go."*

What a powerful message for a child. It's an even more powerful message for an adult who may well have forgotten the basic truth about his own abilities and potential. There is *nothing* you can't do and you decide where to go. With that simple truth in my mind, I drifted off to sleep.

PART FIVE

Masterminding: Thrive and Survive

thrive \thrīv\: to make steady progress; to prosper; flourish

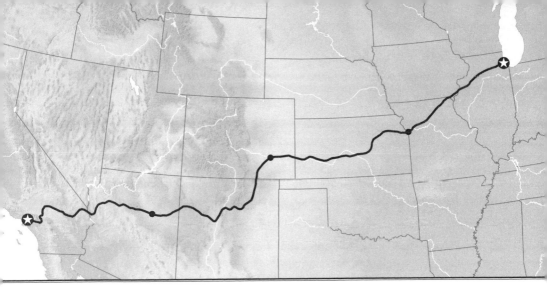

"Satisfactory" Is Not Enough

> "We are what we repeatedly do. Excellence,
> then, is not an act, but a habit."
>
> —Aristotle, Greek philosopher

In order to be happy and fulfilled, you have to put in time, energy, and work. Anything worth having requires you to work at it. A good relationship requires effort and thoughtfulness. You can't just plop down on the couch in front of the TV every night and grunt when your spouse asks you how your day went. You have to look each other in the eyes and really listen to what she is saying. You may not do that every single night, but you must really connect at least a few times a week or your relationship will stagnate very quickly.

The same holds true for your attitude about your career. There are some mornings when you wake up and you just don't feel like putting in any effort. Deep down, you want to give up and throw in the towel, but you know you can't, so you just go through the motions. You do the things you're supposed to do, but it's all done perfunctorily. Your heart just really isn't in it.

As an actor, my professional life is full of myriad opportunities to give less than 100 percent. When you're in the arts, it's up to you to create your own opportunities. If you don't pound the pavement, network with others in your field, follow up on leads, follow through on commitments, and practice your craft, it's not likely that you will find work. Even if you do all those things, there is no guarantee that you will get work, but you'll at least have a better chance of being noticed.

I suppose the same could be said of other professions—even those that at first glance appear to be more traditional and structured. Even if you're working in a corporate environment as a front-office receptionist in the lobby and your goal is to move one day into the corner office on the top floor, it's still up to you to create your own opportunities in order to facilitate that ambition. It's not enough to deliver a satisfactory performance or only to do the tasks that are expected or required of you. You have to give more, do more, be more.

As Daniel Pink says in *Drive*, his excellent book about what motivates people: "Control leads to compliance; autonomy leads to engagement. . . . Gallup's extensive research on the modern workplace shows that in the United States, more than 50 percent of employees are not engaged at work—and nearly 20 percent are actively disengaged. . . . Equally important, engagement as a route to mastery is a powerful force in our personal lives. While complying can be an effective strategy for physical survival, it's a lousy one for personal fulfillment. Living a satisfying life requires more than simply meeting the demands of those in control."

Every time you fail to do whatever you can to keep yourself in the race, to keep yourself chasing your dreams, you shortchange yourself. You're not exactly throwing in the towel, but you're also not moving yourself forward with all your talent and all your heart. The root of the word excellent is "excel." To excel, we must be excellent and vice versa. Satisfactory is not enough.

I, too, have had times that I am not very proud of, times when I didn't do my best. I have done what many of us do when faced with certain obstacles: I've quit. I've quit in that adult way, not like when we were children. We would pout and stomp our feet, or we'd stop playing, take our ball, and go home. **When we quit in an adult way, no one else really knows because we do it internally.** At some point in our lives, we have all had moments when we give up on the inside. Even though others couldn't tell, we secretly knew we'd dropped out of the race.

Over the course of our lives, this sloughing off begins to add up. We quit in increasingly subtle ways. We stop putting forth the effort, the energy, and the creativity required to solve problems because the payoff just doesn't seem worthwhile. It's as if we have lowered our expectations of ourselves. Sometimes we don't even realize that it has turned into something much more serious; we have developed a pattern of giving up before we have even started. Our goals and dreams even begin to atrophy, becoming smaller and smaller.

In some cases, this is a behavior that we've developed for our own protection. Quitting becomes a mechanism by which we can shut off internally and keep from facing things we want to avoid. They may be problems that we've already confronted and conquered, and now we can't believe it has raised its ugly head again. The truth is, most big issues do recur. Small problems can come back in different forms. It's disappointing and frustrating when our original solutions don't hold, and it drains away our valuable energy.

Even if you are doing a line of work you got into because you really enjoyed it, jobs can become stale and repetitive. What seemed exciting to you as a twenty-five-year-old can become dull after five, six, seven, or more years. I love acting, but after seven years of playing the same character on *CSI: NY*, I sometimes feel like I have swabbed fake blood too many times already! But in those moments, it's up to me to find a fresh, energized approach to do what has become very familiar. If we are not careful, experience can trick us into being lazy and not putting forth our best effort.

But who are you hurting most by sailing your career ship at half-mast?

Probably not your employer, because you are still doing a competent-enough job to cover the bottom line. The person you are harming most is yourself. If you lack passion for your work, you pay dearly for that lack of engagement every single day. You have to invest in your career the way you invest in your savings, by building up equity and by putting in the creative effort it takes to really shine. Your boss won't know about the great idea you did not bring up at the corporate retreat because you knew its implementation would fall on you and you didn't want to take on the extra responsibility. But who knows where it could have led? Perhaps to a promotion or joining a different creative team that would have been more to your liking and more compatible with your style and creative energy.

Mark Cuban, owner of the Dallas Mavericks, Landmark Theatres, and chairman of HDNet, has always had creative ideas, a passion for hard work, and tons of energy. When he was twelve, he went door-to-door selling garbage bags. In high school, among other jobs, he gave disco lessons. In the early 1980s, he began selling personal computers. At night, he read everything he could get his hands on and went on to become the number one computer salesman at the company. With a loan of $500 from one of his customers, he started his own computer-consulting business, MicroSolutions, which he eventually sold to CompuServ for $6 million. After taking some time off, Cuban and a college buddy developed a company called AudioNet, later called Broadcast.com, which transmitted radio over the Internet. He sold that business to Yahoo for almost $6 billion in stock.

Not all of us can be the next Mark Cuban, but his story is a phenomenal example of how passion, drive, and pursuing your own best ideas can take you beyond your wildest dreams.

We often avoid work challenges out of fear of additional responsibility and time commitment. Employing real energy into an outside project or "extra credit" task can really rejuvenate one's career or even launch a new career. The next time such an opportunity arises, instead of sloughing it off, try throwing yourself into it, heart and soul. Continuously stretch yourself outside your comfort zone to learn new things and seek out new experiences. If your company offers free classes, take them up on it. Go to that lecture or attend that workshop. You never know whom you might meet in terms of a mentor, colleague, or even someone who's looking to hire an incredibly talented and energetic person such as yourself.

Not all challenges and changes in your work life need to be huge. As Chip Heath and Dan Heath say in *Switch*, change can be less scary if we think about it in small doses. "One way to shrink changes . . . is to limit the investment you're asking for—only five minutes of housecleaning, only one small debt. Another way to shrink change is to think of *small wins*—milestones that are within reach."

Real change doesn't happen overnight. Working incrementally toward your grand design could take months or years. Be prepared at all times to recognize the opportunity that will help take you to the next level. **Preparedness is a key factor in making the most of opportunities**, as is sheer effort and persistence.

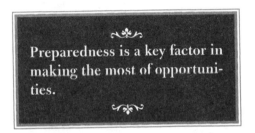

Preparedness is a key factor in making the most of opportunities.

In *The Hungry Ocean*, Linda Greenlaw described how she worked her way up to the job of her dreams over a number of years. "Go to sea I did, every chance I got for the next twenty years. Rarely did a day leave me ashore. I rowed until I inherited an antique outboard motor; I putted around the cove in the skiff until I had courage enough to 'borrow' my Dad's forty-foot powerboat . . . I fished . . . and experimented with nets and makeshift harpoons. Fishing my way through college, I made my first Grand Banks trip at the age of nineteen. . . . My primary job was cooking." Linda eventually graduated from galley chores to helmsman, and by the time she finished college, she was first mate. Four years later, she became a captain and eventually evolved into writing a best seller about her experiences running a swordfish boat.

Like Stephen King, Mark Cuban, and Linda Greenlaw, we can manifest success in our own world by identifying our talents, setting aggressive goals, and then committing ourselves to a plan to achieve them. Even when I was waiting tables and hoping for a callback on an audition, I dreamed big. I wanted to act on TV and in films; work with the best directors and producers; win awards for excellence; and be involved in projects that affected people. By setting specific goals for myself, I eventually achieved my mission, but it took several years and countless rejections before I got my first break.

Although practicing law was never my primary plan, I feared that someday I would have to. My fear was unfounded. It turned out to be False Evidence Appearing Real. **Most of our fears do turn out to be unfounded.** No one was going to hold a gun to my head and say, "You have to practice law." There was no evidence to suggest that I couldn't find employment to keep a roof over my head and feed myself. Shoot, I was a darn good waiter.

We have been taught that just because you have a degree in something, you must go into that area for your career or that you have to go into

Education buys you options.

whatever field would pay the highest salary initially. The point of learning is to have more options, not fewer. Somehow we get that flipped. **Education buys you options. That's incredibly valuable because the more options you have, the better positioned you are to choose a career that will make you happy.**

I t took three years of auditioning after grad school before I got my first big break, not to mention that I had been a part-time actor for last two years of grad school as well. After finishing school, while working as a waiter, I had to jump through so many hoops and auditioned over and over again before that first break, a recurring role on *Married With Children*.

The most difficult aspect of being an actor, by far, is the constant rejection. I can speak with some measure of authority about persevering through a barrage of no's. If you sent out 800 resumes, then you must send out the 801st resume. At that point you should also ask yourself if you need to make some changes and polish that resume. I still deal with rejection, as do most experienced actors. Believe me when I say that there are even movies that

Brad Pitt wanted to do that went to other stars. No matter where you are in this business, you are dealing with rejection. It teaches you a valuable lesson. Some people resort to false ego façades in reaction and become divas; others let it eat them up, and it makes them bitter and angry. In my case, the studios, directors, producers, and casting directors have the power. Having to deal with rejection is part of the journey when you choose a profession where other people decide whether or not you get to do what you enjoy doing.

When you're an entrepreneur, the demand for your product, goods, or services dictates whether or not you can do what you want to do. If the customers don't want your product, then it and you are rejected. That's very similar to being an actor. In both cases, if we want to be successful, we have to figure out how to make what we are offering more attractive to the "buyer." For a product, that could mean improving its quality or improving marketing. For an actor, it could mean getting better at the craft through classes. In neither case is success tied to luck. It's almost always about working smart. I like the term "working smart" much more than "working hard." Because if you are not working smart, you are not being efficient, and if you are working hard at doing the wrong things, you will not reach your desired results. **Let's commit to working hard *at* working smart.**

Speaking of not working as smart as I could and taking a risk when I perhaps shouldn't have, when I finally landed a role in *Married With Children*, I lost it because I went for a bigger part in the movie Smoke. It starred award-winning actor William Hurt. In reading the script, I thought it was an Oscar winner. The only day they could screen test me in New York was on a day when *Married With Children* needed me to work. *MWC* said if I went to New York instead of rehearsing with them, then my character would be written off the show. I chose to go for the film, but I didn't get the part. I also lost the television job. That was early in my career. My representatives at the time had advised me to forget *MWC* and to audition for the film. Now, with more experience in the business, I have come to realize that if people really want you, they will wait for you. You shouldn't necessarily mold yourself around other people's schedules. I could have said to them,

"I am working on something else, but would love to do the project. I can't audition next week, but I'm sure we can make that work out." They probably would have respected me even more if I'd said that. It's like dating—if you're not overly eager, the other person may be more interested. I was so used to hustling for the next opportunity that I rushed out to New York, and I lost the job I had worked so hard to get in Los Angeles. In my book *The Conversation*, I wrote, **"You shouldn't have to chase what you can attract."** I wish I had known that then. That would be working smart.

I kept replaying my decisions over and over in my head. I was depressed for the next two months because I'd worked so hard and had no work. I questioned my choices and blamed myself. When this happens, we need to take a step back and realize that **our lives are a marathon**. Do we think every decision we make on the journey will be correct? **We need to embrace our mistakes** and say, "Thank you for allowing me to make this mistake, because I'll learn from it and not make that mistake again."

We need to embrace our mistakes.

The most painful thing for me at that time was going to see the movie when it came out and feeling that that was my role. Then I realized that the actor who got it deserved it. That was his journey and his role. And ironically, Harold Perrineau, Jr. recently guest starred on *my* show *CSI: NY*, and we are friends today. Whenever we see others doing things that we want to do, we should celebrate and support them rather than be quietly envious. Everything comes back around, and if you stay in it and work smart enough, you will get your turn.

Within a few months I was cast in the Spike Lee movie *Get on the Bus*. Shortly after that, Spike asked me to be in his next film, *He Got Game*. Two major Spike Lee films back to back! Things picked up again, and I felt that my career was on a roll, but I did learn a lot of good lessons from those early rejections and missteps. If I hadn't kept my eyes on the prize throughout the long process, I would probably be spending my days in a law office with a bunch of guys in suits. Education gave me that option—not a bad option to have—but not *my* journey.

Dreaming big, aiming high, and achieving our goals isn't complicated: anyone can do it. Start by mapping out a detailed plan of action—a *blueprint*. Commit yourself to mastering each step along the way with energy and passion—that's building a *foundation*. Perform every interim job at 200 percent—no matter how small or seemingly unimportant—that is the framework, or the *choices* we make. Get to know potential mentors in your field and attend seminars and classes to learn as much as possible about your intended career path—those are the *doors* we must knock on and open. Employing those four components (blueprinting, foundation building, choices, and opening doors) allow us to be what I call "active architects" of our lives. **You can design and build any life you want just as an architect designs and builds a structure.**

Also, it's essential that you tell friends, family, and acquaintances about your intentions and ask for help in terms of contacts within your business. **Don't be silent about your dreams; you never know who's listening.** When you convey your passion for something, others become engaged in your dreams as well. If you are silent about your goals and dreams, you don't give the universe a chance to conspire to help make them manifest. Remember, success, much like courage, is a habit. It's what you do every day, even when no one is looking.

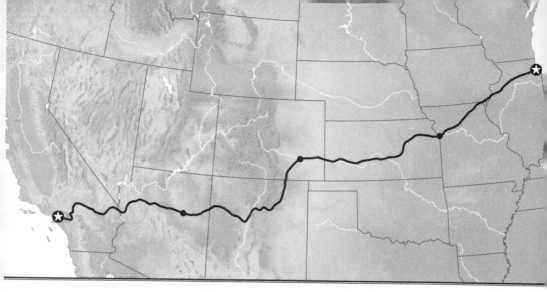

INVESTING IN YOU

"Invest in yourself, in your education. There's nothing better."

—Sylvia Porter

I t is important that we continue learning throughout our lifetime. We never know what new talent or skill will lead our life and career in a different direction. In addition to investing in ourselves by way of a good education and new learning opportunities, we should also make time for our inner life. Reserving quiet time to explore what we want out of life keeps us focused and on track. Having a spiritual life is a supremely important part of investing in oneself, yet it is often an area that we tend to overlook. We feel "too busy" or defer such efforts to "when things slow down." When you've tended your spiritual garden, you will find yourself much better equipped to get through the difficult periods in your life.

A career in acting is often fraught with rejection. The fellowship of church, hearing choirs sing, listening to stories from the Bible, and hearing the pastor preach have all helped me through the more difficult times. The foundational elements of life include money, faith, spirituality, health, and education. I had big goals in a career where there is a great deal of rejection and failure, so I knew that the faith component was essential. You need a strong foundation in faith to be an actor, or the rejection will consume you.

I still haven't attained all of my goals in terms of being an artist and the types of roles I want to play. I have Empire State Building–sized goals and aspirations, so I need an Empire State Building–sized foundation. Often we have skyscraper dreams, but aren't equipped to build the foundation to support them.

We should also invest in our mental health. Since my father was a psychiatrist, and also since I've seen many of my friends' lives affected by depression and bipolar disorder, mental health issues are of extreme importance to me. As a society, we have barely touched the tip of the iceberg when it comes to our understanding of mental illness, and part of that is because we don't discuss it openly. There is no shame to seeking therapy and counseling to deal with depression and mental health.

Money factors in significantly with mental health treatment, and a lot of people don't take the preventative measures they could, or perhaps should, because it is financially inconvenient. When it comes time to tighten the financial belt, people often will remove things like psychotherapy from their budget, because it frees up a lot of money. But what is the long-term cost?

Medication is another financial factor in the treatment of mental health. What's amazing is that it actually costs the country more money not to directly address mental health concerns than it does to address them. The amount of lost wages and lost productivity due to issues like depression is astronomical.

But not addressing mental health issues costs us more than money. In the aftermath of tragedies such as school and post office shootings, it is often discovered that the perpetrators of those violent acts were suffering from mental illness. Depression, the most common and often undiagnosed mental health problem, can often result from financial stress. Being laid off, having bill collectors constantly calling, tax problems, having utility services disconnected, not being able to afford necessities, these are all things that can cause stress that can ultimately lead to depression that can become clinical. Don't cut back on mental health care—it is key to overall health. This is an investment in yourself.

S hane Ward and Shawn J. Ward are two people who are great examples of investing in oneself on every level—monetarily, spiritually, and physically. Shane is creative director and cofounder and Shawn is president and cofounder of Shane&Shawn, a hugely successful shoe company. They told me the story of how they invested in themselves to start their business. It's so inspiring that I want to share it with you.

"When I was a young kid, while my siblings played video games, I was always sketching design ideas," Shane said. "I loved tennis, and I would draw designs for tennis shirts, shoes, shorts; I even had my own company logo. When I got older, I knew I wanted to do something with art, but Shawn and I got a scholarship to Michigan, which wasn't known for its art school. One day during a break between classes, I went into the design building. There were drawings of flashlights, cars, all kinds of things, and it dawned on me that I could be a professional and do this. So I decided to major in design. Shawn chose the mechanical engineering school across the street.

"It's funny, back then when I told people I was majoring in art, they thought I'd wind up drawing caricatures on the street downtown. Actually, I wound up making more money than people in the sciences or business by figuring out what my passion was and then pursuing it.

"Before I graduated from college, I had an interview at Adidas, and they flew me to Portland, Oregon. I didn't have any shoe designs in my portfolio, so I had to come up with something quick. I had one of my younger brothers, who ran track in school, put some masking tape on his bare feet and then run back and forth on the street. Then I looked at where the wear and tear was on the masking tape and designed a cool minimalist shoe that would take some of the wear off of those pressure points.

"I had my interview in Oregon, and they made me a job offer. I had to decide whether or not to move there. Shawn and I are twins. I'd never been apart from him or my family, and I would have to leave my girlfriend back home, too. I had to decide whether or not to stay in my comfort zone. The Adidas offices were fantastic. At that time they had a basketball court in the building, and people were throwing Frisbees and footballs around. I wound up taking the job and moving to Portland.

"By my second year at Adidas, I was a senior designer, traveling around the world to visit the factories and also to take inspirational trips for ideas. It blew my mind, how a passion for design wound up taking me all over the world. I also met with a lot of major athletes to design shoes for them. After four years, I took another job in Philadelphia. After a year with that company, I decided I wanted to go out on my own and start my own business.

"In June of 2001, I moved to New York City and started doing freelance shoe design. I had created a good name for myself in the shoe business. It was before social networking so I just sent out a mass e-mail to everyone I knew in the industry, asking if anyone needed help with design. I got a terrific response, and within six months I had major contracts with FuBu, Fila, and And1."

"I had moved to New York City before Shane," Shawn added. "I was trading in the stock market. We never planned to hook up in New York, but we wound up living in the same place again. Shane was really busy with his freelance work. Since the stock market closed at four, I helped with his business in the late afternoons. I started doing things to grow the company, like adding more clients. Around the end of 2002, we decided that I would do the business plan, finances, logistics, and marketing, and Shane would focus on design. By the end of 2003, we officially started Shane&Shawn, our shoe company."

"At first, Shawn and I bumped heads a lot over decision making, until we decided to totally separate our responsibilities," Shane explained. "Once we decided that I would handle designing the product, choosing the colors, and so forth, and Shawn would handle the marketing and business side, it got much easier. We would discuss various issues, but the final decision was made by the one of us who handled that area of business. That made a big difference in how we got along. The hardest thing about a family business is that you have to change the way you act during business hours. You may be brothers and best friends, but you have to conduct yourself in a businesslike way when you're working."

Shawn elaborated on his brother's point. "One big advantage of working with a family member is the trust factor. You know that the business partner has your best interests at heart, but with an outsider, you have to grow that trust. We had to invest heavily in ourselves when we began our own business from scratch. It wasn't just freelance shoe design any longer. We had to go to China to choose a factory to make our product. We invested half a million dollars in the company, and we also received another five hundred thousand dollars in bank loans. **As with most start-ups, we didn't have immediate success.** It took two years of extremely hard work before we knew that we had a real business. We felt like real players in the market when we got our first big order from Nordstrom. It was very exciting; they shipped our shoes and we did in-store events with them.

"The scariest part of starting a new business was leaving the safety net of the nine to five—the regular paycheck, health insurance, and stability. It's not for the fainthearted. **You have to really believe in yourself.** When you take all of your savings and put it into a company, it's nerve-racking. You just have to have a strong belief that you can accomplish what you want to do and a stronger belief in yourself.

> You have to really believe in yourself.

"For someone who wants to start his own business, my first bit of advice is don't quit your day job yet. First start doing the work you want to do, on a freelance basis, in the evenings and on weekends. Then wait until you have enough cash saved up and can generate revenues to ease the blow of losing your regular paycheck, before you quit your job and go full steam ahead."

"A lot of people e-mail us or come up to us at our speaking engagements," Shane stepped in to tell the story, "to ask how they should go about starting their own business, but many have no experience in the field they want to go into. First you should get a job in the industry you are considering. You learn so much by working in the business—how the industry functions and nuances that you wouldn't realize otherwise. Also you make contacts in your field. People tend to want to skip these steps, but **you need to build a good foundation before you jump off on your own.**

"Another thing we tell people is to e-mail twenty to twenty-five people to try to find a mentor. Shawn and I did this—we sent out a bunch of blind e-mails to anyone we admired and respected in the business. We chose people who were in positions in which we envisioned ourselves in fifteen years. Out of that number, you'll get a couple of people who are willing to help you out, and that is really key.

"Also, you have to invest in yourself in ways other than monetarily. When you have your own business, it's easy to become stressed out and stop eating right, stop exercising, and making time for friends. Being an entrepreneur isn't nine to five; it's twenty-four/seven, three hundred sixty-five days of the year. You have to plan time in your calendar for exercise, friends, and mental health. When I get stuck in one lane in terms of a design I'm working on, I get away from work for a while, and often a good idea will come to me. **I'm a true believer in the concept that when your mind is at rest, not cluttered and blocked with daily work details, it allows room for creativity.**

"You have to keep learning and invest in your education. Right now, in fact, I'm taking a private shoemaking course from an incredibly talented woman in Brooklyn. I've worked in the business since 1996, but I felt that in order to be a true designer, I needed to know how to make a shoe and to understand the challenges that a factory worker faces.

"I have so much respect now for anyone who builds even a small section of a shoe; something like stitching leather is extremely difficult. I've posted about the course on Facebook, and the response has been amazing. **I think you have to keep learning in order to stay fresh, and that's another way of investing in yourself.**"

Shawn took over. "In terms of investing in oneself, a year ago, I started meditating. When you're busy, meditation can feel like having to go to church: How on earth will I have the time? To be effective, you really have to do it every day for fifteen to twenty minutes. **But once you meditate regularly, you see how it makes you so much calmer in times of stress.** It allows me to soak things in and not react emotionally.

"You also have to invest some time in your health. So many great ideas have come to me when I'm out on a nice jog. Physical health is extremely important when you're working hard. You can't afford to let your body fall apart when you're putting so many demands on it. Regular exercise and meditation are the ways I invest in my body and mind.

"Another thing I do is watch biographies on CNBC and Biography. com; it's the way I get inspired. When I see stories of the Astors, the Rockefellers, and other entrepreneurs, it's really helpful to realize that they had many failures as well as successes. You tend to think they were successful from day one, but they all had trials and had to work extremely hard. Watching these bios helps me to stay psyched and inspired."

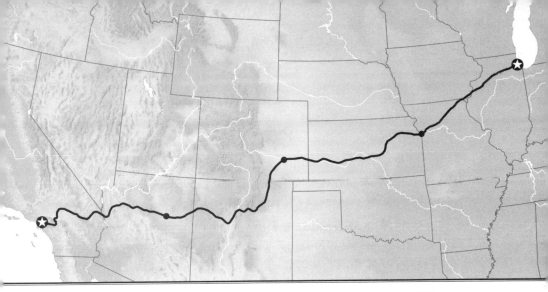

INVESTING IN LIFE INSURANCE, A WILL,
AND AN EMERGENCY FUND

"Health is the greatest gift, contentment the
greatest wealth, faithfulness the best relationship."

—Buddha, spiritual teacher
and founder of Buddhism

Remember how Tracey's and Jarrett's insurance planning smoothed the way for Tracey after Jarrett's untimely death? We all want to take care of the people we love. One mistake that people often make is not having adequate coverage in terms of health, life, home, and automobile insurance.

Possibly the thorniest issue up for discussion in America today is health insurance. At the time of this writing, the entire health care industry is in flux due to changing government agendas. To put this into context, a full 15 percent of Americans did not have any health care coverage as of September 2010 and those numbers could rise if the laws protecting people with chronic illness are revoked.

If you already have health care coverage through your job, then that is probably the least expensive way for you and your dependents to go. Be sure to choose the least expensive option that you feel will give you the best coverage for you and your family's particular situation. Human resources, your office manager, or whoever handles the insurance area of your company should be able to help you if you have questions about which plan to sign up for. The average cost to a company of a health care policy for a family of four is $13,375; for a single person, it is $4,700.

If you are self-employed or work for a company that does not offer health care, you must take it upon yourself to obtain adequate insurance. Many people have made the mistake of thinking, I'm relatively young and in good shape, I don't need insurance, only to be hit with a nasty health crisis that drained their savings or, worse, put them in thousands of dollars of debt. Health care of any kind is incredibly expensive, especially if you need surgery or have to spend even one night in a hospital. Health and wealth are very much related because **medical bills are the number one reason people file for bankruptcy in this country.**

I was never so glad that I had insurance than when I was diagnosed with cancer. My coverage was the result of being a member of a union—the Screen Actor's Guild. It gave me such empathy for people who don't have coverage or not enough coverage in similar situations. It's bad enough to be ill, but to have to worry about not being insured on top of dealing with a medical issue would be exceptionally overwhelming—and people go through it every day.

So if you don't have coverage through work, you should meet with an insurance agent who will direct you to the insurance company most likely to take you on. Group coverage can be less expensive, so check out your professional trade associations as well. Private policies for a family of four can range widely, depending on where you live, how much coverage you opt for, and the deductibles in your plan.

Once you have determined which insurance company you want to sign up with, you will meet with a medical underwriter who will evaluate your health risk. Not being insured is a risk that you cannot take. One big hospital stay can wipe out your savings and ruin your credit for years to come.

Even if you are turned down by an insurance company, you can check out your state's high-risk pool, programs that cover people who are not eligible for private coverage. Not every state has one, and they can be expensive, but do investigate as a last resort.

One way to avoid a financial catastrophe from a medical crisis is to prevent the crisis by taking care of yourself. There are many preventive measures to take to help ensure that you will have a long, healthy life. Giving up smoking is one of the biggest things you can do to improve your overall well-being. Keep in mind that 50 percent of all long-term smokers will die of tobacco-related causes. **About 5 million people die every year because of tobacco use, and smoking will claim a billion lives this century, unless something occurs to halt it.** If that's not enough, secondhand smoke has more than fifty cancer-causing chemical compounds. Eleven of them are Group One carcinogens (cancer-causing compounds). If you haven't yet quit smoking, now is the time to do so.

Another preventive measure that you should consider is making sure you are within the proper weight range. There are scores of online calculators to figure out your body mass index, a good indicator of where you fall in the range of healthy weight. If you're overweight, the most effective long-term weight-loss plans include both eating healthier and less and exercising more. A friend of mine lost forty pounds in a year simply by going for an early morning power walk most days of the week and by cutting out sweets. She has kept off the extra avoirdupois for ten years and saw a dramatic improvement in her overall self-esteem.

Financial health often mirrors physical health.

Quitting smoking, losing weight, eating healthier, managing stress, limiting alcohol intake, exercising, doing yoga or meditating—all of these are simple investments that can reap huge returns when it comes to your health. Combining these things with adequate health insurance will place you on the path to true wealth. By maintaining good health, you potentially save thousands of dollars on medical costs. Those savings become Smart Money that works for you.

A few other aspects of financial literacy that involve investing in oneself are having a will and an emergency fund. Most of us don't like to think about the fact that we will die. You've read about Tracey and Jarrett and the importance of life insurance earlier. An insurance broker can help you figure out how much life insurance you should carry, depending on your income and how much your heirs would need if you passed away. Even if your spouse doesn't work, he or she should also have life insurance, because child care and home maintenance is very costly if you have to pay for it.

You should see a lawyer who handles wills or create an online will and have it documented, so that if you die, your affairs will be handled as you desire. I was shocked to learn that 55 percent of all adult Americans do not have a will. According to a recent Harris Poll, only one in three African American adults and one in four Hispanic American adults have wills, compared with 52 percent of white American adults. For all three groups those percentages are far too low. If you pass away without a will, it's up to the state to dispose of your assets, and you have no control over who among your heirs gets what. To avoid this undesirable outcome, take the time to set up a proper will. And God forbid something did happen to you, you have provided for your spouse or partner and children.

An emergency fund is an extremely important, basic tenet of financial literacy. Experts used to recommend having three months' salary in an accessible bank account, and that means one in which penalties won't apply if you have to withdraw money quickly. Now the recommendation is to have six months' salary saved. With the job market still not recovered from the recession, six months' salary is not an excessive amount when you realize that people are often out of work for a year or more. At the time of writing this book, almost half of all unemployed people are long-term unemployed, meaning that they have been out of work for twenty-seven weeks or more. The six months' savings figure is appropriate.

The specter of unemployment is not the only reason to have such a fund. God forbid you should have a medical emergency, but if this does happen to you or to anyone in your family, you want to be able to pay for the costs not covered by insurance. These costs can really mount up. The average length of a hospital stay is five days, and the average cost is $4,350 per day, or $24,000 for five days. Of course, these are just averages. The cost could be much higher, depending on what is being treated. When you consider potential medical costs, it's obvious that you must have an emergency fund on hand.

Other uses for an emergency fund include large home or car repairs that can't be put off, like a fridge that goes on the fritz. You need a refrigerator, so you will need cash to buy a replacement. Do not use your emergency fund for anything else but spates of unemployment, medical needs, or urgent repairs or replacement of essential equipment. Otherwise, consider it untouchable.

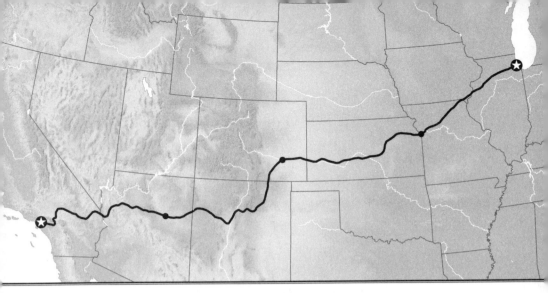

FILLING THE BUCKET

"There are three ingredients to the good life;
learning, earning, and yearning."
—Christopher Morley,
American author and journalist

O ne thing I always find odd is that we are living within a society that
places such an incredible emphasis on money, yet most of us have
never been taught how to hold on to money, let alone make it grow. To
thrive, we want our resources, like money, to expand not contract. Many
of us are taught by our parents to work hard, go to school, and get a degree. When we are in school, our focus is to graduate and land a great-
paying job. Then once we are working, many of us end up mired in debt
because we were never taught how to manage our finances. Families
don't teach it, and we aren't taught it in college.

**Our emphasis on making money, combined with our concurrent
lack of emphasis on keeping it, is like trying to fill a bucket with water**

that has a hole in the bottom. We keep trying to pour more water in the bucket, that is, spend more and more money. The weight of the water eventually makes the hole bigger and bigger. You can never win. The water keeps gushing out, in the same way that your money keeps flowing out. We are puzzled by the fact that even if we earn a good income, often we haven't saved a cent. We wind up deep in debt. We haven't learned how to hold on to the money that we have earned.

Cars and houses are two of the greatest areas of overspending, resulting in a lack of savings. Most money experts say that you shouldn't spend more than 25 percent of your gross income on your house. The cost of your car shouldn't be more than ten percent of income, including loan payments, insurance, gas, and oil changes.

Many people in our country are failing to pay mortgages that are too high. Las Vegas posted one foreclosure for every nine housing units in 2010—five times the national average. A full 67 percent of the homes sold in California in 2009 were sold by sellers who couldn't pay their mortgages. Yet even if you renegotiate your loan with a bank, you might wind up spending far more than 25 percent of your income in order to keep your house. If you're in this situation, selling the house is often a better option than remaining in a money pit for the long term.

You may feel that it will be impossible to sell your house when so many properties are up for sale, but don't despair. In 2010, there were still 321,000 new home sales. So even in the depths of the recession, people were still managing to sell their houses.

"Fort Madison," the conductor yelled. "Fort Madison, Iowa. Next stop."

Fort Madison? No, couldn't be. How could I have not realized that Fort Madison was a stop on Southwest Chief line? When Scott told me that we'd be rolling through Iowa, I didn't realize our stop would be Fort Madison.

This small town is where my father was born. It holds a lot of history for my family. I lived here for a few years growing up and spent most of my summers and holidays on my grandparents' eighty-acre farm. In fact, the train tracks heading into town bordered my grandfather's farm. As kids, we would play in the corn and soybean fields and often flatten pennies on those very same tracks.

As the train pulled into "downtown" Fort Madison, I looked out and saw the banks of the Mississippi where I used to hold my grandfather's hand as we watched the Fourth of July fireworks. Those types of fireworks displays seem almost perfectly suited for small Midwestern towns. I looked at the riverbank right where my grandfather, grandmother, brother, cousins, aunts, uncles, and parents used to picnic, and I was reminded of a story my grandfather told me about how he was able to purchase the land that he had and how he was going to pass a foundation of wealth to the next—my parents'—generation.

My grandfather, a family practitioner, set up a practice in a small shack near the railroad tracks in Fort Madison in the 1920s. The white-owned banks refused to allow him to open a savings account, so he literally had to keep the money he earned under his mattress. In 1928, when the stock market crashed, banks froze assets; people were fearful and needed money. He reached under his mattress and, along with his brothers, purchased an apartment building that spanned nearly an entire city block in downtown Fort Madison. My grandfather and his brothers converted that building into a state-of-the-art medical clinic and lab with residential apartments above. For a number of years it was the number one private medical practice in the state of Iowa. And for nearly forty years, until the end of Jim Crow segregation, African American women from four states would come and give birth in a safe, clean facility built for them and their families.

There were many times that my grandfather would provide services for free if a patient had no money. I also remember him accepting crops and poultry in exchange for medical care. "Hero" and "legacy" are two words that are often overused, but in the case of my grandfather, they could not be more appropriate. He not only found a way to expand our family's financial resources, he also invested by *giving*. And that is a perfect way to "fill your bucket."

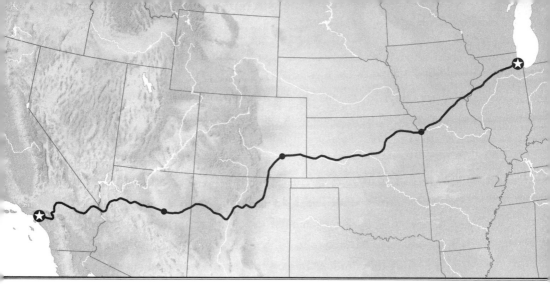

Investing by Giving Back

"Everybody can be great because everybody can serve."
—Dr. Martin Luther King Jr., clergyman, activist, and prominent leader in the civil rights movement

G iving back to your community or to the world at large is a good way to invest in yourself. Donations have been declining during the recession, and charities are feeling the pain. If you have anything in your budget to give, even in the smallest amount, then give it freely to the organizations of your choice. Worthy charities abound. If you have any questions about verifying that a charity is doing what it claims to do, you can check it out on various websites that deconstruct how organizations spend their donations.

If you feel that your monetary contributions would be too paltry, and you are really stretched tight financially, you can always donate your time and energy to organizations like Big Brothers Big Sisters, tutoring, and literacy programs through schools or community colleges, the local food pantry, or the plethora of local and national charities.

When I wrote my first book, *Letters to a Young Brother*, I realized that although it was great to motivate people with a book, individuals need real intervention, too. I founded the Manifest Your Destiny foundation to uplift, inspire, and educate young people who were growing up in the most challenging, underserved situations. I intended to practice what I preached. I helped to start the Summer Empowerment Academy, which takes place at West Los Angeles College. Kids who have finished eighth grade and are going into ninth attend the Summer Academy, free of charge. The program includes free food, motivational training, PowerPoint and other computer training, and ties their future to their education. The kids present a business plan at the end of the program, and they get a college credit for attending. Since the academy takes place on a college campus, it plants a subconscious seed in their minds. They find that they are comfortable on the campus, and they realize that's where they belong.

We have to spread our circle of those for whom we care—not just care *about*. For many years, we were told that our circle of care is our nuclear family, but we are living in world that is global in nature, and we should start thinking of our circle of care in a more expansive way. The dropout rate of most underserved public schools in our country is astronomical. In most cases, you can trace who will drop out after eighth grade. Of kids with a 2.2 average or lower, 90 percent will not make it through high school. Those are the kids my foundation seeks to help. Education is one of the most important elements for future success, so keeping kids engaged is critical.

I was entering the Taco Bell drive-through one day and I saw a 1-800 notice saying BECOME A MENTOR. I know I shouldn't have been eating two chalupas, but in this case, it led to something good. I called the number and signed up and was fortunate to have a little brother from the time he was eight until he graduated from high school. After that, I became an ambassador for Big Brothers Big Sisters.

The most valuable intervention in a child's life is mentoring, and that doesn't cost the government, or anyone else, any money. It's free. It costs only our time. In L.A., there were 850 kids on the waiting list to be mentored. You'd think that in a city with more than ten million people there would be enough adults to mentor these kids. Yet this long waiting list of kids looking for guidance exists in city after city. We need to look in the mirror and ask ourselves if we are willing to expand our circle of care, to do something to help someone outside of our nuclear family. Stop saying it's the government's responsibility, or someone else's responsibility. The buck stops here, with us.

In addition, the time that you put into a group such as Big Brothers Big Sisters will reward you far more than what you do for the organization. There is a great feeling of accomplishment when you have helped a hungry person, for instance, or a child struggling with English or people in need of winter coats. The camaraderie between fellow volunteers is warm and inviting. In addition, participating in the efforts of such charitable organizations is a great dose of reality that makes me appreciate some things I may take for granted, like shelter, food, and a quiet, safe place to sleep at night. Doing so puts complaints such as "My boss doesn't appreciate me" or "I don't have enough time for myself" into perspective. Volunteering really is an investment in yourself. It lifts you up in so many ways.

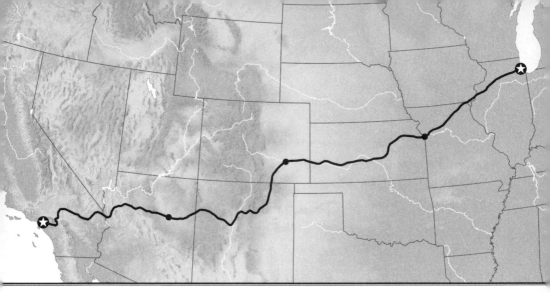

CHI-TOWN BOUND

"New York is one of the capitals of the world and Los Angeles is a constellation of plastic, San Francisco is a lady, Boston has become Urban Renewal, Philadelphia and Baltimore and Washington wink like dull diamonds in the smog of Eastern Megalopolis . . . But Chicago is a great American city. Perhaps it is the last of the great American cities."

—Norman Mailer, American novelist, journalist, essayist, poet, playwright, screenwriter, and film director

T he train was now chugging along toward Chicago.

"Who knows how much longer you would have stayed at your job," I reminded Scott at lunch that afternoon. "Maybe being laid off is what it took for you to really see how far away the life you were living was from the life you wanted to be living."

"Maybe you're right," he said, staring through the huge window.

"I'm not sure if we'll get a chance to chat again before we get off the train," I said as I scribbled my name, e-mail address, and phone number on the back of a sheet of paper. "If what you really want to do is act, don't let anybody or anything stop you. Call me if you ever want to talk, and please let me know if there's anything I can do to help you get on the path you want to be traveling. I volunteer to be a member of your personal board of directors." I handed him the paper.

"Thanks, man." He took the paper from me, set it down on the table, then stood up, stepped into the aisle, and held his hand out for me to shake. We shook and then embraced.

"And remember," I said before turning to walk away, "don't give in to your fears."

"All right. You, either," Scott called out after me.

Just then, the conductor passed by and said, "We'll be in Chicago in about two hours, Mr. Harper. Thanks for riding with us and God bless."

"God bless you, too. It's been an amazing journey."

I returned to my room and sat down on the couch. I had been putting off reading the rest of the packet that Tracey gave me, but it was time to browse through it. I pulled out the envelope and opened it. There were about ten sheets of paper in there, all about Mastermind Circles, which have probably been around since the beginning of time, though Benjamin Franklin is credited as starting the first formal one.

Simply put, **a Mastermind Circle is a collection of two or more individuals who meet regularly for the sole purpose of helping each**

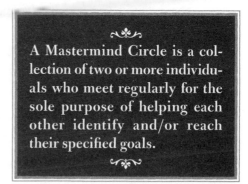

A Mastermind Circle is a collection of two or more individuals who meet regularly for the sole purpose of helping each other identify and/or reach their specified goals.

other identify and/or reach their specified goals. These people are not necessarily friends. They do not have to have any other relationship or connection outside of that group. The meetings are not a forum for complaints but rather a forum for discussion in which you can benefit from everybody's ideas, expertise, and encouragement. It is a forum for empowerment.

In Benjamin Franklin's autobiography, aptly titled *The Autobiography of Benjamin Franklin*, he wrote: "I had formed most of my ingenious acquaintances into a club of mutual improvement, which we called the Junto." The word "junto" is derived from the Latin word *iuncta,* which means to meet or to join. Many ideas came out of Benjamin Franklin's Junto's Friday night meetings, including the very first public library, the first public hospital, the concept of volunteer fire departments, and even the University of Pennsylvania. So many of their transformative ideas now form an integral part of modern America. That Mastermind Circle lasted for forty years. Isn't it ironic that the expression "all about the Benjamins," refers to chasing paper notes and not the actual principles that Benjamin Franklin represented?

There is also another present-day group that uses the name Junto. It's called the London Junto and is modeled after Benjamin Franklin's group. The London Junto is a forum of investment professionals who meet regularly to formulate new financial investment models and strategies. This made me pause for a second. The most influential ideas that came from Benjamin Franklin's Junto seemed to center around collecting ideas and information for community wealth building—hospitals, firehouses, and schools. The new London Junto is centered around the idea of information accumulation for the purpose of individual wealth creation.

Tracey's packet also included information on another famous Mastermind Circle that later came to be known as the Chicago 6. The members included Andrew Carnegie, William Wrigley, Henry Ford, Napoleon Hill, William Hertz, and K. C. Gillette. They began their group in the early 1900s. While only one of the members had a great deal of money initially, within years they each were worth millions, which was a very rare achievement in those days.

Each of the members of the Chicago 6 made a significant impact on the world, particularly in the areas of business and philanthropy. These men helped put Chicago on the map, and it was all as a result of their Mastermind Circle. They met every Saturday in a local restaurant and talked for hours about their goals. They exchanged ideas and helped each other stay focused. Their names were not well known, but now the very idea of these six brilliant, ingenious men in a room together week after week exchanging ideas is incredible. How could they not have become successful?

William Wrigley was the founder of the Wrigley's chewing gum empire and financier of Wrigley Field, where the Chicago Cubs play. K. C. Gillette founded the Gillette Safety Razor Company. William Hertz founded the Yellow Cab Company and his eponymous car rental company. Henry Ford is, of course, known for starting the Ford Motor Company. Andrew Carnegie, who was the only member of means before the Chicago 6 began meeting, made his fortune as an industrialist, and he left behind a legacy of philanthropy. By the time of his death, he was thought to be the richest man in the world, worth more than $500 million.

Carnegie was no stranger to Mastermind Circles. He credited his success and the success of most wealthy businesspeople to the Mastermind process. In fact, he commissioned Napoleon Hill, who also joined the Chicago 6, to speak with and study five hundred successful men and women in order to discover if there was a common formula to success.

Napoleon Hill spent twenty years on this assignment, the results of which he'd promised Carnegie he would publish. Hill kept his promise, and that book is the perennial best seller *Think and Grow Rich*, which was first published in 1937 and continues to enjoy a great readership seventy years later.

In *Think and Grow Rich*, Napoleon Hill writes:

The "Mastermind" may be defined as: **"Coordination of knowledge and effort, in a spirit of harmony, between two or more people, for the attainment of a definite purpose."** Analyze the record of any man who has accumulated a great fortune, and many of those who have accumulated modest fortunes, and you will find that they have either consciously or unconsciously employed the "Mastermind" principle.

It was easy to see how Mastermind Circles could help people create abundance in their lives. The same principles of communion are at the root of treatments and programs like group therapy, Alcoholics Anonymous, and various other support groups. One of the reasons for the success of these groups is their ability to help people avoid distractions and stay on track with their goals. They help people stay focused on the long-term value of the vision that they've created for themselves—a vision of mental health, a vision of sobriety.

I had unknowingly applied this principle when I was a student at Harvard Law School by participating in study groups. People often ask me how I was able to graduate from Harvard Law School *cum laude* and get a master's at the same time, while traveling to New York to audition for plays and doing professional theater in Boston. The answer: two things—the desire to excel in all areas of my life *and* study groups. To this day I encourage the students whom I mentor to form study groups, even with kids in their classes they don't know. I explain to them, whether they are in fifth grade or graduate school, study groups work. If you use study groups, you are employing the idea of working smart as opposed to simply working hard.

Tracey was right to suggest that spiritual wealth was the basis of all other types of wealth, including financial wealth. The Mastermind principle that when two people come together, "a third, invisible, intangible force" is also present reminded me of the Biblical passage Matthew 18:20: "For where two or more are gathered in my name, there I am in the midst of them."

One of the techniques Tracey's Mastermind Circle uses for planning is a goals calendar. For instance, at the start of the year, Tracey writes down all the major goals she hopes to accomplish. Once her goals have been identified, she then takes each goal and turns it into twelve mini-goals, one for each month of the year. Then these mini-goals are further broken down into four smaller goals, one for each week. The weekly goals are then divided into seven smaller goals for each day. In this way, Tracey's daily activities directly connect to her year-end goal.

The one concept that Napoleon Hill emphasizes the most is that in order to be successful, you must find your purpose in life—what I call your North Star. A lot of people don't know what their purpose in life is. The activities you most love will ultimately guide you to your purpose in life. They think it has to be something complex. In fact, some of the most dynamic people in the world claim some of the most simple ideals and goals as their life's purpose.

Deepak Chopra writes, "Everyone has a purpose in life . . . a unique gift or special talent to give to others." When asked what his life purpose is, Chopra responded: "My life purpose is reaching a critical mass of people with a message of healing, personal/social transformation and enlightenment." With that purpose as his guide, Deepak Chopra has managed, through his books, lectures, and other appearances, to help millions of people find uplifting and new ways of looking at themselves and the world.

I understood why Tracey wanted me to know about Mastermind Circles. I kept reading until the conductor announced that we had reached our final destination: Chicago. I gathered my things as we pulled into the station and a peaceful wave of satisfaction came over me. We made it—a three-day journey complete.

I left the Union Station in Los Angeles, traveled more than two thousand miles, and now stood in yet another Union Station. Chicago—also known as the Windy City, Chi-Town, the Second City, the Chill, the Big Onion, and Sweet Home. Chicago is one of the most incredible cities in the world.

I'd gotten so used to the soothing constant rocking motion of the train that it felt odd to be walking on solid ground again. I was in the midst of a throng of people pouring out of numerous trains on multiple tracks.

I've always loved visiting Chicago—except in the middle of winter, when it's frigid and the wind blows so hard that it penetrates your skin and travels through your blood, bone, marrow, and organs. The word "cold" isn't enough to describe Chicago's winters.

When people think of prosperity in America, they tend to automatically think of either coast as being the epicenter. On the East Coast, people think of New York, Philadelphia, Washington, D.C., even Boston; on the West Coast, people think of Los Angeles, San Francisco, Seattle, even Portland. Cities and towns in the Midwest and in the South don't immediately come to mind, which is interesting because that's where much of the real prosperity of America lies.

As I packed up my BlackBerry and laptop, I realized that to have an effective Mastermind Circle, we are no longer limited to in-person meetings. Skype and Google groups, e-mail, and conference calls all make it possible to have an efficient and valuable information exchange using available on-line technology. All the more reason to create a Mastermind Circle in areas where we want to excel. For instance, I could set up a circle for hotel and real estate investors, an area of my life I want to further master.

The information Tracey had given me was a gift that would change my life as it had hers.

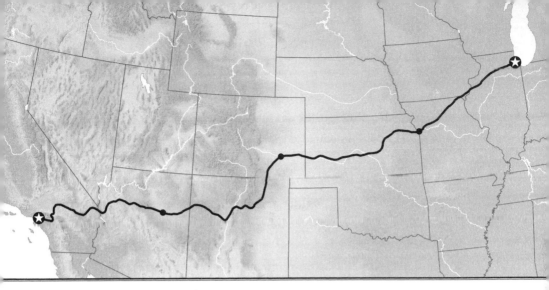

A FAST NICKEL

"It is possible that the scrupulously honest man
may not grow rich so fast as the unscrupulous
and dishonest one; but the success will be of a
truer kind, earned without fraud or injustice.
And even though a man should for a time be
unsuccessful, still he must be honest: better
lose all and save character. For character is itself a fortune."

—Henry Louis Mencken, American journalist

I t was midafternoon, still early, when we arrived in Chicago. While on
the train, I'd had this impulse to go to Wrigley Field. I'd never been
there, and I'd always wanted to visit. It's the oldest National League ballpark in the country—and, hey, it's baseball. What could be more American than that?

Of course, now that I was also aware of the history of William Wrigley,

I was even more moved to visit the ballpark. I was also suddenly interested in seeing the other Chicago, the one that's not as bragged about, but has also helped to define a reputation for the city. I wanted to see the Chicago that was ruled by the desire for something my grandmother used to call "a fast nickel."

Whenever she'd hear on the news about how somebody had gotten into trouble for robbery or some other crime that involved trying to make easy money or get rich quick, my grandmother would warn me, **"The easiest way to get yourself in over your head is by trying to make a fast nickel over a slow dime."** In a way, I feel that this folksy wisdom is the other side of the American dream, the American success story.

In addition to all of the positive things Chicago is known for, the city also has a well-documented history of corruption and organized crime. The fast-nickel syndrome can manifest itself in all sorts of crime, which until lately is the only way I thought it applied. "Hill, I was on the corner selling just trying to make that money to feed my family"—is a refrain that I have heard more times than I can count from young incarcerated men that I have mentored through my foundation. But going for the fast nickel over a slow dime isn't limited to young men on street corners.

What I've noticed, especially of late, is that the fast-nickel mentality also affects ordinary, decent, hardworking citizens who are guilty of nothing more than wanting to create the best lives for themselves and their families.

That's exactly how I would describe the millions of people who signed mortgages and accepted loans that were far too good to be true and then later found themselves either on the verge of losing their homes and life's savings or in the midst of foreclosure, with nowhere to go.

Once after a speaking engagement in Atlanta, I was standing around talking casually with a small group of audience members. One of the women excitedly told us all about how she'd recently bought her first home. The part of her story that amazed me was when she talked about getting her mortgage through a no-down, no-doc loan with rapidly escalating interest payments. Her credit was so good that the lender basically hadn't requested to see a single sheet of paper documenting anything. What was even more shocking to learn was that she was currently not employed and was living off her savings. Worse still, she couldn't tell me exactly when the mortgage moved from the interest-only low initial rate to the higher adjustable rate at full principle and interest. She, not unlike the young incarcerated men I work with, said, "I saw the chance to grab this house, and I took it." The problem is that if she doesn't find a job soon, that house is going to take all of her savings and her good credit.

I worried about this young lady's future. I didn't know her. I'd never seen her before that speaking engagement. Since we were in a public setting and other people were involved in the conversation, I didn't think it was appropriate to begin asking her pointed questions about her mortgage, employment prospects, or whether she had formulated a realistic plan for the future. It would have seemed as though I was calling her out. I encourage risk-taking, but her choice didn't seem to be grounded in intelligent, calculated decisions.

I've always wondered what became of her, whether she was able to find a job and hold on to that house. She only wanted what was best for her and her family. Yet, she *still* made what seemed to be an extremely risky and potentially destructive decision to purchase this home. **Although she didn't do anything illegal, she was potentially stealing from herself.**

So many of us do the same thing. I know that I have made some overly risky and not-well-considered investments more than once. I hoped that this was not going to be her downfall. I pray that she created the opportunity to get employed again and was able to keep her home.

Another reason people fall into the fast-nickel syndrome is because they perceive a lack of opportunities. The volunteer work I do gives me the opportunity to talk to numerous young men who have found themselves at the crossroads of choosing the fast nickel or the slow dime. Usually the fast nickel is more appealing because it seems quick. When it comes to money, many young men are made to believe that it's only what you have in your pocket that matters.

But isn't the style of lending that enabled the woman in Atlanta to buy her first home also the fast-nickel syndrome? It's predatory. When greed and exploitation are watered down and sanitized in the halls of office buildings full of white-collar professionals, people tend to become confused. They fall prey to the illusion, the disguise of sheep's clothing. They don't recognize the wolf for what it is.

The irony, of course, is that the very things that entice people to chase fast nickels are also the very things that inevitably bring their activity to a crashing halt. Whether it's the homebuyers who purchased homes they couldn't afford or the lenders who never should have enticed them with a mortgage in the first place, what usually brings it all crashing down is greed, the insatiable desire for more and more fast nickels.

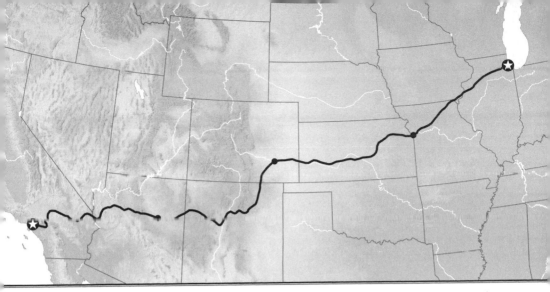

. . . Versus the Slow Dime

"If a man is proud of his wealth, he should not
be praised until it is known how he employs it."

Socrates, Greek philosopher

At the start of my journey, I'd made arrangements to bring Sean with me to have dinner with my friends Janice and Sam. The last time I'd been to Chicago, they'd cooked a wonderful dinner for me at their house, so I invited them out, my treat. Janice accepted the invitation and said they'd get a babysitter for Brandon and meet me wherever I wanted to go.

Since arriving in Chicago and thinking about fast nickels, I remembered Al Capone, one of the most notorious gangsters of all time, who ruled Chicago with an iron fist. I thought it might be fun to see his old haunts. I did a quick Bing search and found out that Capone's old headquarters had been at the Lexington Hotel. I was disappointed to learn that the Lexington had fallen into disrepair and was torn down in the 1990s.

One of Al Capone's other haunts was still open—the Green Mill Jazz Club, an old speakeasy where he and his own crooked Mastermind Circle used to hang out. I called Janice and Sam to ask if they'd mind spending part of the evening there. "Of course. We're from Chicago, we love jazz and blues," Janice replied.

I arrived at the apartment and found a note from Sean on the front door. "Hill, let yourself in. I will be right back!" The door was locked, so I checked under the doormat, and there was a key waiting for me. I walked into the apartment and was surprised to see most of Sean's bags packed. I wondered where he was headed. I continued on to the second bedroom, dropped my bags, and plopped down on the bed, looking forward to a nice, uninterrupted sleep in a bed that was stationary.

As I got settled, I plugged in my laptop. Scrolling through my e-mails, I saw that Andre had sent me another one. It was a short message: "My business is going under. Too many bad mortgages. Can't talk today. I'll call you tomorrow."

I couldn't believe it. Andre's big spending belied the actual state of his finances. After years of success, he had let so much money slip through his fingers. Even when the writing was on the wall, he'd kept on spending. Just like me, my friend Andre was a prime candidate for a Wealth Cure. Birds of a feather, as they say. I decided to help him organize a Mastermind Circle to get him back on track. There was no doubt in my mind that he wouldn't have to look far for other people in his situation in Los Angeles.

A bit frustrated, I decided to distract myself by doing some online reading about Al Capone. What little I knew about him before my Internet searches was from legend and film.

Capone had amassed a large amount of his power and his wealth during Prohibition when he smuggled alcohol into Chicago. He had side businesses like dog racing and horse racetracks. Like most gangsters, he helped himself to other people's territories, businesses, and money. And he was a murderer, who thought nothing at all of taking out whoever stood in the way of his desired goal.

During a turf war, the South Side Italian gang, Capone's people, killed seven members of the North Side Irish gang, which was run by Bugs Moran, a rival gangster. That event, which is referred to as the St. Valentine's Day Massacre, cemented Al Capone's power over the city, and he became unrivaled. Despite all of his violent crimes, it was Capone's greed that eventually brought him down and landed him in prison.

Eddie O'Hare, a lawyer who ran Capone's racetrack, cooperated with the Internal Revenue Service and told agents where they could find all of his organization's financial records. Capone was charged with tax evasion, fined $50,000, and had to pay nearly a quarter million dollars in back taxes. While he was in prison he was apparently haunted by one of the ghosts of a man who was murdered during the St. Valentine's Day Massacre. The articles I read said that the haunting caused Capone tremendous distress. He could be heard screaming in his sleep, begging the ghosts to leave him alone.

It gets frustrating watching people seemingly get away with making fast nickels while you're toiling away earning your slow dime, but over the years I've learned that my grandmother was right: Chasing fast nickels is the quickest way to get yourself in over your head. When that happens, you end up drowning in your own greed and wrongdoing. That is ultimately what happened to Al Capone.

When I read the name O'Hare, I wondered if that was the same person for whom the Chicago airport was named. No, I thought, they couldn't have named the airport after a known gangster. In fact, they didn't. They named it after the gangster's son, Butch O'Hare, a naval aviator who won the Medal of Honor in World War II. No matter what our family legacy, we have the power to determine the course of our lives.

As I was closing my browser windows, I heard the little chime that notifies me that I have a new e-mail. I switched my screen and laughed when I read what was in my in-box. It was a letter addressed "Dear Mrs. Jill Harper." It was from a Nigerian man whose father had died leaving him a significant fortune in his local currency, an amount that translated into millions of dollars. But there was a problem. In order to gain access to the money, he first had to pay some rather hefty fees. In the letter, the Nigerian pleaded with the "kind Mrs. Harper" for her help. If "madam" would forward him $2,500 so that he could clear his father's fortune, in return for her "kindness and humanity" he would not only reimburse her the $2,500 but also give her an additional $10,000 as a token of his gratitude.

In a way, you could say it was a coincidence to get a scam e-mail offering me the chance to make a fast nickel after having spent the last several hours reading and thinking how prevalent and sadly common the chase of fast nickels has become in our society. The very technology that enabled me to spend that afternoon researching Al Capone and past afternoons researching Bernie Madoff's Ponzi scheme, Kenneth Lay and the Enron scandal, predatory lending practices, and Wall Street corruption is the same technology that is used for many of the more insidious scams that prey on good people. Technology-based schemes are the new-era snake oil salesmen.

Not only the greedy and the gullible fall for these types of scams. Intelligent, well-meaning people also fall for them. Sometimes it's difficult to tell the difference between taking a genuine risk, like so many of the people who traveled west did in search of gold or new beginnings, and being foolhardy by jumping at an opportunity that upon closer inspection has obviously been designed to dupe you.

So you see, it really does come down to value and values. It's about knowing what matters most in our lives. It's about being clear about what our life can afford or not afford, and learning to welcome the things that are lasting—the slow dimes—because in the long run, they are the ones that will be worth the most.

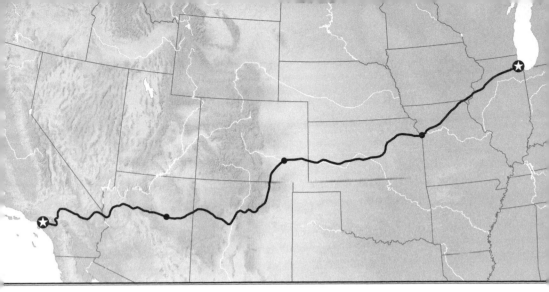

Our Debt to Our Past

"Stop acting as if life is a rehearsal. Live this day as if it were your last. The past is over and gone. The future is not guaranteed."

—Socrates

Just as I was drifting off to sleep, I heard the front door open. It was Sean. Honestly, I was expecting my friend Sean to be unshaven and dejected. But this definitely didn't seem like a depressed, unkempt man. He was looking sharp, and from the looks of it, had just returned from getting a fresh haircut. We sat down at the kitchen table, and I asked that simple question that friends ask of each other all the time. "How you doing?"

"Hill," he said, "I miss her, man. I really miss her. I want my wife back." What he said didn't come as much of a surprise to me, although it sounded as if it came as a surprise to Sean. I asked him as much.

"Yeah, it is a surprise," he told me. "Not that I miss her. I knew that would happen. I just didn't know how much. It's almost like a physical pain, like somebody ripped something out from inside of me, and I need it back to be whole again."

"So what are you going to do?" I asked.

"Hmm." Sean sighed. He tried to explain what had been going on with him, the things he'd been considering over the past several days. The one sure thing he'd arrived at was that he couldn't imagine starting over without Lorraine, not as long as the two of them were alive and able to be together.

Sean had also come to the conclusion that even though he loved New Orleans and that the city would always be his home, it was a home that belonged to history, to the past. He had only been able to live there in his adulthood, because he'd been living *with* Lorraine and their children. Lorraine was his home and his future. His home wasn't the house or a neighborhood or a city; it was her and the life they shared together.

"I keep thinking about what has been drawing me back there," he said, **"and I can only guess that it was this desire to fix what I kept thinking was broken. But it was never broken."** Sean talked about how this push to rebuild had swept him away just as the water from Katrina's broken levees had swept away the homes. During the time that he'd been in the apartment in Chicago, whenever he would think about rebuilding, he was never really sure what it was that he was rebuilding and for what reason. Sure, he could reconstruct his family's house, but then what?

"I got so caught up trying to duplicate what I had in the past that I hadn't even stopped to ask myself what I really want *going forward*. Some things," Sean mused, "even if they were good things, are better left in the past. If we duplicate them and then force ourselves to exist in those replicas, wouldn't that be like living with ghosts?"

I asked him what he felt the alternative would be, for the city and for the residents, especially those who had lost their entire lives, their homes, their property, and, for some, their family. He told me that he now believed that they should build anew, not try to return to the past in some way.

He responded, "Hill, don't get me wrong. I still love the Crescent City and, when I am financially able, will build in New Orleans, not *re*build. It will be a smaller, more efficient, modest home as opposed to replicating our big old family home."

"But years ago you made it a point to move back to New Orleans after you were done with school because you wanted—"

He cut me off. "At *the time*, it was the right decision. It was familiar, comfortable, and safe. It had been home for so long that I thought it was still home. I was so caught up, I was even trying to find the same furniture we had in the house. Rather than having a new plan for our future, I was stuck trying to replicate our past. I didn't realize how much Lorraine resented my spending money trying to rebuild the New Orleans house when I told her we couldn't afford other things. She really opened up about that, and I finally heard her."

"Wow," I whispered.

"Yeah, I'm starting to hope maybe we can meet somewhere in the middle. I think if we come up with a new plan *together*, she will cooperate with me on making a budget and sticking to it. I think she's going to go back to work, too, which would probably be good for her. She's really excited about it. I think she was using shopping to deter her boredom a lot of the time. If we can work things out, I'll be okay with giving up the old New Orleans house."

Sean had always seemed to hold such reverence for his past. I'd admired that reverence. I knew so many stories about his childhood and about the neighborhood, I could write the beginnings of his biography. Now that he spoke of realizing that he'd been trapped within that past, I could see it clearly, too.

"I felt I owed it to my parents not to sell the house. More than that—to stay there and live in it, fill it with a Lombard presence. We've been living in that house for generations. I guess I felt that was my debt to my ancestors, to my past." Sean made me realize that the debt we owe our ancestors is not to replicate their past world but to *build* on the strong foundations they have provided. Creating our own new dynamic legacy. So many sacrifices have been made by so many simply for me to have the opportunities that are afforded me today. The real tragedy would be if I took that for granted and didn't build upon them for the next generation.

There were two things that Sean said during our conversation that I carried with me as we rushed off to dinner with Janice and Sam. I've been thinking about them ever since. The first thing is that concept of owing a debt to your past. What is our debt to our past? Individually? Collectively?

The past can be very tricky. In some ways, it can be empowering and, in other ways, debilitating. Throughout history there have been groups of people who have been wronged in one way or another. Horrific acts have been committed against those groups. Like the Armenian genocide. The enslavement of Africans. The almost complete decimation of Native American tribes. The Rwandan genocide. The Holocaust. The list could go on.

I believe that there is definitely a debt, even it if it is only the assurance of memory, the promise never to forget. There are actions that must be taken to ensure healing, to aid those victims' ability to progress.

In some ways, the issue of an individual's debt to the past is even weightier than that of a group's. In trying to repay perceived debts to their past, people have become bankrupt—financially, spiritually, socially.

Many people are still able to succeed—at least it appears that way on the surface—despite the burden of their perceived debt. In Barbara Walters's memoir, *Audition*, she writes about how she felt a tremendous burden to support her family. She recognized at a young age that her father's reckless risk taking was jeopardizing the family. She knew the responsibility of caring for her mother, father, and mentally challenged older sister would eventually fall on her shoulders.

It could be argued that this fear is what pushed Barbara Walters to succeed, to break barriers, and to forge new ground in an effort to make ends meet for herself and her family. But at what cost? As amazingly successful as Barbara Walters is, she admits that for much of that time, she was not happy.

Whether acting purposely or unknowingly, family members can sometimes use an individual's feeling of indebtedness against them. Some of my friends and acquaintances do quite well financially but never are able to save because they are essentially supporting their extended families. If they try to stop giving in to the constant requests for loans and gifts, they are made to feel guilty, as if they have somehow turned their back on a family that helped them get where they are in life. One of my first major film roles was in the film *Zooman*. Oscar winner Lou Gossett Jr., whom I now call Uncle Lou, played my father in the film. It was right before Christmas, and we were shooting nights. One night, I was sitting in the makeup trailer, and after finishing a heated phone conversation, Uncle Lou walked in, looking very exasperated. He put his phone down, exhaled, laughed, and said, "Hill, it's tough being the richest one in the family at Christmastime!"

These debts are very real in our minds. But even if we do feel obligated to repay them, how do we know when we're done? How do we know when we can call it even? In many ways, I wasn't free of living in the past, just as Sean hadn't been free. A few years before, I had bought thirty-seven acres in Colorado for nearly a million dollars. I had always loved my grandparents' eighty-acre farm in Iowa, where I stayed during holidays and summers. It was a true family meeting place. Relatives and friends came to stay with them from all over the country. Since that generation, our family has become scattered across the country and we come together less frequently. I had a yearning to rebuild this family epicenter. I thought that whenever I got married and had kids, my family could be a part of that. I could create for my family a destination just like my grandparents had.

The property is on a beautiful river, and there's even a bald eagle living there. When I saw it, I thought. This is it. We could fly-fish and hang out, and it would be a great destination for the whole family. My mom had retired in Aspen, and I thought that building a home there would give her a project to work on. I had a grand idea of taking care of my mom and also building a place to last for generations. Buying the land on impulse without really thinking everything through turned out not to be the most prudent way to go about it. Buying it at the time I did and the way I did was a mistake. My heart was in the right place, but I was chasing ghosts, and I put myself in a financially precarious situation in the process. To this day, there is still nothing built on the land, and it costs me over a hundred thousand dollars per year just to hold on to it. Some might say, "Just sell it, then." But it can be extremely difficult to sell a piece of raw land in this real estate market, and there's nothing to rent since there isn't a home on it. I made a decision based on a fantasy from the past, and it keeps me stuck, because I have to make different choices today based on holding this property.

We live with ghosts in so many ways; it can be crippling. As Sean spoke of his realizations, I couldn't help thinking of Lorraine and how her life must have been for all those years that she chose to live with the ghosts from Sean's past because she loved him.

Though knowing Lorraine as I do, I'm certain that she was devastated by all the destruction of Hurricane Katrina. Nevertheless, she must have been relieved that the destruction meant, that she and her family could start something new and leave the ghosts behind. What I remember most from the first visit I paid them in the home they'd rented in Los Angeles was how excited Lorraine was about decorating. It now made sense to me. She'd never, not even as a new wife, had the chance to create a home that the two of them envisioned together. Sean had complained that she was spending far too much money on what he had assumed was a temporary existence, since he didn't plan to stay in Los Angeles. Now I could see how their financial realities were true reflections of what they believed were their deepest desires. In her book *Financial Intimacy*, Jacquette M. Timmons writes, "Let's face it, if you're not able to have significant and substantive conversations about money, what are you able to confront in your relationship?" That had become Sean and Lorraine's reality. And now Sean was determined to change that.

Honor your past by confidently moving forward.

I thought of Tracey as well, and about how deeply she'd loved Jarrett. She'd been able to move through the shock of losing him and their life together and make a commitment to a new life. She'd consciously decided not to live with his ghost, and she'd found a way to honor their past without burdening her future. The dreams that they'd had together, the ones they'd been unable to fulfill because of his sudden death, had been *their* dreams.

When she spoke to me now about her plans, what she intended to do with her life, how she saw it unfolding, it was clear that those were *her* dreams today. Not the dreams she'd once had before she'd met Jarrett and not the dreams she'd created with him. These were dreams that were based on who she was now, emotionally and financially. **She was honoring her past by confidently moving forward.** I recognized the courage and consistency of purpose that it must have taken for her to arrive where she now stood and how the Mastermind Circle had helped her to accomplish this.

One saying that I truly dislike is how a period of time can be referred to as a person's "glory days." A lot of our modern-day marketing is based on that concept. Many of the products that we have are geared toward making us want to be who we once were when we "used to be happy" or who we think we should be in order to "be happy again." In either case, it's False Evidence Appearing Real. Our so-called glory days will always be perfect because they are viewed through the lens of nostalgia.

The problem is that there are huge industries geared toward making people pay to live with those sorts of ghosts. There is the plastic surgery industry, the weight loss industry, the personal training industry, the makeup industry, the fashion industry, the hair-and-nails industry. It stands to reason that many of us buy into these industries because we are unhappy with who we are and, in one way or another, are living with a ghost of a life that no longer serves us.

I am almost certain that I have been living with the ghosts of my parents' marriage and divorce. It has created fears that I've allowed to keep me at arms' distance from certain aspects of a life I truly want. I want to be happy. I want to be in love. I have always wanted the sort of love that Sean described when he was talking about how much he missed Lorraine. Or the sort of love that Jarrett and Tracey shared. I want a family.

I am afraid that I'll never find someone to share that sort of lasting bond with because of the pain of my parents' divorce, but I'm also afraid that I will find that person and then lose her. Although in my head I can say that these are just fears, somehow I end up repeatedly sabotaging relationships because of them.

I once read a story about Coach Wooden I found extremely touching, but that also heightened my fears about finding—or not finding—a woman with whom I can share the rest of my life. Nellie, Coach Wooden's wife of fifty-three years, died of cancer on March 21, 1985. She was the love of his life, the only girl he ever dated.

Until his own death on June 4, 2010, on the twenty-first of every month, Coach Wooden would write a love letter to Nellie. In the letter, he would tell Nellie how much he loved her, how much he missed her, how he couldn't wait to see her again. After he was done writing the letter, he would fold the paper once and place it in an envelope. In his bedroom, on the pillow where Nellie used to lay her head at night, there was a stack of envelopes, all the letters he'd written to her since her death. The stack was held together by a yellow ribbon. When Coach Wooden had finished writing, he'd untie the ribbon and place the new letter on top of the stack, then retie the ribbon.

There were other ways he honored his beloved wife. He only slept on his half of the bed and never slept between the sheets as they had done when Nellie was alive. On a table in the coach's home was a spiral-bound stack of daily inspirational quotes. The quote that remained at the top of the stack until the day he died was the same one that Nellie had flipped over the morning she had to go to the hospital from which she never returned. The quote: **"Oh Lord, make me beautiful within."** It reminds him of Nellie, whom he often said was one of the most beautiful people he had ever known, both outside and within.

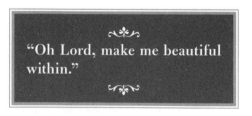

"Oh Lord, make me beautiful within."

When I heard this story, I was deeply moved by the depth of Coach Wooden's love for his wife and his commitment to that love for two and a half decades after she had died. Twenty-five years. It didn't sound as though he was haunted by his love for her or that he was living with her ghost. He still retained his faith, his love of life, and his sense of freedom.

Just as I admired Tracey for being able to honor Jarrett by moving on, I also admired Coach Wooden's ability to honor his wife by holding on. It seemed to me that both of them had found a way to pay tribute to the love that had been in their lives without sacrificing their freedom to live their dreams.

I keep hoping that I'll find someone who could inspire all of those things. I wondered, as Sean spoke about how much he missed Lorraine and explained the fruits of his self-examination, if perhaps I had already found that woman but my fear had kept me from recognizing that truth.

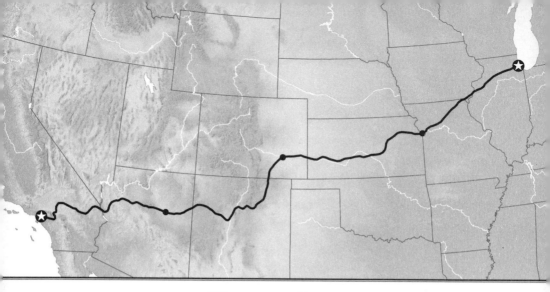

Taking Stock

※

"Your net worth to the world is usually determined by what remains after your bad habits
are subtracted from your good ones."
                              —Benjamin Franklin

We had decided to eat a quiet dinner before going to the speakeasy.
Since Chicago is really Janice and Sam's town, I asked them to
choose, but I wanted it to be someplace they'd always wanted to go but
had never been before. That way, it would be a new experience for all of
us. Everest, the restaurant they'd chosen, is at the top of the Chicago
Stock Exchange Building, on the fortieth floor.

The stock exchange is a world unto itself. It even has its own language.
The average person doesn't have much occasion to use words like "dividends," "shares," "yields," or even "stock." I thought of the symbolism of
having a restaurant located at the very top of that world. It obviously wasn't
by accident, or it wouldn't have been named after the world's highest moun-

tain. Visually, it was a stunning restaurant. With the panoramic views of the city, you certainly felt that you'd arrived at the top of something.

I remember several years ago, a mentee glanced over at a newspaper I'd been reading. It had been left open at the stock pages.

"What is that?" he asked. "What do all those numbers mean?" I tried to explain it to him, but he had a difficult time grasping the concept of individuals owning parts of companies by buying and selling individual shares.

My mentee wasn't the first person I've found myself in a position to explain the stock exchange to. A number of my friends and colleagues, even some who earn decent wages and have mutual funds and utilize the services of small brokerage firms, have revealed that they really don't fully understand the stock exchange, definitely not enough to be able to read about it.

"Look," Sylvia, a young actress friend of mine joked, "until about a year ago, all I had was a driver's license and an Ace check cashing card. My credit was so jacked they wouldn't even let me open up a bank account."

"And now?" I asked, curious to know if her situation had changed—and how.

She told me about how she'd received a call one day from a financial adviser who'd gotten her number from a friend of hers. Sylvia was confused as to why her friend would give her number to a financial adviser.

"It's sweet of you to call," Sylvia told the woman, "and I'm not trying to be rude or anything, but I don't have any use for your services. I don't have any finances for you to advise me about."

What the woman said changed Sylvia's mind and, ultimately, her life. "People like you are the ones who desperately need my services. Maybe the advice I give you will help you *increase* your finances."

Sylvia had agreed to make an appointment with the woman and talk to her. It wouldn't hurt because she had nothing to lose. With the financial adviser's help, Sylvia was able to repair her credit, open a checking account as well as a savings account, and start making small investments.

Even so, the world of the stock exchange was still foreign to her.

"It's like some kind of calculus, and I feel like I'm only at Algebra One," she told me.

I reflected on this as Sean and I made our way up in the elevator to the top-floor restaurant.

I thought we would be late for our reservation because Sean and I had spoken for so long, but Janice and Sam walked in just a few minutes after we arrived. We sat down, and Janice asked me to tell her all about my journey on the train. "Did you meet someone? Did you fall in love?" she asked.

"Why is that the first thing people ask me?" I laughed, assuring her that I had not developed any romantic interests. I told her about Scott and Mabel Macalaster.

"The food here is supposed to be amazing," Sam said, as the four of us scanned the menu.

"Listen to this review. That's how I found out about it," Janice explained. "It was in the *Chicago Tribune*, but they had it posted on their website. 'Chef Joho's plates are the most democratic in Chicago—the side by side pairings of aristocratic and working class ingredients. . . .'" Janice put the slip of paper she'd been reading from on the table. "Isn't that weird?" she wanted to know, "to talk about food like that, in a classist way?"

I thought about that for a second. I'd never heard food referred to as "working class" before.

"Well, I should probably look for the dish with the unemployed people's ingredients," she joked.

I laughed at the joke, but then gave her a quizzical look.

"I'm not working anymore," she explained. Janice worked as a midlevel executive in a corporate office. My first thought was that she, like so many other people I met, had been laid off.

I offered what I thought were words of comfort. "I'm sure with your skills you'll find another position really quickly. They were crazy to let someone as smart and capable as you go."

"Oh, no," Sam chimed in. "She wasn't let go. She quit. They've been begging her to return."

Now that was a twist. Why would someone quit her job in this difficult financial market? Janice was definitely smart and capable. She'd graduated from the University of Georgia, went on to get an MBA from Northwestern, and had been doing fairly well for herself. But I'd met numerous people with just as much education and experience as Janice who suddenly found themselves in dire straits after losing their jobs. It was a good thing, I thought, that her husband also did well. He was an executive at the MillerCoors corporate headquarters in Chicago.

Just then, the waiter brought our drinks, and we placed our orders. Janice ordered the same thing as me—filet of Lake Erie walleye pike, Alsace radish salad, smoked potato, caraway melforjus. We laughed, unsure which were the aristocratic ingredients and which were the working-class ones.

I lifted up my glass. "Well, congratulations to you for making such a bold move. What are you planning to do next?"

Sam and Janice explained, taking turns talking and sometimes finishing each other's sentences in the way that married couples often do, that their son Brandon had recently been diagnosed with Asperger's syndrome, which is an autism spectrum disorder. She didn't want to work at the company anymore. She wanted to be at home caring for their son.

"You should hear the comments I've been getting." Janice laughed. "We've all been so indoctrinated into what we think we should be doing with our lives."

There'd been a nursery and day-care facility at Janice's job, one that the company provided for the benefit of their employees with children. That made it easier for Janice to continue working there when Brandon was little, because she didn't really have to worry about him. She ate lunch with him every day, and she could always pop in to see him.

"But as he got older, we noticed that he wasn't developing socially in the same way as the other kids. He couldn't really hold long conversations. He didn't really have the interest. He would interrupt people while they were speaking. He didn't seem to be developing a functional social filter or learning the difference between appropriate and inappropriate behavior. So we took him to the doctor."

"It has been quite a process," Sam said, taking hold of Janice's hand.

"Brandon's an incredible pianist, a prodigy really," Janice said. "And he knows how to pick a lock or take apart and put together electrical gadgets."

I smiled because I actually knew of another child with Asperger's who had similar talents. Adam Walden was the son of Rosanne and Richard Walden, who started and ran the relief organization Operation USA, which was a corecipient of a Nobel Peace Prize for their efforts in the banning and removal of land mines. The Waldens and I share several friends in common, and I'd heard about how, when Adam was three years old, he opened all the locks on the door and walked outside. He then ran up and down the street ringing all the neighbors' doorbells. Much to their surprise, Rosanne and Richard realized that even at three years old, Adam was adept at picking and opening locks, so they had to reinstall all their locks up especially high, where, even while standing on a chair, he wouldn't be able to reach them. And like Brandon, Adam is also a musical prodigy. He plays the cello.

Janice and Sam enjoyed hearing the story about Adam Walden. They told me that they'd met so many wonderful people and had heard so many wonderful stories about children with Asperger's. In this way, their supportive community of other parents made up their own Mastermind Circle.

"You know," Sam said, in an almost bragging tone. "Lots of famous people, dead and living, have Asperger's. It's been speculated that Bill Gates has Asperger's."

That was news to me, but I wanted to find out more about Janice quitting her job and how that was affecting them.

"Financially," she announced, "it's not affecting us at all."

I wondered how it was possible for them to lose an entire income and not be affected. Even if they were wildly wealthy, surely that would have some impact on their discretionary spending. Sam and Janice explained that once they'd taken stock of all the ways Janice's income was being spent, they realized that they didn't need it after all.

"You have to take into consideration the amount I paid for gas to drive to and from work, the amount I paid for lunch every day and dinner on the days I had to work late, the amount I paid for child care, which was automatically deducted from my paycheck, and the amount that it cost to own and maintain a second car, things like that."

Sam added, "We also got rid of a lot of stuff in our house that we just didn't need. We'd gotten into this habit of buying. We didn't need all the cable stations that we were paying for; we didn't need additional televisions or all the fancy toys we'd been buying Brandon. All of that stuff was actually complicating our lives. Now our lives are much simpler, and we're able to spend time together and enjoy each other."

They talked a lot about how when Brandon was first diagnosed, they'd found out that a high percentage of married couples who have children with autism end up divorcing. They entered counseling, and were advised to take stock of their lives and to write a list of the things they valued and wanted to salvage—in other words, what was important and what was not. That list helped them weed out all the unnecessary things.

"Benjamin Franklin was also said to have Asperger's," Sam said, as if he'd just remembered. "Henry Ford, too."

It clicked immediately in my mind that both of those names had also been in the documents that Tracey had given me about Mastermind Circles. I wondered if, or how, the two things—Asperger's and Mastermind—might lend themselves to each other. Maybe it was just a coincidence that two of the top Masterminders in history also had Asperger's. Or maybe it wasn't.

After dinner, as planned we headed to the Green Mill Jazz Club. It wasn't exactly what I'd expected. I guess I thought I would enter and be taken back fifty years, into a smoky room where people like Billie Holliday, who actually used to perform there, would stand on stage swooning while Capone wannabes sucked on cigars and counted their money at the tables. But there were no such ghosts at the Green Mill. It wore its history proudly, but it was all about what was happening today.

The club had olive-green circular booths, large enough to comfortably fit six people. Without the low lights, the stage, and the sultry voice behind the microphone, it would have felt more like a restaurant than a club. Still,

I liked it. So did Janice and Sam. I was about to tell them a little bit about what I'd read on Capone and his henchmen. Just as I was leaning over to say, "This is where Capone . . ." Janice leaned over and said, "This is where my niece comes to perform her spoken word. She hasn't wanted us to come yet. She says she's not ready to have family in the audience, but I can't wait to come see her."

A waiter came to our table to ask if we wanted to order any drinks or food.

"Um, I don't know," Janice said jokingly, "Do you have anything with working-class or penny-pinching ingredients? I'm unemployed right now." We all laughed.

Given all the changes that Janice and Sam were going through, I decided not to get them involved with my health scare. And I still hadn't told Sean. Instead, I suggested that they might want to find or start a Mastermind Circle with other parents whose children have been diagnosed with Asperger's. They are bound to face many challenges, and they could benefit from the experience of parents raising a child with Asperger's. There have been so many advances in reducing the problems that can result from this developmental disorder. The prognosis is much more optimistic than it had been in the past. Having the support of a Mastermind Circle could make a big difference in Brandon's life.

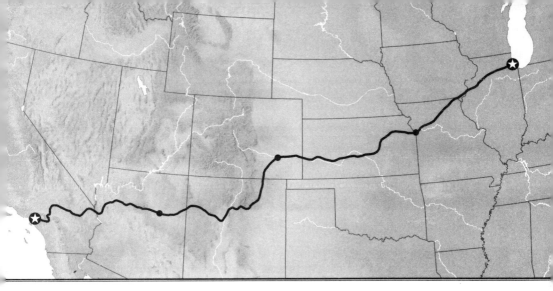

FORMING YOUR MASTERMIND CIRCLE

"In the long history of humankind (and animal
kind, too) those who learned to collaborate and
improvise most effectively have prevailed."
—Charles Darwin, English naturalist

The collective brain is smarter than any individual brain. As I began to look around at the power of the Mastermind Circle, I began to realize they exist in so many areas, yet we don't necessarily call them that. In Hollywood, every television show has a Writers' Room, where multiple writers collaborate and flesh out ideas for each episode. In business, executives often join the popular Worlds Presidents' Organization (WPO), a global organization of business leaders who are or have been CEOs of major companies. In politics, you have political action committees and strategy groups. In school, the aforementioned study groups were the most useful tools that propelled me to high academic achievement. The Mastermind principle is also present in fraternities and secret societies. I think back to filming the movie *The Skulls* about Yale University's Skull and Bones society.

A Mastermind Circle is a resource. Used properly, positive change and improvements can be made to our lives immediately. As I learned from reading Tracey's materials, some of the greatest financial minds in history have used Mastermind Circles. A Mastermind Circle isn't merely a group of people that gets together to brainstorm or to give support to one another. A Mastermind Circle must have a single purpose, and often that purpose is to forward the careers and/or business objectives of every member of the group. But its efficacy is not limited to business alone.

In a Mastermind Circle, each person must participate fully and whole-heartedly. Others in the group provide feedback, help you to discover new possibilities, and keep you accountable so that you stay on track. The group's members share a sense of striving toward a common goal, a terrific support network, and true progress in business and personal life through advice given by the members.

I thoroughly recommend forming a Mastermind Circle in order to build self-confidence, success, and all aspects of wealth. You can rely on a Mastermind Circle to have your best interests in mind, to always have your back. And this is separate and apart from your spouse or partner—they are already part of your life in a different capacity. You formally meet with your Mastermind Circle to discuss various issues that have come up at work or in life in general, and from group members you derive wise counsel, honest feedback, and help in attaining your goals. In today's world, a Mastermind Circle can be a study group, writing group, group of business peers, or a mentoring program. Any such gatherings can foster creative problem solving, give strong referrals, and offer advice in any number of areas.

In order to form a Mastermind Circle, you should seek out people who have similar talents and/or levels of success. All members of the group should want to make the current year a red-letter one, and they should all desire to reach their goals as quickly as possible. It's good for members to have diverse backgrounds, such as being entrepreneurs or working in a certain type of business. They should all want to be supportive of one another.

The optimal number of people in a group is five to eight. The purpose of the group is not for members to compete with but to support one another.

Once you have organized your own group, you can either convene in person, at one another's home, in a café, by conference call or even using online message boards. I prefer to meet by phone or in person. Meetings should be scheduled at regular intervals as agreed upon by the entire group. They could be every other week or monthly. If you find that someone in the group isn't participating or is creating a competitive or negative atmosphere, you should be willing to ask that person to leave, because ultimately that person will drain the energy of the group as a whole. If you bring in someone new to replace the person who has left, everyone in the group should agree that he or she is the right person to fill the slot.

A Mastermind Circle will give as much help and inspiration to each individual member as each person puts into it and more. **When such a group works the way it's supposed to, everyone comes out of the meetings feeling inspired and ready to tackle their most complex problems and paralyzing quandaries.**

One example of how a Mastermind Circle can help is when a member makes a bad investment. Most of us have been there. We didn't listen to that inner voice of warning and plunged into a scheme that promised much more than it gave in the end. It's one of the most common money mistakes, and while falling into such a trap can be embarrassing to admit, you can use the expertise of your Mastermind Circle to provide suggestions for creative ways to get out of the bad investment or scheme. Remember that most of the people in your group have already made similar mistakes. I for one have made more than I'd like to count. At that moment, sitting in the jazz club, I thought back to our dinner earlier that evening and it struck me that Janice and Sam had been sitting with Sean and me in a restaurant on the fortieth floor of the Chicago Stock

Exchange telling us about how they took stock of every aspect of their lives and decided to trade aspects of their life together for things that were worth more to them. I guessed that this was the original, true essence of "stock exchange": to allow people to *increase* their net worth, not only the value of their bank accounts but of their lives.

CONCLUSION

Life Account versus Bank Account

"I challenge you to imbue your money with soul—your soul—and let it stand for who you are, your love, your heart, your word, and your humanity."

—Lynn Twist, American author

The train ride had given me time to reassess my own situation regarding my Wealth Factors and my plans for my own personal Wealth Cure. At this point, I was ready to get back home to pursue the Mastermind Circle concept—and there was that surgery to prepare for.

The morning after our dinner with Janice and Sam, Sean poked his head into my room. "I think we're going to get back together," he said, smiling broadly. "I think we're going to do it. We've had some really good talks on the phone, and she wants me to come back. She's so happy that I'm giving up that house in the Ninth Ward. I never realized what a weight it was on our relationship. I think *I'm* even relieved to be letting it go!"

"That's incredible news," I said. It had been so hard to envision them apart. The whole thing had seemed like a slow-motion nightmare. Their getting back together really felt right, especially if they were both making realistic compromises to make it work.

"Yeah, I feel like I've been given a second chance. We're going to go to counseling to help sort some things out, and believe it or not, that's fine with me. I just want to have my wife back."

"And I'll be glad to have you back in L.A., my friend. And this time we're gonna have to schedule time so we don't go so long between seeing each other," I said. And I really meant it. One thing the trip had made me focus on was the meaning of longtime friends in my life. Friends like Sean provide a wealth that is not easily measured. Friendships like ours come along too rarely not to make the effort to get together often—no excuses.

"Yeah, well, I'll have some time freed up without having to make those trips back to New Orleans," Sean said. "It's funny, sometimes what you thought you wanted was just something you guilt yourself into, all along. If you had asked me last year if I would give up that house, I would have said, 'No way.' It took a real shake-up for me to realize I was holding on to the past in a way that was consuming my future—my future with Lorraine. She *is* my future, Hill." He glanced over at me with a look full of meaning.

"Yeah, I got that. Speaking of the future and the past, I did some thinking about Nichole on the trip," I said, feeling a little shy about bringing her up. Sean had always given me a hard time about our breakup.

"Oh, yeah? What are you thinking?" he asked.

"Just that it was a shame that two people who got along so well had to stop being close. I'm going to write her a really appreciative letter when I get back and just tell her how much she has meant to me. And who knows, maybe I'll wind up back on the East Coast, or maybe she'll see a way to move to L.A. at some point. I guess I just want to keep the doors open. I think I'll send Jade a little something, too; her daughter's adorable."

"Good idea to keep the doors open," Sean said. "Nichole is a real catch."

"Don't I know it," I sighed.

Now that Sean's crisis had a happy ending, I felt easier about giving him the news of my upcoming surgery.

"Listen, when I get back to L.A., I have to have a little surgery—no big deal."

"Why did you wait to tell me?" Sean looked at me, obviously trying to read how worried I was. He knew my family's history. "What kind of surgery?" he asked.

"A biopsy of nodules in my thyroid came back positive. We take it out. They are mostly likely malignant, so the endocrinologist recommended a full thyroidectomy."

Sean was trying to contain his reaction. "You have cancer?" Sean asked tentatively.

"It looks like it, man," I responded.

We sat quietly for a moment, and then Sean said, "We'll just have to beat it, and that's all there is to it." He continued, "I wondered why you took the train here. It's not like you to be so lax about getting from one place to another. How you feeling?"

"I was shaky at first, but I got perspective on the trip." I laughed and said, "Thyroid cancer is the best kind to have. It's treatable. I know I'll beat it." My experiences of feeling my grandfather's presence on the train convinced me of such.

"I don't doubt it, my friend. More than anyone I know, you can do anything you put your mind to." His faith in me was reassuring. "Is there anything I can do to help?"

"That's why I'm here," I answered with a smile. "I'm looking forward to spending a couple of days with you and catching up. Now that you and Lorraine are back together, we have something to celebrate."

And celebrate we did.

I was only in town for a couple of days. It was great to catch up with Sean. As I was packing to return to Los Angeles, he came into the room and handed me his phone. "Someone wants to speak to you," he said.

Money + Wellness = Wealth

Assuming it was Lorraine, I grabbed the phone and said, "What's happening, sister? I'm so glad you'll be staying in L.A."

I heard a familiar laugh. "Hill, it's Nichole. Was that an invitation?" She laughed again. "How are you?"

"I'm doing fine," I replied, surprised and happy to hear her voice.

"Sean told me about your surgery. I want to be there."

A wave of relief swept over me. It seemed so right for her to be by my side for the surgery. It was ironic that a disease I dreaded and feared was bringing us together, affirming the closeness Nichole and I had with each other.

I owed Sean for being such a good friend and knowing what I needed to get over this bump and move on with my life. Nichole and I talked and caught up and finished by planning her trip to L.A. Later that day, I boarded the plane for my flight back to Los Angeles. I took my seat, looked out the window, and, just then, something clicked. I needed a Mastermind Circle to help me deal with my cancer. I was so grateful for Sean's support, and now I needed the help of *all* of my close friends and family as well. I needed my personal board of directors to help me deal with all of this. I didn't have to go it alone.

I am very independent, and I'm not used to reaching out for help. I don't like having to depend on anyone, because what happens if they let you down? Experiencing the unfamiliar feeling of being the person who was now vulnerable and in need rather than the person who always had it together and helping others made me feel so unexpectedly emotional. Tears formed in my eyes as I took out my laptop to draft an e-mail asking Sean, Nichole, Tracey, Andre, Jordan, and my mother to join a Mastermind Circle to help get me through this. I clicked send. I closed my eyes and began to pray.

I thought about all the things I'd learned on my cross-country trip. I realized that we all have our own individual ingredients that make up our personal recipe for happiness. I realized that the two biggest happiness stealers in my life are the areas of health and debt. So I decided to list *my* Wealth Factors:

- To build and maintain a healthy body and attitude; to do some form of exercise daily.

- To live credit-card debt free.

- To not let myself fall into the trap of debt in general and live under the cloud of owing money to various entities.

- To nurture and grow deeper friendships and relationships with loved ones.

- To give back in some way every day, whether through my foundation as a mentor or simple acts of kindness.

- To continue to work toward having a family of my own and having a two-parent, stable, and happy household for our kids.

- To continue to act in and create projects that uplift, inspire, and entertain.

- To take risks and live courageously.

- To approach obstacles and opportunities the same way—with an attitude of gratitude.

- To say "please" and "thank you" even more.

- To give, give, give of my money, time, and talent.

- To remember that money plus wellness equals wealth.

- To be a peaceful warrior, having the energy of a warrior in the spirit of peace.

- To be a purveyor of new ideas and creative solutions to problems, rather than complaining about what "isn't being done" or how things "should be done."

As I approached my surgery, I was happy I learned about Mastermind Circles and was excited that the concept would be a part of my future path. I wanted to put my life in order before the surgery by evaluating my insurance, investments, and savings to be certain I was being as smart as I could be about my money. I also wanted to check out a new film script that my agent said he was e-mailing. First and foremost, I needed to gear up for a great surgery. With the support of my friends and family, that promised to be a lot less daunting. They say that optimistic people do better after surgery, so I was ready and willing to take it on. Cancer was not going to take another Harper.

Just then, despite my illness, I felt so grateful. I felt truly wealthy. All my thoughts about my Wealth Cure came rushing to me with this simple realization: a true Wealth Cure for me is to seek a balanced healthy relationship with all things in my life, especially money.

It was clear to me that one of the best things we can do for ourselves, family, friends, and loved ones, is to have a healthy relationship with money. Honoring the fact that it will flow in and out of our lives like waves in the ocean. Money is a resource that is meant to be used to create wealth, health, and happiness. At this critical time, we have the power to shift the way we prioritize and use money. If we don't, we will perpetuate cycles of fear, greed, and unhappiness. The more we are controlled by money, the more we injure one another in our attempt to collect more of it and this can lead us toward destructive ends.

Unreasonable happiness is not only possible, it's likely if we make collective decisive shifts in our use of money. But collective shifts start with the individual. With you and me. This will be the collective cure. Money can carry anything we assign to it. It can carry our doubts, fears, and greed. It can also carry our love, hopes, and generosity. Money holds power because it *is* energy. Money is everywhere and touched by all of us in differing currencies and amounts. Our healthy relationship with money can be a catalyst for positive change in all areas of our lives. I realized that the most important aspect of living a truly wealthy life is to lead a *balanced life*.

I remembered a thought that had inspired me from *The Game of Life*, a book by Florence Scovel Shinn that offers so much wisdom: "**One must ever hold the vision of one's journey's end and demand the manifestation of that which one has already received. It may be one's perfect health, love, supply, self-expression, home or friends.**" I was determined to hold the vision in that spirit and have a successful surgery. I'm still frightened, but I will pray and allow God and the universe to conspire to protect me. Cancer cannot and will not defeat me. I will be cured. I will go on to live a full healthy and wealthy life. I will love and allow myself to be loved. I will be unreasonably happy. This will be my life, and I will always be thankful for this precious gift of life. I will fly.

I opened my journal, preparing to read over my notes from my journey. I had a newfound sense of purpose and desire for abundance. Once the surgery was over, I'd have plenty of time to address and balance out the other aspects of life and true wealth, such as family, finances, and spirituality—and love. I realized that true wealth is how we feel, and if you can love and feel loved, then you are already truly wealthy. At that moment, and I can't explain it rationally, I felt wealthier than I have at any other point in my life. An internal sunshine brightened my eyes because I *knew* that I had already been cured.

Before my journey, I had an intuition of what true wealth was. But now, I was confident that the wealth my life account provided was so much more valuable to me than any amount of money I would ever have in my bank account.

The plane took off down the runway, and as always, I experienced a moment's thrill as the wheels lifted off the tarmac and the plane gained altitude. I'm always amazed at how a hulking piece of metal weighing up to 870,000 pounds can rise so gracefully and travel effortlessly into the air.

In the same way, we can adjust our attitudes and expectations, our goals and our dreams, so that we, too, can lift off gracefully and purposefully in our lives, and hence take flight.

255

Epilogue
Successful Surgery

"Action is the foundational key to all success."
—Pablo Picasso, Spanish painter,
draughtsman, and sculptor

On July 15, 2010, my wonderful surgeon Dr. Adashek at Cedars Sinai Medical Center successfully removed my thyroid. Three cancerous nodes were discovered inside my thyroid gland. Dr. Adashek and my endocrinologist explained that early detection was key and thankfully, believed that the cancer had not spread to any other areas of my body.

Although I couldn't speak for nearly two weeks and was very hoarse from the surgery, there was no lasting damage to my voice or vocal nerves—which was among my many concerns. I continue to follow up with my doctor and am expected to be fine.

Now that's what I call a cure! God is good, all the time.

"Wealth is the ability to fully experience life."

—Henry David Thoreau

Resource Bibliography

PERSONAL FINANCE

Books

Baritomo, Maria. *Ten Laws of Enduring Success*. New York: Crown, 2011.

Givens, Charles J. *More Wealth Without Risk*. New York: Pocket, 1995.

Greene, Robert. *The 48 Laws of Power*. New York: Penguin, 2000.

Lewis, Michael. *The Big Short*. New York: Norton, 2010.

Lynch, Peter. *One Up on Wall Street*, 2nd ed. New York: Simon and Schuster, 2000.

Miller, Percy. *Guaranteed Success*. New York: Urban Books, 2007.

Orman, Suze. *Suze Orman's Money Kit for the Young, Fabulous, and Broke*. New York: Riverhead, 2007.

———. *The 9 Steps to Fiancial Freedom*. New York: Three Rivers Press, 2006.

Ramsay, Dave. *The Total Money Makeover*. 3rd ed. New York: Thomas Nelson, 2009.

Simmons, Russell. *Super-Rich*. New York: Gotham, 2011.

Stanley, Thomas, and William Danko. *The Millionaire Next Door*. New York: Taylor, 2010.

Timmons, Jacquette M. *Financial Intimacy: How to Create a Healthy Relationship with Your Money and Your Mate*. Chicago: Chicago Review Press, 2010.

Websites

www.buxfer.com

www.daveramsey.com

www.fidelity.com

www.kiplinger.com

www.mint.com

www.money.msn.com

www.msmoney.com

www.suzeorman.com

www.thepennysaved.com

www.wellsfargo.com (My Money Map, My Spending Report, Budget Watch, and My Savings Plan®)

www.wsj.com/personalfinance

ON FINDING YOUR PASSION

Books

Bissonnette, Zac. *Debt-Free U.* New York: Portfolio, 2010.

Boller, Richard N. *What Color Is Your Parachute?* Rev. ed. New York: Ten Speed, 2010.

Gardner, Chris. *Start Where You Are.* New York: HarperCollins, 2009.

Johnson, Tory. *Fired to Hired.* New York: Berkley, 2009.

Lore, Nicholas. *The Pathfinder.* New York: Fireside, 1998.

Miller, Dan. *48 Days to the Work You Love.* New York: B&H Books: 2010.

Rubin, Gretchen. *The Happiness Project.* New York: HarperCollins, 2009.

Websites

www.career-advice.monster.com

www.careerbuilder.com

www.careerkey.com

www.careers.org

www.efinancialcareers.com

INSPIRATION

Books

Albom, Mitch. *The Five People You Meet in Heaven.* New York: Hyperion, 2003.

Bruno, Dave. *The 100 Thing Challenge.* New York: HarperCollins, 2011.

Byrne, Rhonda. *The Secret.* New York: Atria, 2006.

Carlson, Richard. *Don't Sweat the Small Stuff . . . and It's All Small Stuff.* New York: Hyperion, 1997.

Coelho, Paulo. *The Alchemist.* New York: HarperCollins, 2006.

Dittmar, Warren. *Completing the Wheel.* New York: iUniverse, 2010.

Jackson, Harry R. *The Way of the Warrior.* New York: Chosen Books, 2007.

Jay-Z. *Decoded*. New York: Spiegel & Grau, 2010.

Martel, Yann. *The Life of Pi*. New York: Mariner, 2003.

Murray, Liz. *Breaking Night*. New York: Hyperion, 2010.

Pausch, Randy, and Jeffrey Zaslow. *The Last Lecture*. New York: Hyperion, 2008.

Ruiz, Don Miguel. *The Four Agreements*. New York: Amber-Allen, 1997.

Shange, Ntozake. *For Colored Girls Who Have Considered Suicide/When the Rainbow Is Enuf*. New York: Scribner, 1997.

VanZant, Iyanla. *Peace Through Broken Pieces*. New York: Smiley Books, 2010.

Whyte, David. *Crossing the Unknown Sea*. New York: Riverhead, 2002.

——. *The Three Marriages*. New York: Riverhead, 2010.

Websites

www.goodreads.com

www.gratefulness.org

www.gratitudelog.org

www.happiness-project.org

www.inspirationalstories.com

www.lightacandle.org

www.peace.org

www.quotegarden.org

ACKNOWLEDGMENTS

God is the creator of all things (including wealth) and when it comes to acknowledging the gratitude in my heart, for me, it starts with God, from whom all blessings flow. Without guidance, love, and support from my Creator—this creation would not exist.

This, my fourth book (wow, I can hardly believe it!), is the most ambitious book I have attempted to date. There were so many moving pieces, and I am grateful to all the people who helped me put it all together. There are so many individuals that helped me "cure" *The Wealth Cure.*

Thank you to all of my family, friends, and loved ones who teach me daily. I know many of you see yourselves and your stories in these pages and I thank you for allowing me to use "our lives" as the canvas on which this book is painted.

Thank you to my very close collaborator Danielle Caldwell, who I work with daily because she runs my office and—in many ways—runs my life.

Thank you to my friend and amazing author Meri Nana-Ama Danquah for all of your help with the development of the book. To Pastor DeForest Soaries Jr., Rev. Michael Beckwith, Jeanette Perez, Joshua Pianko, Jonathan Diamond, Leslie Wells, Susan Betz, Megan Heintzkill, Diane Reverend, Marilyn Hill Harper, Wayne Federman, Cynne Simpson, Tim Bagley,

Tamekia Strickland, M.D., Cyrus Batchan, Karen Lewis Farrelly, Christina Gomes, Stephanie Covington, Sherman Wright, Marvet Britto, and Jennifer Cohn Beugelmans.

A heartfelt thanks to William Shinker, Lauren Marino, Cara Bedick, and everyone at Gotham/Penguin who have helped shape this book. To Lisa Johnson, Lindsay Gordon, and Adenike Olanrewaju—thank you for your time, dedication, and hard work.

And, of course, very special thanks to the many medical professionals that helped me diagnose, treat, comply, maintain and thrive, especially Dr. Massoud, Dr. Adaeshek, Dr. Braunstein, Dr. Odugbesan and Desert Horse-Grant.

And finally, humble thanks to you for taking the time to read this work. Peace and abundant blessings to all.